Communicating in the Information Society

edited by
Bruce Girard and
Seán Ó Siochrú

UNITED NATIONS
RESEARCH INSTITUTE
FOR SOCIAL DEVELOPMENT

D0097417

This United Nations Research Institute for Social Development (UNRISD) book has been prepared with the support of UNRISD core funds. UNRISD thanks the governments of Denmark, Finland, Mexico, the Netherlands, Norway, Sweden, Switzerland and the United Kingdom for this funding.

Copyright © UNRISD. Short extracts from this publication may be reproduced unaltered without authorization on condition that the source is indicated. For rights of reproduction or translation, application should be made to UNRISD, Palais des Nations, 1211 Geneva 10, Switzerland. UNRISD welcomes such applications.

The designations employed in UNRISD publications, which are in conformity with United Nations practice, and the presentation of material therein do not imply the expression of any opinion whatsoever on the part of UNRISD concerning the legal status of any country, territory, city or area or of its authorities, or concerning the delimitation of its frontiers or boundaries.

The responsibility for opinions expressed rests solely with the author(s), and publication does not constitute endorsement by UNRISD.

UNRISD publications are available from the Reference Centre, UNRISD, Palais des Nations, 1211 Geneva 10, Switzerland; phone +41 (0)22 9173020; fax +41 (0)22 9170650; info@unrisd.org; www.unrisd.org.

ISBN 92-9085-045-0

Contents

Authors

Bruce Girard is a researcher, writer and educator active in development communication and communication rights issues. He is the founder of the Agencia Informativa Púlsar and of Comunica, a network focusing on the use of new information and communication technologies (ICTs) by independent media in the South. He has lectured on broadcasting, information and communication technologies, and communication rights in more than 25 countries. He is a member of the Interim Coordinating Committee of the campaign, Communications Rights in the Information Society (CRIS)*. He is also co-author of the book, *Global Media Governance: A Beginners Guide* (with Seán Ó Siochrú and Amy Mahan, Rowman and Littlefield, Lanham, MD, 2002).

Seán Ó Siochrú is a writer, consultant and activist. He has written several books, the most recent of which is *Global Media Governance: A Beginners Guide* (with Bruce Girard and Amy Mahan, Rowman and Littlefield, Lanham, MD, 2002). He is a member of the CRIS* Campaign Strategy Working Group, and is the chairperson of Community Media Network and Dublin Community Television in his home country, Ireland. He works as a consultant on media and ICT issues for international bodies such as the United Nations Development Programme (UNDP), International Fund for Agricultural Development (IFAD) and the European Union. He is also director of Nexus Research, a non-profit research organization.

Fackson Banda is director of Panos Southern Africa and is in charge of the overall running of the institute in Southern Africa. He was formerly director of communications and social justice at the Christian Council of Zambia and part-time lecturer in mass communication at the University of Zambia. He has a B.A. in mass communication from the University of Zambia, and an M.A. in mass communication from the University of Leicester. He has recently obtained a Ph.D. in communication from the University of South Africa.

---

* Communication Rights in the Information Society (CRIS) is an international campaign working to ensure that communication rights are at the heart of the information society. CRIS is active in the WSIS process at every level, collaborating with NGOs with similar aims; it also promotes communication rights at the World Social Forum and other events, and through national-level campaigns. CRIS was initiated by the Platform for Communication Rights, a coalition of NGOs involved in media and communication around the world. See www.crisinfo.org.

James Deane is executive director of Panos London and one of the founding members of the Panos Institute. He was formerly director of Panos' Communications and Social Change Programme, and author of several publications on new information technologies and developing countries. He has advised and been a consultant to many international organizations including the Rockefeller Foundation, the World Bank, the Department for International Development in the United Kingdom and the United States Agency for International Development (USAID). He has an M.A. in International Communication and Development and is a visiting fellow at the London School of Economics.

Kunda Dixit is a Nepalese journalist and publisher of the newspaper, *Nepali Times*, in Kathmandu. He is a graduate of Columbia School of Journalism in New York, has worked for the BBC, Inter Press Service Asia-Pacific and was regional director of Panos Institute South Asia. He is the author of *Dateline Earth: Journalism as if the Planet Mattered*.

Jean-Claude Guédon is a historian of science by training and a professor of comparative literature (University of Montreal). He has spent the last 10 years of his life studying the social and cultural effects of the Internet, as well as the evolution of scholarly publishing in a digitized and networked context. He has worked with the Internet Society, several francophone organizations, and, more recently, with the Open Society Institute. Actively engaged in the open access movement within scholarly publishing, he is also involved in the promotion of open source software. He is a member of various boards or steering committees, such as the Networked Digital Library of Theses and Dissertations (NDLTD), Canadian National Site Licensing Project (CNSLP), Electronic Information for Libraries (eIFL) and Open Source Initiative's (OSI) Information Sub-Board.

Cees J. Hamelink has been professor of international communication at the Universiteit van Amsterdam since 1984, and since 2001, he has also been professor of media, religion and culture at the Vrije Universiteit in Amsterdam. He has a Ph.D. from the University of Amsterdam, where he studied theology and psychology. Professor Hamelink is the editor-in-chief of the scientific journal *Gazette*. He has written 16 books on media, ICTs and human rights.

William McIver, Jr., is assistant professor in the School of Information Science and Policy at the University at Albany in the United States. His areas of research are database systems, and social and community informatics. He co-edited the book, *Advances in Digital Government:*

Technology, Human Factors, and Policy (with Ahmed K. Elmagarmid, Kluwer, Boston, 2002). He is a member of the Information Technology and International Cooperation research network of the Social Science Research Council. Professor McIver has a B.A. from Morehouse College and a Ph.D. from the University of Colorado at Boulder, both in Computer Science.

Njonjo Mue was regional director of Panos Eastern Africa from June 2001 to July 2002. He is a lawyer by profession and an advocate of the High Court of Kenya. He studied at the University of Nairobi and Oxford University, where he was a Rhodes scholar. He has held various human rights jobs, including as legal adviser to the freedom of expression group, Article 19. In 2000, he was named Jurist of the Year for his work in defence of human rights, democracy and the rule of law in Kenya.

Dafne Sabanes Plou is a freelance journalist and social communicator from Argentina. She has been a member of the Association for Progressive Communications Women's Networking Support Programme (WNSP) since 1994. At present, she is regional co-ordinator for the WNSP for Latin America and the Caribbean, and regional co-ordinator for the field testing of the Gender Evaluation Methodology (GEM) in Latin America. From 1991 to 1999 she was chairperson for the Latin American region of the World Association for Christian Communications (WACC), and from 1992 to 2000, she was chairperson of the Latin American and Caribbean Communications Agency (ALC). She is the author of several articles, papers and books, including *Global Communications, Is There a Place for Human Dignity?* (WCC, Geneva, 1996) and *Peace in Troubled Cities* (WCC, Geneva, 1998).

Antonio Pasquali is a highly respected communication scholar in the Spanish-speaking world. In his writings, from *Comunicación y cultura de masas* (1962) and *Comprender la comunicación* (1974), to *La comunicación cercenada* (1990) and *Bienvenido global village* (1998), he combines scholarly reflection with experience in politics and in the field. Between 1974 and 1975, he presided over the Venezuelan ministerial commission that worked on the Venezuelan Radio and Television Project (RATELVE), an initiative in favour of a new policy for public communications. From 1978 to 1989, he held high-level positions at the United Nations Educational, Scientific and Cultural Organization (UNESCO), including Assistant Director-General for Communication.

Marc Raboy has a Ph.D. from McGill University and is full professor and head of the Communication Policy Research Laboratory in the Department of Communication, University of Montreal. He is also senior research associate in the Programme in Comparative Media Law and Policy at the University of Oxford. He has written and edited 15 books and more than 100 journal articles or book chapters, as well as research reports for national and international, public- and private-sector organizations including UNESCO, the Japan Broadcasting Corporation (NHK), the European Broadcasting Union, the Government of Canada and the Quebec Ministry for Culture and Communication. His current research focuses on issues and sites of communication policy making in the context of globalization.

Silvio Waisbord is a senior programme officer at the Academy for Educational Development in Washington, DC. He was associate professor at Rutgers University between 1995 and 2003. He has written and co-edited several books and articles on media policy in Latin America, development communication, media globalization and journalism. He received a Ph.D. in sociology from the University of California at San Diego.

Foreword

The United Nations Research Institute for Social Development (UNRISD) has been supporting research on the interaction between societies and informational developments since it held the Information Technologies and Social Development Conference in Geneva in 1998. This has resulted in a range of publications on many aspects of information-related change. However eclectic their subject or origin, a number of common themes have emerged. One is recognition of the multiple interplays between societies, and the adoption, appropriation and development of informational technologies: interplays that refute any simplistic notion of technological determinism. Another, consequently, is the necessity for critical thinking, debate and the transparent and accountable making of choices if appropriate informational strategies are to be adopted in any society.

It therefore seemed fitting, on the occasion of the first World Summit on the Information Society (WSIS)—which is also the first UN-sponsored world summit to specifically seek the formal participation of civil society—for UNRISD to emphasize the importance of societal perspectives on information society debates. It invited Bruce Girard and Seán Ó Siochrú of Communication Rights in the Information Society (CRIS), a civil society organization active in the WSIS process, to select and edit a collection of essays on what they saw as core issues. I am very pleased to present the result, along with an introduction from the editors, which makes clear both the rationale for the selection of individual contributions and the questions they, as a collection, pose for the ongoing debate.

And the debate is ongoing. WSIS 2003 in Geneva will lead to WSIS 2005 in Tunis, and who knows what beyond. In the meantime, individual nations and agencies will be developing their information-related strategies and making large investments accordingly. If few now argue that information and communication technologies (ICTs) alone will solve their problems, not many articulate a clear vision of what ICTs can contribute to internal social and economic development, as distinct from their role in enabling globalization. Three decades ago, in the 1970s, UNRISD research brought to light the social and developmental inadequacies of an earlier revolution that was led by technology: the Green Revolution. This time I would hope that the ongoing debate will be enriched by sufficient disinterested research on informational developments within societies so as to avoid such disappointing discoveries in the future.

I would like to thank the government of the Netherlands for its particular interest in and support for UNRISD's work on the social impacts of information technology. I also acknowledge the support of that government and the governments of Denmark, Finland, Mexico, Norway, Sweden, Switzerland and the United Kingdom, which provide UNRISD's core funding.

Thandika Mkandawire
Director
UNRISD

November 2003

Acronyms

ABC	American Broadcasting Corporation
ABN	African Broadcasting Network
AIDS	acquired immune deficiency syndrome
ALC	Latin American and Caribbean Communications Agency
AOL	America Online, Inc.
APC	Association for Progressive Communications
ASL	American sign language
AT&T	American Telephone and Telegraph
ATM	asynchronous transfer mode (in "Locating the information society within civil society")
ATM	automatic teller machine (in "A community informatics for the information society")
AWORC	Asian Women's Resource Exchange
BAZ	Broadcasting Authority of Zimbabwe
BBC	British Broadcasting Corporation
BCE	Bell Canada Enterprises
BMC	BioMed Central
BOAI	Budapest Open Access Initiative
CAP	Control Advisory Panel
CBC	Canadian Broadcasting Corporation
CD	compact disc
CD-ROM	compact disc—read-only memory
CEE	Central and Eastern Europe
CIRA	Community Informatics Research Application Unit
CIRC	Community Informatics Resource Center
CNN	Cable News Network
CNSLP	Canadian National Site Licensing Project
COTS	commercial off-the-shelf
CPSR	Computer Professionals for Social Responsibility
CRIS	Communication Rights in the Information Society
DeCSS	Decryption of Contents Scrambling System
DMCA	Digital Millennium Copyright Act
DNA	deoxyribonucleic acid
DOS	disk operating system
DVD	digital versatile disc
EC	European Commission
ECOSOC	United Nations Economic and Social Council
eIFL	Electronic Information for Libraries
EU	European Union
FCC	Federal Communication Commission
FEMNET	African Women's Development and Communication Network
FIRE	Feminist Interactive Radio Endeavour
FM	frequency modulation
G-8	Group of Eight
GA	United Nations General Assembly
GDP	gross domestic product

GIS	geographic information systems
GPS	global positioning system
HIV	human immunodeficiency virus
HTML	hyper-text markup language
ICANN	Internet Corporation for Assigned Names and Numbers
ICASA	Independent Communication Authority of South Africa
ICCPR	International Covenant on Civil and Political Rights
ICESR	International Covenant on Economic, Social and Cultural Rights
ICT	information and communication technology
IDRC	International Development Research Centre
IEC	International Electrotechnical Commission
ILO	International Labour Organization
IMF	International Monetary Fund
INCP	International Network on Cultural Policy
IP	Internet protocol
IPRs	intellectual property rights
ISO	International Organization for Standardization
IT	information technology
ITU	International Telecommunication Union
IWTC	International Women's Tribune Center
LBC	Lebanese Broadcasting Corporation
LDC	least developed country
MB	megabytes
MDG	Millennium Development Goal
MIS	management information systems
MIT	Massachusetts Institute of Technology
NDLTD	Networked Digital Library of Theses and Dissertations
NEAR	National Electronic Archive Repository
NGO	non-governmental organization
NIH	National Institutes of Health
NWEO	New World Economic Order
NWICO	New World Information and Communication Order
OAI	Open Archive Initiative
OECD	Organisation for Economic Co-operation and Development
OI	organizational informatics
OP	Optional Protocol
OSI	Open Source Initiative
PANA	Panafrican News Agency
PBS	Public Broadcasting Service
PDF	portable document format (Adobe Acrobat)
PEN	Poets, Playwrights, Editors, Essayists, and Novelists
PLoS	Public Library of Science
PrepCom	preparatory committee
PRSP	poverty reduction strategy papers
RAP	Reform Advisory Panel, International Telecommunication Union
RATELVE	Venezuelan Radio and Television Project
SABC	South African Broadcasting Corporation

SCI	Science Citation Index
SLETP	Sri Lanka Environmental Television Project
STM	science, technology and medicine
TAMWA	Tanzania Women's Media Association
TCP	transmission control protocol
TDD	telecommunications devises for the deaf
TIA	Total Information Awareness
TNC	transnational corporation
Tulip	The University Licensing Programme
UDHR	Universal Declaration on Human Rights
UMTS	Universal Mobile Telecommunications System
UN	United Nations
UNCSW	United Nations Commission on the Status of Women
UNDAW	United Nations Division for the Advancement of Women
UNDP	United Nations Development Programme
UNESCO	United Nations Educational, Scientific and Cultural Organization
UNIFEM	United Nations Development Fund for Women
UNRISD	United Nations Research Institute for Social Development
UNU	United Nations University
UNU/IIST	United Nations University/International Institute for Software Technology
UNU/INTECH	United Nations University/Institute for New Technologies
USAID	United States Agency for International Development
W3C	World Wide Web Consortium
WACC	World Association for Christian Communication
WCCD	World Commission on Culture and Development
WENT	Women's Electronic Network Training
WHO	World Health Organization
WiFi	wireless fidelity
WIPO	World Intellectual Property Organization
WNSP	Women's Networking Support Programme
WSIS	World Summit on the Information Society
WTO	World Trade Organization

Introduction[1]

Seán Ó Siochrú and Bruce Girard

The contributions in this book cast a spotlight into dark, often neglected, corners of the "information society" as articulated in the World Summit on the Information Society (WSIS). Several very different layers are illuminated, from the philosophical underpinnings of the role of information in society, to the context and manner in which the concept has recently emerged into global consciousness, to how it can be deployed in practice to maximize benefits to society. An edited volume is well suited to covering these diverse ways of thinking about the topic as it offers the opportunity to bring together authors with different backgrounds and approaches.

All the authors display a degree of healthy scepticism toward the information society, which is partly why they were selected. There was considerable unease when WSIS was first announced in mid-2001, regarding its concept, focus and purpose. Subsequent developments did little to allay the widely held suspicion that it was hastily conceived, and that its central tenets were perhaps taken too much for granted. The information society had become common coin before it had earned it. Only a thin veneer covers the cracks that, left unattended, could open up deep fractures with the potential to undermine any enduring utility. This publication raises some such issues, exposing areas where some further thought and work is needed.

In many ways, the information society is an unfortunate term. It is unfortunate in its genesis as a smokescreen for the narrow liberalization and privatization policies pursued by the European Union in the 1990s, designed to suggest a social dimension that barely transpired. It is unfortunate because "information" is an insubstantial substitute for "knowledge", lacking a certain depth and sagacity, pointing more in the direction of computers and information technology than in the direction of the breadth of human experience and capacities. Some thus argue for the term a "knowledge society". But it is especially unfortunate because information and hence an information society seems static, non-interactive, and lacking in social and human dynamism. "Communication" and "communicating" are dynamic terms that necessarily involve people and communities in a cycle of exchange and mutual interactivity: by comparison, information and even informing ("informating" simply is not a word) are bureaucratic, half-hearted and indifferent. As Antonio Pasquali puts it in the final chapter of this book:

---

[1] The editors would like to thank Amy Mahan, Cynthia Hewitt de Alcántara, Mike Powell, Suroor Alikhan and the contributing authors for their work in producing this book.

information categorically expresses a less perfect or balanced communicating relationship than does communication, and tends to produce more verticality than equality, more subordination than reciprocity, more competitiveness than complementarity, more imperatives than indicatives, more orders than dialogue, more propaganda than persuasions.

It is no accident that we have been saddled with such a term. The most recent and ardent propagator of the information society—the International Telecommunication Union (ITU) as the lead UN agency for WSIS—has a mandate and history of promoting the extension of infrastructure. It is not an organization that has been associated in the past with communication or interaction. Although the ITU has occasionally and commendably referred to the "right to communicate", this tends not to go beyond the laudable but limited goal of achieving universal access to information and communication technologies.[2] It could have been worse. The other contending title of the mid-1990s was more revealing still of the narrow vision of its promoters: the technological-determinist and asocial "Global Information Infrastructure" promoted by the United States.[3]

But things might also have been better. In August 1996, the Executive Board of the United Nations Educational, Scientific and Cultural Organization (UNESCO) began planning a Conference on Information and Communication for Development, to be held in 1998, which would:

> focus on development issues to which information and communication can make a meaningful contribution and would provide a forum for all who wish to contribute to the search for international consensus in these matters (UNESCO 1996a).

In November the Executive Board agreed that:

> The possibility of coorganising the conference jointly with other bodies within the United Nations system, such as ITU, would be actively explored (UNESCO 1996b).

The idea, however, was dropped, and UNESCO was not centrally involved as a co-organizer with ITU of the summit. Indeed, it might have ended up as the World Summit on Information and Communication for

---

[2] The Maitland Commission of 1984 was the last time the ITU attempted a broad interpretation of telecommunication (see Independent Commission for Worldwide Telecommunications Development 1984).

[3] Al Gore, opening remarks at the World Telecommunications Development Conference, Buenos Aires, 21 March 1994.

Development, a far more attractive title. Many believe that the outcome of WSIS would have been improved had UNESCO been a co-organizer. The cultural and communication brief of the event, as well as relations with civil society, would have been enhanced in the WSIS process.

Having said this, WSIS has given the regrettable term the "information society" new legs, and it appears that we must live with it for some time. This book is about infusing it with some of its missing meaning, missing not only in its history but in its current incarnation in WSIS.

Inertia in WSIS

The substantive issues raised by the WSIS process include some on which progress is blocked, with powerful governments ensuring that nothing will be done beyond confirming the current status quo as exercised outside of WSIS. Thus a number of "inert" passages in its declaration are intended as no more than markers that certain topics are off-limits.

One passage in particular goes further, in that it not only reaffirms the status quo, but gives the game away as to the direction in which the powers that be would like to move. This passage refers to who owns and controls the rights to use information, which is a key area for the information society. A perverse notion that what we need is the "protection" of intellectual property by means of exclusive monopoly rights given to owners is pursued. A typical formula is:

> Intellectual property protection is essential to encourage the innovation and creativity in the Information Society. However, striking a fair balance between protection of intellectual property, on the one hand, and its use, and knowledge sharing, on the other, is essential to the Information Society. This balance is reflected by protection and flexibilities included in existing Intellectual Property agreements which should be maintained (Paragraph 33, Draft Declaration, 25 September 2003).

Expressed like this, the idea of "intellectual property protection" is nonsense, historically, legally and logically. Intellectual property rights (IPRs), the collective term preferred by industry for copyright, patents, trademarks and so on, are basically monopoly usage privileges granted by society to their creators (later, their "owners") for a given period, before such intellectual creations go into their natural habitat in the public domain. This is proposed as a means (among several possible means) to ensure that the creative process is rewarded and thereby encouraged to continue. Logically, to protect intellectual property thus

3

refers at least equally to ensuring that it finds its way into the public domain, as it does to protecting the monopoly usage-privileges temporarily granted. Furthermore, the "fair balance" to be struck is thus rendered nonsensical: there is simply no balance to be struck between the protection of intellectual property and its use and knowledge sharing. The best way to protect creations of the intellect is to allow them to be used—this constantly reproduces them. Only in exceptional circumstances and for very specific reasons (and there are some) should they be withheld for a period from the public domain.

In fact, this language is logically consistent only if it is presupposed that *the only right recognized is the right of the party that is granted the temporary monopoly usage*. And of course this is the intention (though not necessarily conscious) of those drafting this paragraph. It assumes that only owners have rights over intellectual property, just as only owners have rights over the disposal of a physical object, or indeed of a piece of land. It is this application of exclusive rights associated with physical ownership (that not everyone agrees with in any case—ask any indigenous people) to the rights associated with products of the intellect that is the basic error in this way of thinking. It ignores the several and fundamental differences between intellectual products and physical products, as well as the entire economic and legal history of copyright, patents and other forms of protection since their invention.

But do they care? The goal of the copyright industries, it seems, is to keep the IPR railroad moving, with the World Trade Organization (WTO) as the engine and the World Intellectual Property Organization (WIPO) aboard, trampling earlier agreements, human rights treaties, national laws and any other barriers encountered. The copyright industries, including print, television, press, film, music and software, are simply trying to create facts on the ground, the fact that the only legitimate rights are those of IPR owners. Paragraph 33 simply reveals this fact through the WSIS Declaration process, which has already, whether naively or disingenuously, adopted the language, though at a price.

Jean-Claude Guédon's chapter on scientific and scholarly publications makes the case that the information society is most certainly seen as an opportunity in these circles—an opportunity to diminish even further the possibility of exercising rights to fair use, the term used in treaties for legitimate use of copyrighted material, and to dispense altogether with the obligation of "balance" through the introduction of licensing schemes governed by contract law. It is a compelling example of what happens when a particularly sterile profit maximization dynamic is allowed free reign in an area of special social and development value.

There are other blind spots that, though less revealing, are no less important.

The role of media in the information society is one. In general, the media are given short shrift, appended as a sideshow rather than a central and defining feature. Few would deny that media play an increasingly constitutive role in society, in the self-constitution of the individual through childhood, in the formation of culture, identity and community, and in political and democratic processes. There is even general agreement regarding the need for diversity and freedom of the media. And more and more are beginning to realize that these critical functions of the media are under threat, less in the traditional form of state control (which persists) but in the form of centralization of corporate media control at the global level and the commercialization of media intent only on maximizing profits. Most disturbing are signs of unholy alliances between the media industry and governments (future or actual) in countries as diverse as Italy, Russia, Thailand, the United Kingdom, the United States and Venezuela. But such issues have remained largely unacknowledged in the WSIS process, which goes to pains to avoid ruffling the feathers of powerful corporations and governments. The vital role of the media to service the public interest is glossed over, with public service and non-commercial media barely mentioned.

Another area where substantive progress eludes the WSIS process is the identification and reining in of growing surveillance and control of electronic space. There is growing evidence that the United States, the European Union and many others are using the terrorist attacks on the United States on 11 September 2001 as a pretext to take control of this space. A plethora of hastily drafted laws, treaties and other instruments were pushed through in a climate of fear, and "purpose creep" is extending their implementation beyond even the often draconian original intent. Yet at the surface level, this is barely visible in the WSIS process. While giving a nod to protecting privacy, it talks of promoting "a global culture of cyber-security". It makes little reference to the myriad ways in which commercial and state control of electronic space is growing ever tighter, where civil society, non-commercial and non-military interests are expected to live with the leftovers.

So when it comes to key aspects of any information society, and indeed key elements in encouraging open, creative and free communication within that society, WSIS is so far found wanting. Critical questions are not satisfactorily addressed, around the corralling of intellectual creations into pay-as-you-enter ranches; growing corporate control over the main means of communication; and the gradual but inexorable loss of the freedoms in electronic space.

Several factors explain these lapses. The inexperience and background of the ITU is one. Many governments are also uncertain of whether WSIS is about telecommunications and infrastructure, or about content, media and culture, or solely about development, which has resulted in delegations of very different experience and orientation; some from telecommunication ministries and regulators, others from foreign affairs and aid-related ministries, and a few from substantive areas that can yield specific benefits in health, education and so forth. An understandable general confusion was thus evident especially at the earlier stages of WSIS. But as the confusion clears, a few factors come into relief.

The tendency persists of reducing the "information society" to an ahistorical and technical question of extending telecommunication infrastructure and services, driven by technological innovation. The WSIS process has not led to a deeper exploration of what, if anything, the information society means, but instead to the opposite. Its meaning-deficit is now taken for granted and indeed has become invisible to many.

A number of powerful actors are determined to ensure that WSIS does nothing to question or interrupt the global neoliberal agenda across all sectors. Some even see in it an opportunity to eliminate what they regard as constraints on corporate goals in the digital era as, for instance, in relation to copyright.

There is a risk that, on the coattails of growing unilateralism and fragmentation of global governance structures, some governments may to use this as an occasion to justify increasing surveillance and control over electronic space.

Why "Communicating in the Information Society"?

The selection of contributors to this volume was driven by a keen awareness of the above issues, cast up repeatedly in so many of the forums during the early days of the WSIS process, though we cannot claim to cover them all or from every angle. We believe that the outcome of WSIS can be enhanced if the debate proceeds on the basis that there are shortcomings, and that it is better to face up to them than to ignore them. Our goal required writers of very different styles and backgrounds, some in touch with the WSIS process, others far removed from it. We sought contributors with a Southern as well as a Northern perspective, some from non-governmental organizations (NGOs) and others from academic institutions, each with their own take on the key questions. With somewhat less success we also sought a gender balance, although the importance of the gender issue is acknowledged with a contribution dedicated to it.

It is hoped that such diversity will offer the reader new vantage points from which to view the information society. As WSIS proceeds to 2005 and beyond, we hope to encourage the reader to maintain a critical eye on the question of *which* information society we are building, and who will benefit most from it.

The contributions range from practical, down-to-earth advice on concrete implementation of an information society, through strategies to enrich the potential of WSIS, to philosophical ruminations on the etymology of the central concepts. They all, in one way or another, support the idea that the process of communicating must be at the centre of an information society.

The book begins, quite deliberately, not at the lofty end of the discussion but with some very practical and down-to-earth analysis and advice on priorities in implementing an information society, relevant no matter how we conceptualize it. Dafne Sabanes Plou and William McIver, Jr., focus on two groups of users who are absolutely critical to designing and implementing an information society that empowers instead of divides, and whose needs and potential are so often ignored: women and local communities. Neither group is particularly attractive to commercial interests, yet the extent to which their needs are addressed and their potential realized is probably as good a measure as any of the sincerity of claims for an inclusive information society. Building on the Beijing Platform for Action, Sabanes Plou makes the case for gender mainstreaming in WSIS. Failure to act positively will replicate existing problems in emerging spheres, further embedding discrimination and exclusion. McIver lays down the principles and practice of "community informatics", concerned with the design, deployment and management of information systems by communities themselves, designed to solve their own problems.

Light is cast on the media blind-spot in two very different but complementary contributions, underlining the powerful dynamic of "traditional media" and pointing to WSIS as an opportunity. James Deane and his co-authors offer a timely reminder of that "other information revolution" in the countries and regions of the global South. The frequent funnelling of debate on the information society into the development potential of the Internet ignores what has been happening in television, newspapers and radio, whose impact is more pervasive and potentially even more far-reaching. Wresting control of much media from the clutches of self-perpetuating and oppressive governments has been a major positive development, weakened or swept aside by a media liberalization maelstrom that has wrought massive and deep change almost everywhere. Yet a new set of challenges, perhaps even more intractable, is emerging as commercially driven media begin to drown out or obstruct the emergence of public interest media. Journalists and media activists, who have fought for years to escape government control, are rightly suspicious of government-led policy responses. Yet the need for action to place the public interest at the centre is pressing—to do nothing is not an option. The authors identify a key role for civil society actors in terms of pressuring both media industry and governments to build a regulatory and policy space that pursues the sectarian interests of neither group, and instead serves the broader public interest.

Marc Raboy follows this by exploring what is needed to build such an enabling framework at the global level. After briefly framing media in a historical context, he focuses on the last decade or two, pointing out that media issues are increasingly transnational and hence must be the subject of international conventions and other instruments. Taking the UNESCO World Commission on Culture and Development and the follow-up intergovernmental conference as a key event, and as a lesson in the balance of forces, he situates WSIS as a direct successor. Offering an opportunity to broker the interests of the state, the broadcasting industries and civil society, he argues that WSIS can be, if not a milestone, then at least a moment in the establishment of the new global media framework within which media can flourish and contribute to democratic public life and human development. He notes that such a framework can both enhance freedom of expression *and* promote in practice the right to communicate.

Cees Hamelink addresses directly the issue of the right to communicate—a controversial one in WSIS—and makes a case for it. He introduces the concept of informational developments, denoting the growing significance of information and related technologies and dynamics, and points out that the international community over the years has established a broad set of human rights standards for how informational developments should interact with society as a whole. The problem is twofold. First, the existing standards are simply not implemented in practice—people have only very limited means to vindicate their information-related human rights. And second, current human rights provisions focus exclusively on information and ignore communication. And if anything characterizes the momentous changes of the last half-century, it is the need to encourage and democratize communication as an interactive and participative process. He suggests several remedial roadmaps, and concludes with a call on WSIS participants, governmental and non-governmental, to broadcast a strong signal of their intention to mobilize around achieving the right to communicate. In between, the main body of the chapter covers some very valuable terrain, identifying the full panoply of human rights and instruments that relate to informational developments, sorted under technological, cultural, political and economic dimensions, as well as the means for and obstacles to their enforcement.

Jean-Claude Guédon's point, mentioned above, on scientific and scholarly publications is in fact just one strand in a much more complex and layered study. It proceeds from an examination of the sometimes contradictory evolving relationships between scientists, the creation of symbolic values, the institutions that translate into various rewards, librarians, and, at the fulcrum, commercial publishers. He identifies how since the late 1960s, a narrow, conventional and profit-maximizing trend has created an institutional elite and highly profitable business through ever more tightly policed gateways for accessing scientific knowledge. Digitization threatens to change that, but the question is whether it will be for better or worse. Against the traditional approach that would deepen control is a free or open-access approach promoted by civil society. Simplifying a nuanced argument, such an approach requires a sustainable model—which implies some borrowing from the "business" approach to the information society and an alliance with more progressive publishers. The plot thickens further when he generalizes the argument to the area of free and open source software, and to discussion of the commons and the public domain in general. This in turn leads to the claim that drawing a clear distinction between infrastructure provision and service activities, and developing strategies around it, is more fundamental than the commercial/non-profit dichotomy. His ultimate conclusion (hence we can decipher the title of his contribution) is that the tendency of the phrase information society to convey the idea that social problems are best resolved "scientifically"—away from the fray of politics—must be overturned, and that civil society, with its focus firmly on the social and political, is best placed to lead this. The capacity of civil society to network in a distributed manner is what is needed to exploit the fullest potential of the information society.

Finally, posing as a (highly select) glossary of the information society, Antonio Pasquali's contribution returns from a different vantage point to many of the same points. His first chosen term is "human relations", an apparently self-explanatory term that he deploys to restate the need to resist the strong tendency of reducing the information society to a purely technical or economic discourse. Taking us back to the etymological roots in ancient history, he says: "The words communication or information always, and necessarily, refer to the essence of community and human relations". If WSIS allies itself with the current trend of moving decision-making powers from consensus-based bodies of the United Nations into power-based bodies such as the International Monetary Fund (IMF) and World Bank—and it seems set to—then that key domain will favour technological and economic, rather than social, approaches to issues. He rescues other terms from their vague and ambiguous usages which suit discourse that reduces social development to a technical matter. In arguing for rigorous and judicious use of "deontologies", "morals" and "ethics", he is at the same time laying the groundwork for a rights-based approach. Then he tackles "informing" and "communicating" together, concluding that while they are inseparable, the latter must always be chosen over the former, instrumentally in terms of favouring certain media as well as sociopolitically in terms of choosing reciprocity, pluralism and democracy over, for instance, efficiency. A robust defence of communication rights is followed by an interpretation of its supposed erstwhile mortal enemy, free flow of information. The latter sits uncomfortably alongside the reality of a communication superpower that alone can turn off the information tap of others; the free-flow of paedophilia and pornography; growing global surveillance; and the violation of the new holy grail of intellectual property rights. He still manages to defend free flow in a reconciliation with communication rights as "a beautiful positive principle that we must defend in conferences and in real life, though we must unceasingly denounce abuses of dominant positions committed in its name". Then "access" and "participation" are rendered mutually reinforcing as, respectively, the capacity to receive, and the capacity to produce and transmit.

He signs off with his account of the term information society. We leave this to the reader, adding that the chapter rounds off the book nicely but could equally well serve as the introduction.

References

Independent Commission for Worldwide Telecommunications Development. 1985. **The Missing Link**. Report of the Independent Commission for Worldwide Telecommunications Development (chaired by Sir Donald Maitland). ITU, Geneva.

UNESCO. 1996a. **The Challenges of the Information Highways: The Role of UNESCO**. Decisions Adopted by the Executive Board at its 150th session, 16 August. UNESCO, Paris.

————. 1996b. **Decisions Adopted by the Executive Board at its 150th session** (Paris, 14–31 October). UNESCO, Paris.

What About Gender Issues in the Information Society?

Dafne Sabanes Plou

Abstract

Despite the work of many gender and information and communication technology (ICT) advocates from different stakeholders around the world, scant reference is made to several critical gender and ICT issues when information society issues are discussed at any level. A fully informed gender perspective should encompass the diversity and specificity of concerns of different sectors of women both in the North and in the South. This chapter seeks to emphasize that the principle of gender mainstreaming should be adopted when discussing women's role in the information society, taking into account their communication rights and their demand for full participation in ICT development more widely. This includes challenging their portrayal in the new media, considering their labour rights in the ICT work market, making radical changes in education policies, ensuring women's participation in science and technology, encouraging their access to decision making and working toward equitable redistribution of available resources in the ICT field.

ICTs are one of the fields where gender relations take place, sometimes reinforcing old roles, sometimes changing them, but making us aware that the social and cultural context has an impact in ICT development and use, and that it is not possible to think of new communication technologies as gender neutral. The absence of women's voices and perspectives in the information society also shows us that power relations in the new media replicate in many ways those in conventional media. The globalization of communications produces new challenges and impacts that must be considered in relation to gender equality. Women's access to information sources and communication channels are crucial if they are to attain democratic participation, respect for their human rights and an equal voice in the public sphere.

Convinced that ICTs can be an empowering tool for resistance, social mobilization and development in the hands of people and organizations working for freedom and justice, the women's movement has become an active participant in the preparatory process for the World Summit on the Information Society (WSIS). Women are struggling to ensure that gender is a cross-cutting principle when discussing ICT policies at all levels, international, regional and local. They encourage democratization of policy processes within the ICT sector, including use of ICT tools to support this process, and to formulate and implement ICT policy using principles of openness and fair participation. This collective participation in the communications field is also an essential element for women's empowerment.

Introduction

Despite the work of many gender and information and communication technology (ICT) advocates from different stakeholders around the world, scant reference is made to several critical gender and ICT issues when information society issues are discussed at any level. A fully informed gender perspective should encompass the diversity and specificity of concerns of different categories of women both in the North and in the South. This chapter aims to emphasize the fact that a principle of gender mainstreaming should be adopted when discussing women's role in the information society, taking into account their communications rights and their demand for full participation in ICT development, which includes challenging their portrayal in the new media, considering their labour rights in the ICT work market, making radical changes in their education and participation in science and technology, encouraging women's access to decision making, and the equitable redistribution of available resources in the ICT field.

One of the achievements of the global women's movement was the consolidation of Section J on Women and the Media in the Beijing Platform for Action during the preparatory meetings to the United Nations Fourth Conference on Women. The relation between the media, new communication technologies and the advancement of women became one of the critical areas of concern discussed during the conference, thanks to the activism and efforts of thousands of women worldwide. They felt that the lack of gender sensitivity in the media and in the emerging ICTs had to be addressed in order to involve women in an expanding industry and field of knowledge with an increasing social and cultural impact and influence in development policies.

The two strategic objectives stated in the Platform for Action in 1995 have become the basis for women's advocacy work in communications and their struggle for the advancement of women in a field where they had felt excluded and manipulated. These objectives are:

- Strategic objective J.1: Increase the participation of women in expression and decision making in and through the media and new technologies of communication.
- Strategic objective J.2: Promote a balanced and non-stereotyped portrayal of women in the media.

Eight years later, the need to reaffirm these aims is urgent as the rapid growth of telecommunications, digital, cable and satellite technologies, the emphasis on speed and the miniaturization of technologies that enable people to carry last generation communication devices in their pockets, frame people's behaviours, thinking and way of living (Gill 2003).

New communication technologies are a vehicle of a process of globalization that takes place on unequal terms, and that often increases social and economic inequality, between and within countries and people; at the same time, these technologies can be an empowering tool for resistance, social mobilization and development in the hands of people and organizations working for freedom and justice.

Gender relations in ICTs, whether they reinforce old roles or change them, highlight the impact of the social and cultural context on ICT development and use, and the fact that new communication technologies are not gender blind. The absence of women's voices and perspectives in the information society also shows that gender power relations in the new media replicate in many ways what has happened in conventional media.

A human-rights approach is framing the debate on women's rights in the information society. The women's movement believes that women's rights to information and communication can enhance opportunities for democratic governance, the exercise of citizenship and full participation in development for all (UNCSW 2003a:2, paragraph 3). On the other hand, to focus the debate and the political activism in and for ICTs within a frame of human rights and human development encourages women's involvement. When women associate ICTs with the struggle against poverty, unemployment, violence, racism, discrimination and the consolidation of democracy and economic growth, their participation in ICT programmes and policies gains force, impact and social relevance (Bonder 2002).

Between 1998 and 2000, the World Association for Christian Communication (WACC) organized a series of regional conferences around the world on Gender and Communication Policy. Communicators from women's and feminist organizations met to discuss their role in the information society and called for making women's right to communicate a reality in order to construct civil processes and strengthen democracy. Participants in the Latin American regional conference considered that for women's right to communicate to be made effective and real, it must include:

- freedom of expression and the free circulation of ideas;
- the right of access to information and the right to be properly informed;

13

- the right of access to communication channels as sources of information, as expressions of self-identity, and as active subjects in the construction of democratic citizenship;
- the right for women to have their own channels and to produce communication messages;
- the right to count on legal frameworks, and economic and technological conditions for women's development in this sphere; and
- the right to participate at decision-making levels in communication organizations both public and private (WACC 1998:5).

Could ICTs Open New Channels for Women's Participation and Decision Making?

Is it possible to use Internet communications and other ICT tools to modify the situation of women's citizenship and the standing of their rights? Could we say that ICTs open new channels for participation and decision making in the social and public spheres? Past experience tells us that access to the media can modify the power structure in society. Control over knowledge and information is an important source of power and that is where the media are relevant. It is always striking that women, who make up half the world's population, have to struggle to get their voices in the media. According to a feminist, "Globalization also means patriarchy becoming more powerful, more entrenched" (Bhasin 1994:5).

One of the most successful women's information networks in Latin America was born out of an urgent need to produce news and information with a gender perspective to strengthen the national women's movement, affirm women's right to communicate, and break the dominating discourse in the media that distorted the real issues in the debate on reproductive rights. In 1992 the Mexican women's movement was starting to participate in the preparatory process for the UN Conference on Population and Development that would take place in Cairo, Egypt, in two years' time. It was evident that information was concentrated in only one place, Mexico City, and strongly influenced by a few voices, mainly belonging to patriarchal power structures wanting to keep their control on women's bodies and their decisions on their sexual and reproductive health. Women's organizations in other Mexican states felt isolated from all the information generated in the women's movement, the debates, political analysis, up-to-date news and the planning of future strategies and actions. Women could not afford communication by telephone or fax, and the post was too slow. A feminist activist, who was working at the time in the state of Yucatan, felt that isolation and lack of communication were weakening all initiatives. The need to link women's organizations nationwide became a priority, and she decided to launch the creation of an electronic communication network. With a minimal infrastructure and some previous training on the use of electronic mail, a group of women started Modemmujer, an information and communication network that aimed to strengthen women's participation in this process. During the first years of work, in combination with well-established technologies (radio, fax, print media) and repackaging information available online, Modemmujer was able to bridge the distance between women's organizations and decision-making processes (Sabanes Plou 2000).

The need to strengthen their political participation encouraged Indonesian women's activity in the field of ICTs. In 1998, when women's organizations that had been demanding the end of the Suharto regime came together to work for democracy in their country, they saw that in order to influence the new political process and have a voice in decisions on the country's future, they had to build their own communication strategy. They wanted to share their ideas and proposals with as many other women activists as possible. With women's organizations spread across the many islands of the extensive archipelago, it was crucial to identify a means of distributing and exchanging information speedily at the lowest cost. A Web-based free mailing list service became a feasible option. The Rumpun email Perempuan (Women's Mailing List) was launched in July 1998 with a handful of subscribers, which had multiplied by 10 in two years. The mailing list covered action alerts, announcements, news clips, statements, press releases and discussion topics strictly on women's issues and activism. By putting into practice their right to communicate, Indonesian women were able to build together strong positions on issues of national interest (Buntarian 2000).

How can women better the development of their communities or play an informed role in public life, without access to pluralistic information, the means of public expression and sharing knowledge? How can women work toward a new geopolitical order governed by norms of peace and mutual respect without channels of communication for dialogue and exchange of information? When ICT policy is linked to women's human rights issues, as stated in the Beijing Platform for Action, it can be seen that ICTs offer a potential for the defence and advancement of these rights. Women worldwide are using ICTs to monitor the promotion and protection of their human rights, using the Internet to denounce violations, send alerts and campaign for their rights. They are also using ICTs to facilitate communication among organizations, thus empowering the networks that work to ensure that women have equal rights. Gaining access to legal information (law and other legal instruments, new legislation and legal recourse, and accountability procedures) via the Internet enables them to discuss human rights issues with authority and thus further their struggle against any sort of discrimination either under law or practice (IWTC 2003).

In a successful use of the Internet in campaigns against violence on women, the Kenya-based African Women's Development and Communication Network (FEMNET), launched the Men to Men Initiative in 2001 to mark the Sixteen Days of Activism Against Violence on Women. The campaign targeted men to promote male involvement and action to combat gender-based violence at the regional level in Africa. In Costa Rica, Radio FIRE (Feminist Interactive Radio Endeavour), the first Web-based feminist radio station in Latin America, organized a 25-hour marathon in 2000, broadcasting a special programme on 25 November, the International Day for the Elimination of Violence against Women. FIRE asked women from all over the world to contribute material for the programme and invited other radio stations worldwide to link in simultaneous broadcasting. For this effort, Radio FIRE received the Peace Builders Award during the IV World Encounter on Non-Violence (WomenAction 2000 2001).

The globalization of communications produces new challenges and impacts that need to be considered in relation to gender equality. Women's access to information sources and interchange channels are crucial for their democratic participation, the respect for their human rights and for intervening with an equal voice in the public sphere.

Gender Issues in the Information Society

"Old" patterns in the "new" media?

The "new" ICTs already reflect many of the gender patterns (in relation to power, values, exclusion and so on) that have been evident for decades in relation to the "old" media. Indeed these patterns cannot be divorced from patterns of gender relations in society as a whole. Neither old nor new media by themselves can offer solutions to this problem. Their structures reflect much wider social, economic and political relations in which women tend to be marginalized. For instance, the new media—just like the old ones—are primarily vehicles for the transmission of ideas, images and information. An issue for women, in relation to both old and new, is who decides on access, content and control. In essence, many of the issues are the same as they have always been since they refer to questions of power and power relations in the context of gender.

At present, women's organizations feel that, although more women with university degrees are in the communication field and more grassroots women are trained in communication skills, little has been gained when it comes to access to decision-making bodies, breaking the glass ceiling in private or public communication companies, or even taking part in policy making at the local or national levels. During the Beijing+5 revision process, women communicators in Latin America issued a document entitled *We Met Our Commitments, Did You?* (WomenAction 2000 2000) in which they described the achievements of the women's movement in the region in meeting Section J objectives. They also questioned governments and the private sector about their efforts and achievements in the area, which were very limited at the time and have not advanced much since then.

Although there are thousands of Web pages belonging to women's organizations or alternative media that give space to women's issues and concerns, newspapers and news agencies using the Internet maintain the same policies as in their print versions. Technology has changed, but the fundamentals remain the same. Women's absence from information is crucial because today the media play a decisive role in the building of the public agenda. The media highlight certain agendas or issues by prioritizing some and ignoring others, or by conferring a voice or an image on some social actors and not on others. As a consequence, the media (and its presence on the Internet) disseminate an image of the world in which women are portrayed in a discriminatory and disempowering manner, or simply do not exist. Their invisibility as social actors results in the fact that their viewpoints and concerns are under-represented in the debate that defines the public policies that rule our societies.

Women's portrayal in the media is an urgent challenge that needs to be addressed across all regions and all types of media (Spears et al. 2000). There is still a sexist and stereotyped portrayal of women in the media, and there is a need to work with media professions to create a media environment that promotes gender equality by fostering positive images of women and women's views. Several women's organizations in different parts of the world have developed strategies for lobbying and advocacy in the area of gender-based violence. In 1998, the Tanzania Media Women's Association (TAMWA) organized workshops to sensitize journalists as part of a campaign to lobby for amendments to the Law of Marriage Act which, according to research commissioned by TAMWA, condones domestic violence, denying women and children their rights. The workshops mobilized media coverage and helped women in their advocacy for review of the law. In Nepal, Sancharika Samuha (Forum of Women Communicators) has focused on using the media to address violations of women's human rights. They challenged the mainstream media campaign against granting women the same rights to inherit property as men. The group was able to place articles on equal property rights in the press, produce and air radio jingles and television advertising, distribute posters and hold workshops with journalists and

NGOs. As a result there is a new awareness among journalists and the general public of women's side of the story (Gallagher 2001).

Another issue to consider is that the image of women on the Internet often reproduces a model that reinforces stereotypes and prejudices that already exist in society and shape the role of women as social actors and their capacity to influence public life and in the discussion of public issues. The Internet is not free from sexist images and rhetoric. It is also being used increasingly to spread violent pornography and paedophilia, and for the trafficking of women and girls. The women's movement believes that policies that seek to redress this use of the Internet should under no circumstances be used for centralized control of all other content development on the Web (GSWG 2003). There should be policies to encourage the corporate sector to eliminate the violation of women's rights online and the Internet service providers to undertake efforts to minimize pornography, trafficking and all forms of gender-based violence online by re-examining their own editorial/user policies from a gender perspective (IWTC 2003).

Defining ICT development from a gender perspective

Access to ICTs is typically divided along traditional lines of development resulting in unequal access that has become known as the digital divide or digital exclusion. This divide is often characterized by high levels of access to technologies—including the Internet—in developed countries, while infrastructure in less developed nations is at a very low level due to problems of poverty, lack of resources, illiteracy and low levels of education. Access for people in the developing world continues to be marginal because of the high cost of connectivity resulting in their exclusion from the emerging global system being built around information and knowledge. Women are particularly marginalized since the majority have no buying power and no access to modern means of communication. That women are in the deepest end of the digital divide has been the main message of gender advocates working in ICT development (APC WNSP 2001).

A key priority that has guided the women's movement in the last decade is the intersectional approach. This takes into account the diverse needs and perspectives of women coming from different geopolitical, historical, class-based, racial and ethnic contexts. The women's movement considers that strategies and solutions for achieving gender equality, including ICT development, must strike at the root of unequal power relations—not just between men and women, but more funda-mentally between rich and poor, North and South, urban and rural, empowered and marginalized (GSWG 2003).

Women are under-represented in all ICT decision-making structures, and ICT policy currently rests on the assumption that information and communication technologies are gender neutral and that women must adapt to technologies, rather than have ICT policy specifically formulated to meet the interests and needs of women. It is becoming clear that without active intervention by gender activists, new ICTs are unlikely to make a positive contribution to gender equality, sustainable development and democratization of communications.

Experts in gender and ICT issues consider that "there is substantial evidence to support the contention that policy making in technological fields ignores gender issues" (Hafkin 2002:3). Gender analysis has advanced substantially in social and economic fields, but is rarely used when it comes to the consideration of information and communication technologies. Gender differences and disparities have been ignored in policies and programmes dealing with the development and dissemination of improved technologies. As a result, women have benefited less from, and been disadvantaged more by, technological advances. Women, therefore, need to be actively involved in the definition, design and development of new technologies in order to avoid new forms of exclusion and ensure that women and girls have equal access and opportunities in respect of the developments of science and technology (APC WNSP 2001).

An evaluation of gender relations in a telecentre in an underprivileged neighbourhood found that parents did not want their children, especially girls, to go to the telecentre, because they considered it a "den of ruffians"—the telecentre had a special programme for out-of-school youth. Less than 2 per cent of users were girls. Evaluators saw that these girls hardly used the computers. Instead, they sat beside the boys and watched how they surfed the Internet, played games and worked on the computer. All of the trainers, managers and technical support staff of the telecentre were males; there were two female members of the staff who provided administrative and logistical support. The management realized that the lack of participation of girls in the telecentre was indicative of the initiative's failure in meeting the needs of the community and young people. New programmes and services for girls and young women are being planned to overcome this situation. This is an example that should be looked at in a wider context: what should policy makers do to ensure that the gender gap will be closed in the ICT field?

Educational programmes fostering the use of ICTs among women, particularly girls and young women, are highly instrumental and gender insensitive. There is a need to develop educational projects that stimulate critical and creative skills, and encourage greater participation of women in the design and production of new technologies. Lack of acknowledgement of gender inequities in all the social areas, and in the technological and scientific fields in particular, is responsible for the absence of gender-fair policies in this area. Many women lack the educational and cultural capital to administer the immense flow of information that the Internet offers and that cannot be provided through mere access to computers. Intelligent and selective connection demands much more time than women usually have, because of family and work duties. The lack of infrastructure and technological skills prevent women from becoming producers of new content and formats that are attractive and powerful from the communicational point of view (Bonder 2002).

> Education is the single most important factor for increasing the ability of women and girls to participate fully in the new information society at all levels. This requires a comprehensive set of interventions raging from quality public education for all, through scientific and technological education and research (Global Unions 2003).

Unfortunately, several studies show that, when it comes to computer studies, teachers pay more attention, and dedicate more time and encouragement, to boys rather than girls. It has been observed that most girls feel tense when they have to work with computers in the presence of other people, especially of boys. This has to do with the pressure from boys, who sometimes make the girls feel ridiculous in order to dominate or show off their own skills. It is also known that male students in university computer labs often send pornographic messages to their female classmates or even post the messages on the walls. In spite of protests against this kind of sexual harassment, university authorities have not put in place any policy measures to stop this behaviour. If girls and young women show little interest in computer studies, is it because of some sort of "natural" technophobia or is it because a male-dominated cyberculture acts to reject them, or even to offend them? (Bonder 2001).

> Sometimes, collateral cultural factors, other cultural attitudes based in gender bias, and not the immediate gender identification of technology use, prevent young girls and women from accessing and using ICTs (Hafkin 2003:5).

Research carried out by the Commission on Technology, Gender and Teacher Education of the American Association of University Women (AAUW) Educational Foundation came to the conclusion that girls are critical of the computer culture, not computer-phobic. Sherry Turkle, professor of sociology at the Massachusetts Institute of Technology (MIT) and co-chair of the commission, said that results showed that instead of trying to make girls fit into the existing computer culture, the computer culture must become more inviting to girls. Some of the commission's major conclusions show that girls find programming classes tedious and dull, computer games too boring, redundant and violent, and computer career options uninspiring. Girls also show clear and strong ideas about the kinds of games they would design: games that feature simulation, strategy and interaction. The girls' critique points to a more inclusive computer culture that embraces multiple interests and backgrounds and that reflects the current ubiquity of technology in all aspects of life. In this framework, to be technologically literate requires a set of critical skills, concepts and problem-solving abilities. Based on its findings, the commission is working on a new definition of computer literacy and equity. It acknowledges that obtaining gender equity in this field means using technology proactively, being able to interpret the information that technology makes available, understanding design concepts and being a lifelong learner of technology. In its recommendations, the commission states that girls should be educated to be ICT designers and not just users. Educators and parents should help girls imagine themselves early in life as designers and producers of technology, stimulating deeper interest in ICTs and providing opportunities for girls to express their technological imaginations (AAUW 2000).

Many of the concepts underlined by the AAUW are evident in feminist uses of ICT. In feminist use, women are not seen as consumers; rather, they are encouraged to develop content where analytical skills, computer concepts and innovative uses of technology play an important role. Women's electronic networks have created opportunities for women to learn about ICT tools in order to maintain dynamic relationships, which empower and allow them to build strategies and policies for the advancement of their rights.

"This issue of the role of women in creating the knowledge embodied in ICT networks is a key educational one" (Kirkup 2002:11, see paragraph 1.8.3). Women in their daily electronic networking have been able to create multiple points of access to ICT literacy. These practices have allowed them to recognize themselves in the culture of computing and have helped them to overcome barriers created by gender bias. Women have found an instrument for their empowerment and emancipation in communication technologies. The Internet has allowed the voice of ordinary citizens and organizations lacking strong financial resources to be heard. As the Internet provides a unique public sphere where decisions that shape people's lives can be freely debated and considered, small groups and individuals, men and women—previously working in isolation from one another—have been able to communicate, network, share information and prepare actions in ways they were never able to before (APC WNSP 2001). While more women are now taking part in this new technological practice, the dangers of deeper exclusion for those who do not have access to ICTs are, unfortunately, only too real for the majority of women, especially in developing countries.

In Africa, Latin America and Southeast Asia, community telecentres have become friendly environments for women's access to ICTs. The use of open source software with low technical requirements and training in local languages encourages women's interest in ICT access in areas and social groups with scant technological resources. Women can find opportunities there to merge newer technologies with other technologies in which they have experience (such as radio and video), as well as indigenous and traditional forms of communications (WomenWatch and WomenAction 1999). In community telecentres women can be trained not only in technical aspects, but also in the strategic uses of digital technologies for social change. In one of the telecentres that Chasquinet sponsors in a neighbourhood outside Quito, Ecuador, women came together to organize a micro-business that would help them to market their production of marmalade. The fact that they learned how to use computers to organize a marketing plan and advertise their products on the Web was only one side of the experience. They were also able to create a community of interests and exchange, paying attention to other needs in the neighbourhood that were demanding their participation. "The best ICT projects are those that are not introduced as ICT projects to give women access or get them connected, but are integrated seamlessly into those women's lives and concerns" (Gill 2003:7).

Overcoming language barriers and lack of local content have also been a concern when encouraging women's use of ICTs in rural and poor communities. The high number of illiterate women and the fact that most of them work in the informal economy to provide for their families puts forward an important challenge for those working in ICT development with a gender perspective. An interesting experiment in the Nakaseke Multipurpose Telecentre in Luweero District, central Uganda, showed that technology by itself could not have achieved the expected results without an accompanying tool produced in the local language, Luganda, and with content geared to women's needs and interests. The use of a CD-ROM in Luganda to enhance women's skills in the economic field has opened the way for women participating in the local telecentre to learn more, undergo training and train others in the use of this new tool. Anastasia Namisango, a 70-year-old woman who has become a trainer and successful poultry producer, thanks to the use of ICTs, said in an interview that she teaches other women and men how to use the CD-ROM because "I don't want to see women crying about poverty when they have all the resources" (Women's Worlds 2002). The CD-ROM entitled *Ideas for Making Money* was developed by the International Women's Tribune Centre (IWTC), based in the United States, with the support of the United Nations Educational, Scientific and Cultural Organization (UNESCO), and the East and Southern Africa Office of the International Development Research Centre (IDRC).

ICTs and women's working lives

ICTs offer new job opportunities for women in communication centers, telemarketing, mobile telephones and the software industry. Thousands of women now work in data processing, for example. Women also have good self-employment opportunities as teleworkers, using ICTs from their homes. In developing countries, ICTs even alter the pattern of production in the informal sector, which recruits women in large numbers. According to a report from the International Labour Organization (ILO 2001), the role of women in the digital era is concentrated in the area of information and online work. Women's income in this new economy is higher than normal. However, gender discrimination exists, because men usually get the better positions and women carry out less-skilled tasks. The report notes that the diffusion of the technologies is according to skills and therefore accompanied by rising wage inequalities. Although there is pay inequality between those with ICT skills and those without, pay polarization also exists within ICT use itself and this polarization is often gender-based.

But the gap is also present among women themselves. Class, education and age restrain most women from getting higher positions in the ICT job market. Women also complain about working conditions in the area of telemarketing, call centres and data banks, where they are the majority. They are concerned about possible health hazards brought about by repetitive work in high-pressure working environments. And while wages and conditions of work in call centres appear to vary widely, the worst of them have been called the "sweatshops of the digital era". Teleworking has also raised some concerns. While it has created new employment opportunities for women, it could also have potential negative effects on the quality of working life. Women could find themselves excluded from better career possibilities because, instead of finding a balance between family and paid work, they could get caught in a difficult situation with new demands on top of the old. The ILO report recommends the formulation of adequate policies to protect the labour rights of women workers in the ICT industry.

When formulating policies on ICT work, the challenges that women face in adjusting to the new demands, and their responses and organizing strategies when confronted with such challenges, should be taken into account. According to Swasti Mitter (Mitter et al. 1995), radical thinking about training in ICTs that takes into account the obstacles that gender and class pose to a trainee will be essential in using human potential to the full. Women play an unconscious role in reproducing the gendered nature of society and of the wider ICT sector. They still need to overcome internal barriers and conquer technophobia. In order to do this, women need to maintain a political perspective (Hafkin 2002). However, important progress is being made in the "soft" side of technical knowledge, such as communications and user-producer interaction. Women in this sector are doing much better than in traditional technical professional work, like engineering. Positive advances could enable women to achieve greater economic and social opportunities.

Working for engendered ICT policies

One of the most important points of intervention for women working in ICT is the policy arena. ICT policies at the international, regional and national levels must be addressed in order to create an appropriate technological culture and adequate policies for women. Without a gender perspective on the issue, new ICTs will continue to develop at a rate and in a direction that is bound to alienate women.

There is a lack of acknowledgement on the part of governments of gender inequities in social areas, and particularly in the technological and scientific fields. As a result, there is an absence of gender-fair public policies. There are very few gender activists, researchers and educators involved in this field, and those who are working on the issue have not really co-ordinated their efforts, which could help them influence national and regional policies. Taking these facts into account, during the United Nations Division for the Advancement of Women (UNDAW) Expert Group Meeting in Seoul, Korea, in 2002, it was agreed that two things are crucial when working on ICT policies with a gender perspective:

- sensitizing policy makers to gender issues, and
- sensitizing gender advocates to information technology issues (Hafkin 2002).

With these two needs in mind, women should work for gender representation in the power and decision-making arenas of ICTs, in ICT privacy and security as it impacts gender, and gender representation in the ICT industry and labour force. A gender perspective should be present when working on policies in technological fields; tackling issues such as access to infrastructure, social and cultural issues; financial resources; content that meets women's information needs; advocacy/ networking activities; and participation in business, entertainment and education. The gender gap will be bridged:

- if women also have the means to access knowledge necessary to be actors in development, and not just objects of development;
- if women and women's concerns are present at all levels of development, from grassroots to board rooms and cabinet tables; and

- if gender dimensions and consequences for all decisions are taken into account, including those issues that are not obviously women's issues (Malcom 1999).

The Asian Women's Resource Exchange (AWORC) was formed in 1998 to respond to the challenge posed by the need to access ICT knowledge and encourage women's key participation in development policies. Since then, AWORC has grown to be an active and energetic Internet-based network of women's organizations and resource centres, developing co-operative approaches and partnerships to increase access to, and applications of, new information and communication technologies for women's social and economic development. In 1999, AWORC held the first Asian Women's Electronic Network Training (WENT99) in Sookmyung Women's University in Korea. More regional workshops were held in the following years and in 2002, WENT national workshops took place in Malaysia and the Philippines. WENT regional trainers have started to work with nationally based women's organizations and ICT trainers to develop and run WENT-modelled training workshops, which are designed to reach out to women and organizations interested in raising their capacity to use ICT for their social action and advocacy work. The workshops also aim to enhance women's training skills and their capacity to develop and run ICT training for nationally based and/or community-based ICT training for women and their organizations. A similar event took place in Africa for the first time, with a WENT workshop organized by the Association for Progressive Communications (APC) Africa-Women in Cape Town, South Africa, in April 2003. Participants and trainers worked together to share skills, and discuss gender and ICT policy issues. Networks such as AWORC and APC Africa-Women, equipped with working experience as well as a theoretical understanding of women and ICT, are ready to participate in the ICT policy development to ensure that these policies fully adhere to the needs and realities of women (Cinco and Garcia 2000).

Karat, a coalition of women's NGOs in Central and Eastern Europe (CEE), is leading an ICT project to better understand women's economic rights and the impact of economics, employment and social policies on women. The project aims to produce information and initiate debates on women's economic rights and the gender impact of policies to improve gender standards, and their implementation in the CEE. Karat members say that, while the enlargement of the European Union has been getting a lot of coverage in the CEE media, there has been little civil society information and understanding of the enlargement process, little citizen involvement, and no organized women's participation to address women's rights and gender integration. They believe that CEE women's groups need to become more active in addressing women's rights in the context of European integration, and that there is a strategic opportunity for partnership with European Union women's organizations to reinforce the commitment to gender equality standards. With the support of the United Nations Development Fund for Women (UNIFEM), Karat has been able to create an active network that shares electronic news reports and joint bulletins, teaches advocacy by example, disseminates information about gender equality and EU accession, and produces alternative reports and information kits for parliamentarians and the media. They have also been able to hold training workshops for activists from CEE countries (Karat 2002).

Mainstreaming Gender in the WSIS Process

Convinced that ICTs can be an empowering tool for resistance, social mobilization and development in the hands of people and organizations working for freedom and justice, the women's movement has become an active participant in the preparatory process for the World Summit on the Information Society (WSIS). By participating in the discussion of the main documents, it has contributed relevant input to the debate that civil society encourages around the main WSIS topics.

> The information society should be based on principles of gender equity, human dignity and gender justice, and should be geared towards the eradication of gender disparities in education and training, socio-economic status, civic and political decision-making (APC WNSP 2003).

One of the main demands by women's movements has been the adoption of a principle of gender mainstreaming throughout all aspects of the WSIS Declaration and Action Plan. This has not happened, and women's organizations working in the WSIS process want official documents to recognize the centrality of gender inequality to the broader social inequality.

Women's organizations are also concerned about women's participation in the decision-making processes on ICTs policies. They know that unequal power relations and other social and cultural aspects have contributed to differential access, participation, control over and access to resources and status for men and women. They would like WSIS to take into account a number of commitments made by governments in the Beijing Platform for Action, like article 13 in the Beijing Declaration that reads:

Women's empowerment and their full participation on the basis of equality in all spheres of society, including participation in decision-making process and access to power, are fundamental for the achievement of equality, development and peace (UN 2001).

Discussions and policy development on gender equality on the one hand, and on ICT and media and communication systems on the other, tend to be carried out in parallel and are almost never interconnected at the international, or even the national, level. ICT decision making is more commonly considered a technical rather than a political or social issue. In March 2003, the UN Commission for the Status of Women discussed the issues of participation and access of women to the media and information and communications technologies. Government representatives encouraged a high participation of women in WSIS and reiterated the strategic objectives of the Beijing Declaration and Platform for Action and the outcome document, *Gender Equality, Development and Peace in the Twenty-First Century*, that resulted from the UN General Assembly Special Session to review the Beijing conference (Beijing+5) in 2000 (UN 2001). They also recalled the UN Millennium Declaration, which

resolves to promote gender equality and the empowerment of women as effective ways to combat poverty, hunger and disease and to stimulate development that is truly sustainable, and to ensure that the benefits of new technologies, especially information and communications technologies, are available for all (UN 2000).

The Commission urged governments to take action, to prioritize

the integration of gender perspectives and ensure women's early and full participation when developing and implementing national policies, legislations, programmes, projects, strategies and regulatory and technical instruments in the area of information and communications technologies (ICT) and media and communications (UNCSW 2003b:2).

It also recognized the need to build constituencies for gender equality in ICT developments within civil society and governments. Monitoring and evaluation of such developments should also include gender impact analysis.

But no policies can be planned or implemented without proper financing. Women's organizations recommend in their proposals that WSIS should

- develop and implement gender planning and budgeting guidelines for the allocation of public and public-private partnership resources with respect to investment in ICT infrastructure, projects and programmes;
- encourage investment in the development of low-cost technologies and non-text-based computer interfaces using iconographic software and voice recognition to facilitate ICT access for poor, illiterate women; and
- take steps to finance open source technologies and software that will facilitate women's access to ICTs (APC WNSP 2003).

Women activists are struggling to ensure that gender is a cross-cutting principle when discussing public policies and have committed themselves to take a gendered approach to all activities, including information and communications. They encourage democratization of policy processes within the ICT sector, including use of ICT tools to support this process, and to formulate and implement ICT policy using principles of openness and fair participation. This collective participation in the communication field is also an essential element for women's empowerment.

After three decades of feminist research, theorizing and analysis, women are in a better position to confront the problems thrown up by ICTs than they had been in relation to the old media, which they critiqued in a fairly simplistic way, at a time when feminist analysis was still in its infancy. Also, in some respects—although in different ways—both governments and civil society now recognize (some of) the claims of the women's movement, rather than dismissing (or ignoring) them as they tended to do 20 years ago.

During the African Regional Preparatory Meeting for WSIS, in Bamako, Mali, in May 2002, women representatives from NGOs and other communication organizations met by invitation of UNIFEM and organized the Gender Caucus which now meets during the regional conferences and the preparatory committees (PrepComs). It released a declaration in Bamako that brought up relevant issues of concern for the women's movement, which were rapidly adopted by women activists globally to lobby in the national, regional and international processes concerning WSIS. The declaration was addressed to the United Nations system and agencies, regional organizations, national bodies and public sector, African private sector, private, public and community media, the research community, civil society and the women's movement. They were urged, among other things, to:

- work toward ratifying treaties and protocols that recognize women's human rights including the right to communication;

- develop training and capacity development programmes that can raise awareness of the gendered nature of the information society and identify strategies for ensuring fair and equitable participation by men and women;
- increase access to ICT facilities through making arrangements that support achievement of universal access targets and defining specific targets for women's access to ICT;
- ensure that gender equity is a cross-cutting principle and commit themselves to take a gendered approach in all activities, including planning, implementation, monitoring and evaluation, and in the structure of civil society organizations themselves;
- promote cultural diversity in the implementation of national ICT strategies including through active use of local languages and provision of information on strategies in various media including community radio and non-electronic media;
- ensure that there is gender equity in education, specifically by providing opportunities to increase girls' literacy, and by providing access to fair and equitable participation in science and technology education and training at all levels;
- support use of ICT for women's empowerment including through application of ICTs in health, education, trade, employment and other women's development arenas;
- promote national languages and local content to ensure the widespread participation and inclusion of women;
- ensure that local knowledge, including local gender knowledge, is given importance in media content, and steps are taken to establish standards of reporting which include gender dimensions (Gender Caucus 2002).

On many occasions, women's organizations have declared that they favour a communication system at the national and international levels, based on democratic principles, that limits the monopoly in the globalization of telecommunications. They have also worked toward information and communication societies where development is focused on fundamental human needs and clear social, cultural, economic and environmental goals; where priority is given to the alleviation of poverty and other inequalities in a way that is environmentally sustainable. Achieving control in communications and in the ICT field is important to ensure that the resources and benefits of the information and communication society are distributed equally between women and men.

References

American Association of University Women (AAUW). 2000. **Tech-Savvy: Educating Girls in the New Computer Age**. Educational Foundation Commission on Technology, Gender and Teacher Education, AAUW, Washington, DC.

Association for Progressive Communication Women's Networking Support Programme (APC WNSP). 2001. **ICTs for Social Change**. www.apcwomen.org/gem, accessed in October 2003.

————. 2003. **Comments on WSIS Documents** (21 March 2003). www.apc.org/english/news/index.shtml?x=12233, accessed in October 2003.

Bhasin, Kamla. 1994. "Women and communication alternatives: Hope for the next century." **Media Development**, Vol. 41, No. 2.

Bonder, Gloria. 2002. **From Access to Appropriation: Women and ICT Policies in Latin America and the Caribbean**. Paper presented at the Expert Group Meeting (EGM ICT/2002/EP.3), UN Division for the Advancement of Women (Seoul, 11–14 November). UNDAW, New York.

————. 2001. **Las nuevas tecnologías de la información y las mujeres: Reflexiones necesarias**. Paper presented in the experts meeting on Globalisation, Technological Changes and Gender Equity (São Paulo, 5–6 November). CEPAL/University of São Paulo, São Paulo.

Buntarian, Nani. 2000. "Indonesian women find a virtual space of their own." In Pi Villanueva (ed.), **Women in Sync—a Toolkit for Electronic Networking, Vol. 3: Acting Locally, Connecting Globally—Stories from the Regions**. APC WNSP, Philippines.

Cinco, Cheekay and Chat Ramilo Garcia. 2000. "The Asian Women's Resource Exchange." In Pi Villanueva (ed.), **Women in Sync—a Toolkit for Electronic Networking, Vol. 3: Acting Locally, Connecting Globally—Stories from the Regions**. APC WNSP, Philippines.

Gallagher, Margaret. 2001. **Gender Setting**. Zed Books, London and WACC, New York.

Gender Caucus. 2002. **Gender Caucus Statement**. For inclusion in Bamako 2002 Declaration, African Regional Preparatory Meeting for the World Summit on the Information Society, Bamako, Mali, May. www.geneva2003.org/bamako2002/doc_html/finalstatementgendercaucus-en.html, accessed in October 2003.

Gill, Rosalind. 2003. **Participation in and Access of Women to the Media, and Information and Communication Technologies and Their Impact on and Use as an Instrument for the Advancement and Empowerment of**

Women. Paper presented at the UN Commission on the Status of Women, 47th Session. UNCSW, New York.

Global Unions. 2003. **Statement of the Global Unions**. Presented to the 47th Session of the UN Commission on the Status of Women. UNCSW, New York. www.union-network.org/uniindep.nsf/0/787ec2009c3e0375c1256ce 70032681d?OpenDocument, accessed in October 2003.

GSWG (NGO Gender Strategies Working Group). 2003. **Submission by the NGO Gender Strategies Working Group to the Second Preparatory Committee (PrepCom 2) on World Summit on the Information Society (WSIS)**, (Geneva, February). www.genderit.org/wsis/wsis_process.shtml, accessed in October 2003.

Hafkin, Nancy. 2002. **Gender Issues in ICT Policies in Developing Countries: An Overview**. Paper presented at the Expert Group Meeting (EGM ICT/2002/EP.1), UN Division for the Advancement of Women (Seoul, 11–14 November). UNDAW, New York.

ILO. 2001. **World Employment Report 2001: Life at Work in the Information Economy**. ILO, Geneva.

International Women's Tribune Center (IWTC). 2003. **Women and the Information Society: Women Engendering Policy at the WSIS**. IWTC, New York.

Karat. 2002. **Gender and Economic Justice in European Accession and Integration**. www.karat.org/links/pages/Detailed/74html, accessed in October 2003.

Kirkup, Gillian. 2002. **ICTs as a Tool for Enhancing Women's Educational Opportunities**. Paper presented at the Expert Group Meeting (EGM ICT/2002/EP.6), UN Division for the Advancement of Women (Seoul, 11–14 November). UNDAW, New York.

Malcom, Shirley. 1999. **Knowledge, Technology and Development: A Gendered Perspective. Women in Global Science and Technology**. www.wigsat.org/malcom.html, accessed in October 2003.

Mitter, Swasti and Sheila Rowbotham (eds.). 1995. **Women Encounter Technology: Changing Patterns of Employment in the Third World**. Routledge, London. www.unu.edu/unupress, accessed in October 2003.

Sabanes Plou, Dafne. 2000. "Electronic networking in the women's movement." In Pi Villanueva (ed.), **Women in Sync—a Toolkit for Electronic Networking, Vol. 3: Acting Locally, Connecting Globally—Stories from the Regions**. APC WNSP, Philippines.

Spears, George, Kasia Sydegart and Margaret Gallagher. 2000. **Who Makes the News? The Global Media Monitoring Project 2000**. WACC, London.

United Nations. 2001. **Beijing Declaration and Platform for Action with the Beijing+5 Political Declaration and Outcome Document**. Department of Public Information, New York. www.un.org/womenwatch/daw/beijing/platform/, accessed in October 2003.

————. 2000. **UN Millennium Declaration**. www.un.org/millennium/ declaration/ares552e.htm, accessed in October 2003.

UNCSW. 2003a. **Panel Discussion on Participation in and Access of Women to the Media, and Information and Communication Technologies and their Impact on and Use as an Instrument for the Advancement and Empowerment of Women**. Summary submitted by the moderator (E/CN.6/2003/CRP.5). 47th Session of the Commission on the Status of Women. UNCSW, New York.

————. 2003b. **Participation in and Access of Women to the Media, and Information and Communication Technologies and their Impact on and Use as an Instrument for the Advancement and Empowerment of Women**. Agreed Conclusions, Advance unedited version, 14 March, as adopted at the 47th Session of the Commission on the Status of Women. UNCSW, New York.

World Association for Christian Communication (WACC). 1998. "Declaration of Lima." **Media and Gender Monitor**, No. 2, Spring.

WomenAction 2000. 2001. **Mujeres y Medios para el Cambio Social— Iniciativas de Comunicación en el Mundo**. Co-ordinated by the Centre de documentation sur l'education des adults et la condition feminine. Les Éditions du remue-ménage, Montreal.

————. 2000. **We Met Our Commitments, and You? Latin American NGO Declaration**. www.mujeresaccion.org/docs.php3?id=20, accessed in October 2003.

WomenWatch and WomenAction 2000. 1999. **Report of Online Discussion on Women and Media (Section J, Beijing Platform for Action)**. 8 November–17 December.

Women's Worlds 2002. 2002. **Granny Who is a Computer "Whiz Kid"**. Newspaper published at the 8th International Interdisciplinary Congress on Women, Uganda. 26 July, p. 3.

A Community Informatics for the Information Society

William McIver, Jr.

Abstract

Community informatics is an emerging, interdisciplinary field concerned with the development, deployment and management of information systems designed with and by communities to solve their own problems. From academic and policy-making perspectives, community informatics is now concerned with developing a coherent theory and methodology drawn from a now significant history of projects and the ever-increasing efforts to use information and communication technologies to solve life-critical community problems.

Community informatics might be considered analogous to the well-established discipline of management information systems (MIS), where the former is tailored to the unique requirements of communities and the critical problems they pose for developers of information systems. These requirements and problems are significantly different from those faced in MIS, thereby warranting a unique disciplinary focus.

The goals of this paper are to:

- motivate the need for a community informatics in the context of the World Summit on the Information Society (WSIS);
- give an overview of conceptual and methodological issues; and
- propose the parameters of a community informatics sufficient for addressing development goals established in recent United Nations initiatives, including the Millennium Declaration and the ICT (information and communication technology) Task Force, and, in particular, the forthcoming WSIS.

Many of the concepts and issues discussed here are the results of research and practice in the developed world. Nonetheless, an effort is made in this paper to link community informatics to the realities of communities in developing countries, as well as disadvantaged communities in highly developed countries. Suggestions for new areas of research are also made. A set of related resources is listed in the annex to this paper.

The Basis of Community Informatics

That technological systems are neither value-neutral nor infallible should no longer be in dispute. What should also no longer be in question is the fallacy of information and communication technologies (ICTs) as *a priori* solutions to societal problems. Yet, recent high-level policy discussions concerning the introduction of ICTs into society have often not clearly acknowledged this. Technocentric solutions have been pushed without a critical analysis of potential and realized impacts of technologies and without proper acknowledgement of the historical processes responsible for the social and economic inequalities for which ICTs are being proposed as solutions. This is not to mention the "technofilia" and "cyber-fetishism" that seem to be rampant in popular discourse.

Community informatics is an acknowledgement of more than the non-value-neutral and fallible nature of ICTs. It is a recognition that the idea of purely technical solutions to societal problems is a fallacy and, further, that the seeking of technical solutions must necessarily be a social process. Mumford (1934), in his seminal *Technics and Civilization*, showed that technology is technique based on interactions between people and environment, and thought and creation, in order to achieve a specific goal. Of course these interactions have often not been positive. For these interactions to benefit people or communities that will be impacted by the resulting artefacts, the design process must be participatory. Kristen Nygaard, a computer scientist, pioneered the practice of participatory design in the 1960s when workers raised concerns about the potential for ICTs being introduced into their factories to eliminate their jobs. Because new systems invariably introduce unforeseen changes into organizations, often with bad consequences, Nygaard called for user involvement throughout the life cycle of a system (its design and operation). He also showed that ICTs should be viewed as only part of an overall system, with humans being major components of systems (Hausen and Mollerburg 1981). Nygaard's insights have come to be supported by other research. Benjamin (1999), in the context of post-apartheid South Africa, has shown how community-based ICT projects have failed due to non-participatory approaches being used.

Participation is a necessary but insufficient condition for community informatics to be effective. Among the greatest threats of new technologies is that they have the potential to perpetuate and expand existing power relations and inequalities, as well as to enable new forms of state repression. To empower communities to respond to and avoid these threats, community informatics must enable a fully democratic process. That is, it must be more than political democracy embodied in a participatory approach. Community informatics must allow people to share control of the decision making around the economic, cultural, environmental and other issues regarding ICT-based projects. More fundamentally, community informatics must empower communities who contemplate ICT-based solutions to develop their own productive forces within the information society so that they can control the modes of production that evolve within it and, thereby, have the possibility of preventing and responding to its threats. The open source and free software movements as modes of production are prime examples of the necessary elements of a community informatics that can enable communities to develop their own productive forces.

Finally, a participatory approach must also respond to the diversity of users and needs that exist within communities. User communities cannot be viewed as homogeneous. This principle is embodied in the universal design approach discussed later in this paper.

While this paper emphasizes methodological issues within community informatics, references to design, deployment and analysis in the following discussion must be understood to be grounded in the participatory and democratic perspective articulated above.

The Potential of ICT Impact, and the Role of Community Informatics

Given the potentially serious threats that ICTs pose to communities, their putative benefits must be constantly challenged and weighed carefully against the risks. A critical insight here in locating reasons to consider ICT-based approaches in communities is that the relationships between technology and society are non-linear. A cyclic interplay is often possible. For example, while ICTs have the potential to fortify socially unjust power relations, they can sometimes offer entities in civil society flexibility in responding to their conditions. The potential benefits of ICTs can be seen at a base level within the responses of communities to social and economic problems. Communication research has shown that people in economically and socially marginalized communities spend an inordinate amount of time and energy seeking and managing information related to survival and security. Information and the ability to communicate it—to receive and impart it—are necessary (but not sufficient) conditions for communities to develop and for inhabitants to thrive within them. Appropriately designed ICTs can fulfil such needs. Research has also shown that economically and socially marginalized people spend an inordinate amount of energy negotiating geography and time. Recent work in the area of digital government, for example, has revealed the lack of appropriate access points to and integration of US government information systems, which hinders the provision of social services by forcing individuals—often the poor—to travel long distances between offices (Bouguettaya et al. 2001, 2002). ICTs in this context offer the possibility of introducing more flexibility into people's lives in terms of time and space. Specific advantages of ICTs are discussed below.

The potential impacts of ICTs in least developed countries and developing communities

The United Nations Millennium Declaration (2000) contains a series of goals for the improvement of human society by 2015 and 2020. The goals can be categorized under the areas of poverty and hunger eradication, universal education and literacy, reversing major diseases and improving health care, environmental sustainability, and gender equality.

In examining the specific potential impacts of ICTs in addressing poverty in the developing world, Accascina (2000) has argued for a broader definition of poverty, one that includes information poverty. Community informatics in this view would, thus, be concerned with facilitating access to information independent of specific technologies.

Accascina provides a useful taxonomy for viewing the potential impacts of technological interventions. Impacts are considered along dimensions of geography and type of benefit that could potentially accrue to developing communities and, consequently, to individuals living in them. Potential impacts on poor individuals and communities are seen as originating from local or regional, national or global initiatives. For each, impacts may be either direct or indirect. Examples, including those cited by Gurstein (2000) and Finquelievich (1999) in the context of rural communities and non-profit organizations in both developing and developed countries, are given in table 1.

Thus, a community informatics can potentially make contributions at multiple levels in a society and through a variety of direct and indirect development relationships. In particular, community-based ICTs can be seen as contributing to the following Millennium Development Goal (MDG) areas:

Poverty and hunger eradication: Poverty and hunger eradication might be partially addressed through improved local access to information that impacts on local food production or other sectors of local economies such as tourism. Training in ICT-related skills can prepare people to take advantage of certain types of higher paying jobs in their countries, if and when they should become available.

Table 1: Potential benefits to communities from ICT interventions

Geographic span	Potential direct benefits	Potential indirect benefits
Local or regional	• Access to local or regional market information for small producers • Access to information about social and health services • Facilitation of customer-to-customer or community-to-customer transactions (for example, tourism) • Improve spatio-temporal relations for NGO work	• Employment in ICT-sector or jobs requiring ICT skills for family members • Better leveraging of human resources in response to community problems
National	• Access to Information about legal or policy information • Access to information about jobs facilitating business-to-business transactions	• Overall improvement in human development and poverty indices
Global	• Participation in ICT-based systems (for example, trade) • access to services provided by international NGOs	• Overall improvement in human development and poverty indices

Education and literacy: The supplementation or improvement of primary education might also be facilitated by ICT-based solutions. This is arguably the case for societies whose teaching pools are already inadequate to meet MDGs or whose adult labour forces have been devastated by major diseases, such as HIV/AIDS. While not pedagogically ideal, a limited teaching pool might be extended "virtually" through the use of ICTs in different modes of distance learning. ICTs provide various means by which educational content could be captured, stored and managed for use in other locations. The content could be delivered live or in recorded form. Subject matter experts could also be shared for teaching higher level courses across wide geographic areas.

Illiteracy is another major factor in the MDGs, as well as human development in general, that could potentially be addressed through the application of advanced ICTs. Adult literacy rates remain below 60 per cent in many of the world's countries, with rates below 50 per cent in the least developed countries, or LDCs (UNDP 2002). Both video and audio modalities can now be supported through relatively low-cost computing platforms and some other types of ICTs. These could potentially offer alternate means of delivering information that would otherwise be inaccessible to illiterate adults. Additionally, the dual use of audio or video with text might be explored as one means of reducing the rate of functional illiteracy in adults. This is being explored in the context of iconic human-computer interfaces (Noronha, no date).

Reversing major diseases and improving health care: The delivery of life-critical health information might also be facilitated and improved through ICT-based solutions (Driscoll 2001). Lack of access to information and communication has been identified as a critical factor in public health crises around the world (Garrett 2000). Garrett suggests that providing citizens of underdeveloped countries with community-level points of access to health information would be a critical starting point for addressing health care crises. However, such access points should support more than one-way flows of information (for example, from expert to community or patient). Communities must be allowed to participate in the selection and creation of communication flows that they find useful and necessary to address health care (for example, between local health professionals and between patients). Examples of current efforts in this area include the dissemination of HIV/AIDS information using CD-ROM, diskettes and other types of ICTs in Africa, and a Web site, sponsored by the United Nations Development Programme (UNDP), for HIV/AIDS in Southeast Asia (Driscoll 2001).

Environmental issues: Dwindling water supplies, fresh air and sanitation have all been threatened by trends and pressures brought to bear by development. ICTs are seen as a component of solutions to such problems. One ICT-based approach to improved environmental stewardship is community-based natural resource management (Bhatt, no date). As with other issue areas, ICTs can facilitate improved delivery, co-ordination and analysis of information about environmental issues and strategies. One example here is the Sri Lanka Environmental Television Project (SLETP), which integrates television, video and the Internet to deliver information to broadcasters, educational institutions and individual homes.

Gender equality: Jansen (1989) and others have pointed out that technological designs and processes used to deploy them often reflect society's gender biases (see also Muller et al. 1997 and Sabanes Plou in this volume). This has unfortunately been the case in gendered attitudes toward advanced ICTs and opportunities afforded women and girls to learn information technology (IT) skills in many parts of the world. The potential of ICTs to address this area of the MDGs is, thus, less linear than the other issue areas discussed above. That is, the application of ICTs themselves cannot be viewed as improving gender equality. Rather, it is argued that significant, positive reinforcement cycles toward gender equality can be created in a society through improved IT-related opportunities for women and girls. It is further argued along this same line that improvements in other MDG areas beyond those likely to be realized through IT-related opportunities for men can be achieved by providing the same opportunities to women and girls. There are several arguments for this claim. Munya (2000) pointed out that most critical, culturally situated knowledge resides with women and, therefore, enhancement of the abilities of women to continue to exchange such information are a necessary part of any development that is to be realized in a community or region. In addition, Munya points out that women in the developing world are often central to agricultural production, and they expend more of their income on their families than men do. Thus, it can be reasoned that women are likely to better leverage the potential benefits of ICTs in all of the MDG issue areas discussed here.

The Need for a Distinct Informatics for Communities

The pressing nature of the problems outlined above calls for every tractable and useful strategy to be brought to bear to solve them, including the application of ICTs. It might be argued that traditional organizational informatics have long existed and are readily available to guide the development of ICTs in pursuit of MDGs and other types of community development. Organizational informatics (OI) is taken here to mean the traditional development of ICTs in resource-rich, high-capability settings, such as corporations or governments. This encompasses the application of disciplines such as systems analysis, software engineering and management information systems (MIS). The need for a community informatics as distinct from organizational informatics has been motivated by recognition of two realities. First, organizational informatics is itself known to be very difficult and the site of many failures. An overwhelming majority of government ICT projects fail, for example (McIver and Elmagarmid 2002). Second, the characteristics of communities are highly unique relative to organizations and, therefore, the development of ICTs for communities warrants a special focus: community informatics (Gurstein 2000, 2002).

Disciplines such as computer science and mathematics periodically list "grand challenge" problems, a set of problems whose solutions are necessary to make major progress in the field and which possibly offer applications that would advance society. The identification of technically feasible candidate solutions to meet goals such as those in the Millennium Declaration is relatively easy in the context of an organization informatics approach. In community informatics, however, the grand challenge is to develop technological solutions for communities that are economically, socially and culturally appropriate and that are operationally and economically sustainable. This is especially true for developing countries, where resources and training may be even scarcer than in most communities.

The economic, social and cultural appropriateness of ICT designs factor in to the grand challenge in that they must address significant differences and deficits in knowledge and experience in the communities they are to benefit. Systems analysis and development is often done poorly even in well-funded, high-technology organizations in high-income countries. A number of realities suggest that communities in developing countries are likely to do worse without a special approach. The general history of technological development in organizations and for the consumer market is replete with cases of failure. Most are attributable to poor design practices. Systems analysis and design, software engineering, usability engineering and the other related disciplines that make up the constellation of generally recognized best practices all demand people with special training and experience. Communities without a proper educational framework and knowledge base are not likely to have access to such people. Based on the history of ICT development in an organizational context, it can also be argued that communities are not likely to arrive at nor apply best practices on their own. Thus, special community-level training in these skills is needed. The processes involved, as traditionally practiced, can also be costly. Consequently, communities may have to forgo best practices. Thus, alternate, cost-effective approaches to ICT development for communities must be developed.

Evidence suggests that the viability of technological designs for communities in the developing world is far more sensitive to the use of best design practices in general, and attention to economic, cultural and social dimensions of appropriateness in particular. Potential adopters of technologies in communities may be less able to withstand the economic and social impacts of poor designs. The costs of failure in ICT-based projects are on average high, relative to the size of an organization. Communities in developing areas are probably least able to withstand such impacts. In addition, social and cultural norms about the appropriateness of various facets of a given application of technology may differ significantly between communities and thereby impact the viability of a system. Such facets could conceivably be the functionality (or lack thereof) provided by a system, methods of interaction required to use it or the user interface metaphors that it employs. A major reason for poor designs is a failure to adequately involve the target user community in the design process. This is a common oversight in organizational settings (Landauer 1995; Norman 1998). Without proper training, it is likely that communities would also fail to employ user-centred design processes. Finally, research suggests that the general level of technical literacy of a system's users can have a significant impact on its perceived usability, with experts being less sensitive to problems of design. This suggests that communities in the developing world, whose citizens likely have a low level of technical literacy or experience, may have an even lower tolerance for poor designs than in developed countries, which would make the need for a sound and practical community informatics in the developing world critical. More research and practice is needed to better understand the needs of communities in developing countries in all the respects discussed here. However, it is clear from experiences in the broader world of ICT development that developing countries need methods of systems analysis and design that are geared specifically to their economic constraints, experience and training needs.

The operational and economic sustainability of ICT designs factor in to the grand challenge in that they must address significant deficits in investment capital, infrastructure and experience. The economics of a community will often preclude individualized solutions that are the norm in developed nations, such as home-based Internet access. Instead, approaches to developing group-based solutions must be sought. In addition, the remoteness of many communities will preclude certain modalities of communication, such as broadband. Instead, novel approaches to using wireless telephony, radio, satellites or low-power television will be necessary. In general, a community informatics must be open to using alternate design approaches and technologies. This includes the use of open hardware standards and open source software, the creative appropriation and adaptation of existing technologies of infrastructure, and use of traditional ICTs (such as print and radio). In addition, the use of open technologies—as opposed to custom commercial or commercial off-the-shelf (COTS) solutions—requires people in the community who have sufficient expertise to develop, operate and maintain systems. This is an added challenge for developing communities, where such expertise may be difficult to find and afford. A community informatics must, therefore, establish methodologies that empower communities to build the capacity and knowledge to sustain technological solutions. Communities that are to be properly involved in the development and sustenance of their own systems must also develop an educational foundation for their work.

In summary, the need for a community informatics exists in stark contrast to the domains of MIS, and science and engineering applications for which large bodies of knowledge and best practices have been developed. These practices generally assume an abundance of resources and expertise. The characteristics and needs of communities are significantly different from those of business and technical organizations and, thus, require different approaches to design, development, deployment and operation. The next section develops a canonical view of a community informatics necessary to adequately address the challenges discussed above.

Conceptual and Methodological Issues in Community Informatics

Community informatics is an interdisciplinary field concerned with the development, deployment and management of information systems designed with and by communities to solve their own problems. It is arguably a part of social informatics, which has been defined by Kling (1999) as "the interdisciplinary study of the design, uses and consequences of information technologies that takes into account their interaction with institutional and cultural contexts". Social informatics research has three principal areas of focus.

- *Theories and models:* The development of models and theories that explain the social and organizational uses and impacts of ICTs.
- *Methodologies:* The development of methodologies that address the social impacts of the design, implementation, maintenance and use of ICTs.
- *Philosophical and ethical issues:* The study of philosophical and ethical issues that arise in the use of ICTs in social and organizational contexts.

Thus, community informatics should be seen in the context of social informatics as a disciplinary site focusing on the development information technologies for communities, which takes into account research from social informatics, as well as MIS, software engineering and other technical fields. It might also be argued that the definition of community informatics should include that part of traditional MIS practice where the public's interests are properly considered. Examples here include publicly funded ICT development where democratic participation and oversight by citizens can help reduce traditionally high failure rates and address negative social impacts.

Classes of community-based systems

A wide spectrum of technologies—both hardware and software—can be considered for use within community-based systems. These include technologies that "externalize" non-governmental organizations (NGOs) or government by enabling people to interact with processes inside of these organizations, and those technologies that can be used to improve internal processes within organizations that benefit communities. The former type of technologies will be referred to as externalizing systems and the latter as internal systems. The prime examples of externalizing systems technologies are the Web-based services that provide government services, which have become prominent in the past few years in the developed world. Internal systems technologies include novel applications of computing techniques in communication, geographic information systems (GIS), database management and image processing to solve critical tasks within government or NGOs. Of course, many externalizing systems employ the services of internal systems. The architectures of systems in both the categories of externalizing and internal systems are in most cases database-centric.

The dominant vision of externalizing systems for most organizations has become—like many other areas of the information technology sector—Web-centric. Commercial Web service offerings have clearly raised citizens' expectations of the level of service provided over the Web (Cook 2000). These systems can generally be characterized along two dimensions: the architectural relationship they have with their clients and the type of service they are capable of providing for their clients. Architectures include intranets to support intra-organizational processes, public network access to facilitate organization-citizen interactions, and extranets for supporting interactions between organizations (for example, government-to-business, government-to-NGO, NGO-to-NGO).

Four basic types of Web architectures are seen among current externalizing systems, each corresponding to a level of service (McIver and Elmagarmid 2002).

- *Level 1 externalizing services:* These services provide one-way communication for displaying information about a given agency or aspect of an organization.
- *Level 2 externalizing services:* These services provide simple two-way communication capabilities, usually for simple types of data collection, such as the registration of comments or requests with an organization.
- *Level 3 externalizing services:* These services extend on level 2 services to provide the ability to carry out complex transactions that may involve intra-organizational work flows and contractual procedures. Examples include voter and motor vehicle registration, and brokering systems between third parties (see Gurstein 2000).
- *Level 4 externalizing services:* These services are characterized by the emergence of portals that seek to integrate a wide range of services across whole sectors, regional bodies or geographically distributed organizations. The eCitizen portal developed by the government of Singapore is a prime example of this type of system.

A wide spectrum of technologies can be considered to fall within the category of internal systems, including those that perform tasks common to large organizations, such as financial management, document processing and communications (for example, email). The development of novel systems that would likely have benefit for communities would fall generally into two categories.

- *Integrative and communicative systems:* These are systems that provide support for interorganizational integration and co-operation. These types of systems can enhance the sharing of data and the co-ordination of processes in and among organizations.
- *Domain-specific processing and knowledge management systems:* These are systems that provide support for processing and interpretation of data within ontologies that are unique to an organization, community or government. These include the processing of agricultural statistics, management of community assets, co-ordination of social services policies (that is, rules) and data, and management of geographic images from government geological surveys.

Principle issue areas in community informatics

As discussed above, community informatics might be considered as analogous to MIS. The following are the principle issues that community informatics must address and which set it apart from MIS.

Prioritizing social requirements: Community informatics differs from MIS in that it must, in the interest of social and cultural goals, be open to creative solutions for communities that may be outside the orthodoxy of traditional MIS solutions or cost-benefit analyses.

Accessibility, universal design and participatory design: Community informatics must also have a commitment as a matter of principle—and law in many countries—to the development of ICTs for communities such that the widest range of citizens can enjoy their benefits, particularly those with disabilities (Glinert and York 1992). The concept of universal design has evolved out of the objective of designing systems that are accessible to people with disabilities. It has been recognized, however, that universal design benefits all people, not just those who have disabilities. General principles for universal design have been developed by a number of organizations. Universal design principles have also been developed for the specific software engineering domain of Web applications (W3C 2001). Finally, universal design must take into account literacy and linguistic barriers.

Sociotechnical geographies: Communities are geographically situated and, thus, there are often significant geographic components to their problems. For example, rural communities worldwide have historically faced major geographic barriers in gaining access to infrastructure necessary to use ICTs, including electrification and telephony.

Technology lifecycle constraints: Communities also often face tighter financial constraints than business or governmental organizations in attempting to address their problems in terms of the costs of implementation and long-term maintenance. The seeking of IT-based solutions must, therefore, include consideration of low cost, public domain or open source solutions. The development process must also include training of community members and the development of local capacity to participate in the design process and to provide ongoing technical support for their own systems.

The development of technology for communities without due consideration of the unique requirements cited above has often had unfortunate consequences (Rudolph 2002; Margonelli 2002). Community informatics as a discipline, therefore, must develop a coherent body of theories and methods to address the issue areas above. Each of these areas is examined in greater detail below.

Prioritizing social requirements

In community-based ICT projects, social and cultural issues have greater priority than they might in organizational informatics. In the interest of social and cultural goals, therefore, community informatics must be more open to creative solutions for communities. Candidate solutions might be considered for communities that exist outside the orthodoxy of traditional cost-benefit analyses likely to be used in an organizational setting or user expectations that might exist in a consumer context (for example, individual Internet access).

A commonly cited example here is the argument about digital divide strategies, which is that it makes little sense to prioritize the introduction of advanced ICTs in a developing country where major deficits in Human Development Index components remain. In particular, it could be argued that it is not reasonable to implement individual Internet access in a society where literacy rates are low, and public health and other basic services are lacking.

In this context, advanced ICTs such as the Internet must be considered only "candidate solutions"—in the parlance of systems analysis—within a community informatics approach. They must also be viewed as only potential components of overall solutions to a given problem, where other non-technical and social components are assumed to play major roles. The overriding concern then should be to select technologies that are suitable and appropriate to a community, given social, cultural, sustainability and economic factors. To achieve this, it is necessary to be open to the full range of communication modalities and technologies, including analogue broadcast technologies, interpersonal communication methods, and institutional mechanisms such as libraries.

What must also be realized in prioritizing social requirements is that most telecommunication technologies can be deployed at granularities appropriate to a community's needs and resources. That is, a number of advanced ICTs can be deployed in a range of access scopes, from community-level access down to the individual. This perspective sets community informatics apart from an organizational or consumer approach in many applications in the developed world in that expectations are often oriented toward individualized access.

Accessibility, universal design and participatory design

A community informatics approach must ensure that the widest range of people are able to enjoy the benefits of ICTs. The particular concern here is for those who have disabilities, and those who face linguistic and literacy barriers to accessing information.

The concept of accessibility encompasses not only the direct human-ICT interactions used to conduct transactions, but also factors that limit citizens' physical interactions with organizations or individuals. Barriers to physical interaction include both disabilities and disabling conditions, and problems of geography and time, independent of disabilities, that prevent people from travelling to sites where community-based services and information are offered. The integration of telecommunication and computing technologies has, of course, served greatly to reduce barriers of geography and time, though many infrastructure issues remain.

The Trace Center for Research and Design at the University of Wisconsin, United States, identifies four major categories of disabilities or impairments.

- *Visual impairments:* Visual impairments range from low vision to blindness. Some visually impaired people are able to see light, but can discern no shapes; the vision of some people is dim or fuzzy; some people cannot differentiate between certain colours; and others can see no light at all.
- *Hearing impairments:* Hearing impairments range from partial hearing impairment to deafness.
- *Physical impairments:* Two major types of physical impairments exist: skeletal and neuromuscular. Those with skeletal impairments may have a limited range of movement for certain joints or they may have small or missing limbs. Those with neuromuscular impairments may have paralysis in all or part of their body or they may have poor neuromuscular control.
- *Cognitive / language impairments:* Cognitive/language impairments include problems with memory, perception,

problem solving, conceptualizing, and comprehension and expression of language.

Often people have multiple impairments. Responding to all of these types of impairments will be critically important in areas of the world where people suffer from war injuries.

ICTs are the basis for a wide array of solutions for accommodating people with disabilities. Solutions include text-to-speech and speech-to-text conversion devices and software, text magnification features offered in desktop operating systems and applications, voice-activated controls for computer applications, telecommunication devices for the deaf (TDDs), closed captioning for video data, and computer-based Braille devices for the blind.

Approaches to accommodating specific types of impairments (or combinations thereof) are not always obvious and, therefore, deserve the attention of specialists. For example, many hearing-impaired people in the United States use American sign language (ASL) to communicate. It cannot be assumed, however, that ASL speakers understand English, as it is a completely different language from ASL.

The concept of universal design has evolved out of the objective of designing systems that can accommodate people with disabilities. The goal of universal design is to develop systems that can be used by the widest possible range of people without special design modifications. General principles for universal design have been developed by a number of organizations. Universal design principles have also been developed for the specific software-engineering domain of Web applications (W3C 2001). Web site accessibility is discussed later in this section.

Two points must be stressed in motivating the use of universal design. *First, it is critical that universal design principles be applied from the inception of a project.* Accessibility features can be made more useful and easier to use when they are made into integral parts of the design. It is also usually far more cost-effective to include accessibility features into a design than to retrofit them into a completed system. Second, *universal design benefits all people, not just those who have disabilities.* Techniques developed to provide those having a specific type of impairment with access to some system are often found to be useful to others. For example, text-to-speech conversion has been found to be useful for "hands free" applications, such as having email messages read to people as they perform other tasks. Closed captioning is useful not only to those with hearing impairments, but also to hearing people working in noisy environments.

The National Institute on Disability and Rehabilitation Research in the United States (Connell 1997) has developed the following universal design principles:

- systems should accommodate a wide range of user abilities and preferences;
- it should be easy to adapt systems to a broad spectrum of user preferences and abilities;
- system interfaces should be intuitive and simple to use;
- systems should be able to employ different input and output modes according to user abilities and ambient conditions;
- systems should be designed to minimize hazards and to be tolerant of user errors;
- systems should be usable with minimum physical effort; and
- the size and spatial placement of system elements should accommodate a wide range of body size, posture and mobility.

Special attention has been paid to accessibility in the context of Web content. Different aspects of markup languages pose unique problems for various adaptive systems. Some text readers, for example, have difficulty processing HTML tables. Guidelines for designing accessible Web content have been developed by the World Wide Web Consortium (W3C) and are continuously revised as markup languages evolve (see W3C 2001). A number of tools are available for validating Web content against these and other accessibility guidelines.

Specialized browsers and devices have been developed that provide alternate ways for people to use the Web. These include special browsers for the visually impaired that allow Web content to be read aloud or displayed on devices such as Braille bars; general screen-reader devices and software that allow users to have any on-screen content read to them; and other adaptive technologies, such as voice input systems, telephone-based Web browsers, and systems that transform or filter existing Web content to make it more accessible.

User-centred and participatory design

Landauer (1995) has pointed to the "failure to design well" as the central cause of problems with usefulness and usability of computer-based systems and processes. These failures, he points out, are often due to a lack of focus on users in the design, development and operational phases of systems.

Landauer also cites some other major factors as impacting usefulness and usability.

Hardware and software limitations: Usefulness and usability are often limited by the functional limitations of software systems and, in some cases, the technical limitations of the hardware systems that they control. The case literature is replete with examples of software systems that overly constrain the ways that tasks can be performed or that do not allow them to be performed at all. Media-rich Web sites often tax the limited processing power and bandwidth limitations of many users' hardware. Bandwidth limitations will remain of particular concern to community informatics practitioners working in the developing world.

Unreliable systems: Systems fail due to software errors, user errors and hardware failure, with the first two factors being the most common. Landauer assigns responsibility for user error to computer systems. They should be designed so as to prevent users from causing erroneous conditions. The production of technologies that meet this latter requirement is likely to be far more difficult in communities, where people have little experience using advanced ICTs.

Incompatible systems and data types: While standardization of software systems and data types (for example, file formats) has become widespread, particularly in the context of Web technologies and desktop environments, incompatibility problems continue to limit the usefulness and usability of many systems. Though Web clients (such as browsers) have brought about a significant improvement in the interoperability of data sources from different applications and operating systems, the use of data sources such as PDF files and RealAudio streams requires clients to support special adjunct software systems (for example, plug-ins). Compatibility problems due to this issue are likely to be more acute for economically disadvantaged citizens and community organizations (for example, schools and libraries) that cannot upgrade from older or relatively low-end equipment.

Negative ergonomic and social impacts of computer systems: Computer systems are now recognized as potential sources of ergonomic problems such as repetitive stress injuries and fatigue. Many negative social impacts have been attributed to the deployment and use of computer systems. These include impacts on work and work life, privacy, culture and the natural environment.

Landauer and many others have long recommended user-centred approaches to design, development and deployment as necessary to the creation of useful and usable computer systems. Using these approaches, designers, developers, procurers and maintainers of systems would engage in iterative processes of systems analysis, implementation and operation, with each process having users as their central focus. Unfortunately, these approaches are not used often enough. Financial and time constraints are common reasons for forgoing user-centred processes.

Designers working in a community informatics framework would work continuously in direct interaction with users in the design phase to gain an in-depth understanding of their needs and to explore possible approaches to meeting them. In the development phase, developers would engage in iterative cycles of implementation, evaluation of usability, and design modification based on test results. Once a system is ready for operation, user-centred processes would be used to determine how best to integrate it into human work flow processes, to determine what skills are necessary to use it, and to periodically monitor its usefulness and usability. Deployment, including procurement of software systems and hardware developed by other organizations, would also be user-centred, having inputs from the people who would use and manage such systems.

Sociotechnical geographies in the information society

Information and communication technologies have come to be seen as spatial systems that change space and time relations to create new "virtual" geographies (Gillespie and Robins 1989; Kitchin 1998). These include geographies defined by communication, economics and social formations.

Geography presents significant problems in many community-based ICT development projects. Analyses of the needs of users in domains such as e-government, for example, have revealed serious geographic barriers in providing social services. Situations have been identified where people seeking particular types of social services are often required to travel large distances between various social service and health agency offices (Bouguettaya et al. 2002). Such barriers can be eliminated through availability of online services and local access points (such as computer terminals, telephones, and automatic teller machines, or ATMs).

An effective community informatics must be concerned with facilitating access to a geographical area in which access points or other appropriate telecommunication infrastructures exist. Such geographies include work environments, libraries and schools where access points likely exist.

Less obvious are the relationships between the deployment of these technologies and urban planning by both public and private sectors. Both urban and rural geographies must either have an evolving infrastructure to provide telecommunication services sufficient to sustain community informatics projects, or policies that allow communities to appropriate newer ones (for example, licensing structures that permit the deployment of wireless fidelity, or WiFi). Characteristics of emerging technologies are allowing community informatics projects to "leap-frog" older telecommunication technologies to build infrastructure at lower costs.

Access to knowledge has traditionally required access to the physical geographies in which the desired information exists. Such geographies include not only technological access points, such as records or books, but, most importantly, points where human agents who possess knowledge can be reached and from which they can transmit. It is in this latter context that community informatics projects may have the most profound impacts toward the MDGs. Automated information delivery will not suffice in meeting MDGs on education, health care and other domains in which human expertise must be consulted continuously— unlike the provisioning of engineering artefacts such as water or environmental technologies.

Managing technology lifecycle constraints

The design, development, deployment and operation of ICT systems have traditionally been viewed as a lifecycle in that such systems undergo iterative processes cycling between their birth and their modification or replacement. This type of perspective is important in managing the complexity of designing systems, putting them into operation, and responding to faults or changes in system requirements. Many articulations of the life cycle model exist. The ISO/IEC 12207 standard is a widely recognized version.

The information technology software life cycle processes defined by the International Organization for Standardization and the International Electrotechnical Commission under standard ISO/IEC 12207 (ISO/IEC 1995) contains the following primary processes: acquisition, supply, development, maintenance and operation (Moore 1998). The life cycle may be viewed in figure 1.

Figure 1: ISO/IEC 12207 Life cycle

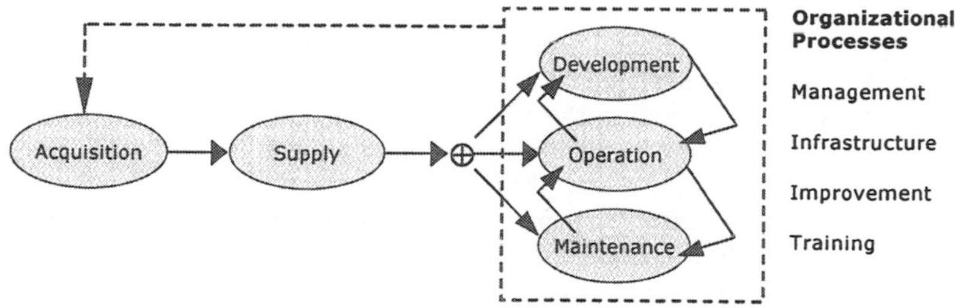

Several key relationships must be examined between traditional views of life cycle processes and the development of a community informatics.

Primary processes

Acquisition: This process involves identification of system requirements, analysis and design of the prospective systems, and the identification and acquisition of its components or services necessary to develop the components. That is, acquisition could involve commercial off-the-shelf components or contractual agreements with developers.

Communities often face tighter financial constraints than business or governmental organizations in attempting to acquire technologies and other resources required to implement ICT-based solutions. Public domain and open source technologies offer potential approaches to mitigating acquisition costs. This is discussed below.

Supply: This process involves the delivery of system components, intended to satisfy the system requirements, which were contracted for during the acquisition process. Supply can involve several possibilities or combinations of the following: commencement of the development process to produce a unique system, or commencement of the operation process using a turnkey system or a third-party service.

This process is complementary to acquisition and as such it too may be impacted in a community informatics context by the financial constraints that communities face. Additionally, supply involves the enforcement of contractual arrangements and co-ordination of their delivery. In a community informatics context, unlike an organizational one, this should be supported by appropriate oversight and governance mechanisms.

Development: This process involves the production of a new system. This occurs either through the integration of existing components or the implementation of hardware or software (for example, programming), or some combination of these two types of activities.

Maintenance: This process involves either the correction of faults in an operational system or its enhancement in order to realize new requirements. New requirements might be new features desired by users, tasks that are mandated by new legal requirements, or some other fundamental change desired in the operation of a system.

Operation: This process involves the ongoing activity of setting a system into a functioning state: that is, into a state where users can begin to realize its benefits. This process may be arrived at through one of several paths: when the development process has been completed; upon completion of a maintenance process; or directly from the supply process, in which case a service has been contracted. In the third case, no development is necessary since an existing system is being used (that owned by the service provider).

In a community informatics approach, the development, maintenance and operation processes all require training and capacity building in communities if they are to be supported adequately by community members. To be done properly, this requires a formal set of activities carried out in a highly disciplined manner. Along with the costs required to perform these processes, the skills required to do so constitute the major elements of sustainability in community ICT projects.

Organizational processes

The ISO/IEC 12207 standard also includes sets of supporting processes and organizational process. The primary and organizational processes are of greatest importance here. The organizational processes are management, infrastructure, improvement and training. Organizational processes are processes that are necessary to administer the primary and supporting processes.

As with development, maintenance and operation, communities must have the ability to perform these processes themselves if projects are to be truly sustainable. Again, training and financial resources are key here.

Selected Cross-Cutting Issues in Community Informatics

Issues discussed here intersect with many of the key conceptual and methodological issues discussed above.

The potential of existing and emerging technology frameworks

As Innis and others have shown, ICTs and transitions to new types of ICTs have historically had profound impacts on communities (and whole civilizations). In addition, he has shown how characteristics unique to different media have determined the natures and biases of the impacts they were able to make in terms of space and time (Innis 1964:3–32, 33–60). It is reasonable, therefore, to look proactively at new and existing technological areas in considering general systems design approaches within a community informatics approach.

Media and data convergence

Many NGOs are currently arguing for attention to traditional ICTs (for example, radio and television). While this approach is prudent for various reasons in a community informatics context, the unique properties of the technologies that enable the Internet cannot be underestimated in terms of their potential contributions to community-based ICT projects. The properties of the enabling technology for the Internet must be examined in a community informatics since they offer solutions for bridging traditional and advanced ICTs, as well as supporting different modalities of communication. Its technical characteristics have enabled unique dispersion possibilities, and it supports almost all earlier forms of communications.

The packet-switching nature of the Internet allows a distributed infrastructure, which distributes set-up and access costs to different organizations or communities, and amortizes infrastructure development costs. Use of packet switching is also independent of the physical transmission medium—copper, fibre optics, radio or satellite. Its store-and-forward means of operation allows it to support multiple modes of transmission: continuous, discontinuous, synchronous and asynchronous. These technical characteristics have made its dispersion potential high. In fact, dispersion has taken place over many types of infrastructure.

At the application layer, packet switching has provided a nexus for different forms of communication. The Internet is, therefore, able to support all components of J. Richstad's framework for communication: interactive, participatory, horizontal and multiway communications (Richstad 2003). The implication of this for community informatics exists at the application layer, in that it can enable the integration of all elementary forms of communication: text, audio, images and video, and most communication technologies: postal services, telephony, radio, film and television, and collaborative applications. In this way, the Internet is now able to serve as a bridging technology between new and older forms of communication (for example, broadcast radio to Internet). Thus, while it is prudent to retain traditional ICTs in a palette of technologies to be considered in developing community-based systems, a strong focus on deploying packet-switch data communications (for example TCP/IP/Internet) should be stressed.

Wireless data communications

Wireless data communications, including WiFi, is widely viewed as having significant applicability in the developing world. Wireless data communications has offered developing countries the possibility of leap-frogging the developed world in terms of acquiring advanced communication infrastructures. The high costs of deploying landline infrastructures required in traditional telephony have been an econ-omically intractable barrier for many countries. The deployment of wireless data communication infrastructure, on the other hand, requires fewer material resources (for example, wires and poles) and is far less labour intensive. Wireless data communications also makes possible the distribution of communications over wide and rugged geographies where landline approaches may not have been possible. Finally, some wireless data communication standards can be deployed and scaled in an incremental and distributed way. WiFi, for example, can be used to build an evolving network, where individuals or organizations contribute to the expansion of a network as they acquire and make new nodes operational (for example, installing WiFi service on their platform). A community informatics approach must maintain a focus on deriving maximum benefits from technologies for financially constrained communities by leveraging technologies such as these.

Open source and public domain development

Open source can potentially enable communities to be self-sufficient in replicating, maintaining and enhancing ICT-based development projects. This approach allows a community to have complete access to the internal workings of the technologies (for example, software and hardware). Many open source technologies are also public domain, alleviating developers of much of the cost of acquiring technologies.

Open source is of great interest among NGOs involved in the World Summit on the Information Society (WSIS). At the second preparatory committee (PrepCom 2) of WSIS in February 2003, for example, a partnership with African NGOs initiated an open source technology project. The goal is to foster greater development throughout Africa through the diffusion of free, open source technologies. Many participants from civil society have consistently declared their desire for the creation of a global commons for this very purpose in statements to WSIS. Also, the United Nations Educational, Scientific and Cultural Organization (UNESCO) started a Web portal in 2001 to promote free and open source software. See the annex below for more information.

Low-cost hardware

On the hardware side, an effort was initiated in 2000 to create an open, public domain design for an affordable computing device for the developing world. The approach taken was to create a non-profit trust in which many people volunteered to produce a design. The result is called a Simputer. In its current version, it has 32MB of memory and has a Linux-based operating system. It is handheld with a pen-based interface and it runs on three AAA batteries. It is now being offered for sale by several organizations, including Simputer.org, PicoPeta, and Encore Software of India. Its current cost is approximately $200. While this cost may be prohibitive in many areas of the world, it is a beginning and the general approach taken to its development should be factored into the development of a community informatics approach to meet the MDGs.

Public involvement in information society governance

Democratic policy, accountability mechanisms and socially responsible practice by computer professionals are necessary for communities to ensure that ICTs are designed and deployed appropriately. It is the case, in fact, that citizens and NGOs like Computer Professionals for Social Responsibility (CPSR) have historically played major roles in defining and implementing not only the technical structures of various parts of the information society, but also in making and enacting policy recommendations concerning their operation. This includes Internet governance through the Internet Corporation for Assigned Names and Numbers (ICANN) and Internet standards development. For a community informatics to be truly meaningful, these types of mechanisms must be strengthened and maintained.

The role of international organizations

The need for a community informatics can be motivated by the goals and imperatives established in human rights frameworks. The Universal Declaration of Human Rights articulated rights that can be directly linked to social implications raised by information systems and to technological advancement in general, Article 27, section 1 states: "Everyone has the right freely to...share in scientific advancement and its benefits" (United Nations 1993).

Community informatics is arguably a necessary means, given the existing economic dynamics of ICT development, for enabling "a social and international order in which the rights and freedoms set forth" in the declaration "can be fully realized", as Article 28 states, for those communities who are not able to negotiate the marketplace of advanced ICTs. Many communities will have to acquire or develop their own technologies.

A major area of contention in the development of an information society through a community informatics will be in defining and enforcing the rights of all stakeholders as well as the particulars of its governance. Critical issues in addressing rights and governance are:

- democratic management of international bodies dealing with ICTs;
- information and communication rights of governments, business and citizens;
- privacy and security policies and rights;
- censorship and regulation of content;
- the role of the media;
- defining, identifying, and responding to criminal activities within an information society;
- the application of ICTs for government and decentralization (McIver and Elmagarmid 2002); and
- media ownership and concentration.

A major emphasis here for civil society and some governments has been to establish support for the empowerment of citizens. The relationship here is non-linear, as in gender equality discussed above, in that many view an information society as enabling the reform and strengthening of democracy, which in turn will presumably improve citizens' participation in community informatics processes. Mueller (1999), Hamelink (1999) and others have shown the importance of structures of accountability and participation for the maintenance of the public's interest in the development and use of ICTs.

Finally, international organizations such as UNESCO, the United Nations Research Institute for Social Development (UNRISD), and others can continue to play a role in supporting the development of community informatics in a way analogous to the International Telecommunication Union's (ITU) role in the telecommunication sector. For example, UNESCO now maintains a Web portal for free and open source software use and development. A number of programmes within the United Nations University (UNU) have mandates to perform training and research in information technology in developing countries, as well as study the social and economic impacts of new technologies. These include the International Institute for Software Technology (UNU/IIST) and the Institute for New Technologies (UNU/INTECH). UNRISD's project on the Information Technologies and Social Development has been playing a critical role in supporting research on the role of policy making and institutional factors affecting "the likelihood that new information and communications technologies can be used to improve the lives of large numbers of people in developing countries".

See the annex for additional information about community informatics resources, both within UN organizations and the NGO community.

Recommendations

Community informatics offers promise in helping to achieve the MDGs. However, it is still an evolving meta-discipline, and additional research and experience is required to make it more effective. International organizations can play a major role in making progress in this area. The following recommendations are made toward this end.

Support for research: Research geared toward evolving community informatics must be supported. This would include the development of a research agenda among practitioners, scholars and communities; the cataloguing of community informatics projects and identification of factors for both failure and success; and support for research projects and systems trials.

Support for a conference: An ongoing, international conference in community informatics is required. This would create a centre of focus and a forum in which researchers, practitioners and communities could exchange results and maintain a coherent, field-wide research agenda, as is done in other fields.

Develop standards: ISO, IEC and other relevant bodies must be involved in the development of standards that are tailored to community informatics. This might include an examination of the ISO/IEC 12207 life-cycle standard.

Establish governance mechanisms: WSIS and similar processes must establish global information society mechanisms of governance that empower citizens to apply and manage community informatics processes in meaningful ways. This would include the creation of intellectual property mechanisms that protect and encourage the use of open source technologies and development processes. In addition, it would provide mechanisms that ensure that the public interest is taken into account when community informatics processes involve the private sector.

Annex: Selected Community Informatics Resources

This section provides a list of selected community informatics organizations and projects.

Community Informatics Research and Applications Unit (CIRA): CIRA is located at the University of Teesside, Middlesbrough, in the United Kindgom. CIRA is a multidisciplinary entity in which the social and economic impacts of ICTs on communities are studied. An emphasis is placed on studying the growth of the Internet and "the consequences for community development, economic restructuring and social inclusion" (www.cira.org.uk).

Community Informatics Resource Center (CIRC): CIRC is a programme within the Rural Policy Research Institute at the University of Missouri, United States. It attempts to provide an environment in which the "implications of issues impacting rural America can be more effectively visualized, analyzed, queried and mapped" (http://circ.rupri.org).

UNU/INTECH: The Institute for New Technologies of the United Nations University (UNU/ITECH) in Maastricht is a research and training centre of the United Nations University. It conducts research and policy-oriented analyses and performs capacity building in the area of new technologies. In particular, the research examines new technologies with respect to their diffusion characteristics; the opportunities they offer; and the economic and social impacts they present. Emphasis is given to developing countries (www.intech.unu.edu).

UNU/IIST: The International Institute for Software Technology of the United Nations University (UNU/IIST) in Macao has a mandate to help "developing countries strengthen their education and research in computer science and their ability to produce computer software". In particular, IIST works with universities in developing countries on curriculum development in computer science and software engineering, as well as the development of research programmes (www.iist.unu.edu).

Jiva Institute: Jiva is an organization that attempts to develop sustainable technology projects in India (www.jiva.org).

The UNRISD Project on the Information Technologies and Social Development: This project has been playing a critical role in supporting research on the role of policy making and institutional factors affecting "the likelihood that new information and communications technologies can be used to improve the lives of large numbers of people in developing countries". In particular, the project supports research on trends and patterns of concentration within the global IT industry, new developments in international regulatory policy impacting IT development, and research by people from the developing world on "specific uses of information technologies" in their countries (www.unrisd.org).

The Simputer Trust: The Simputer Trust was established by academics and industry experts to develop a public domain design for an affordable computing device called the Simputer (www.simputer.org).

UNESCO Free Software Portal: UNESCO maintains a Web portal that serves as a publicly accessible repository of documents and Web sites that promote the "Free Software/Open Source Technology movement." It also provides ancillary resources for users and developers of free software (www.unesco.org/webworld/portal_freesoft/index.shtml).

References

Accascina, G. 2000. "Information technology and poverty alleviation." **SD Dimensions**. Food and Agricultural Organization of the United Nations (FAO), Rome. www.fao.org/sd/CDdirect/CDre0055h.htm, accessed in November 2002.

Agada, John. 1999. "Inner-city gatekeepers: An exploratory survey of their information use environment." **Journal of Information Science,** Vol. 50, No. 1, pp. 74–85.

Barbour, I.G. 1993. **Ethics in an Age of Technology**. Harper Collins, San Francisco.

Benjamin, P. 1999. "Community development and democratisation through information technology: Building the new South Africa." In R. Heeks (ed.), **Reinventing Government in the Information Age: International Practice in IT-Enabled Public Sector Reform**. Routledge, London.

Bergman, E. and E. Johnson. 1995. "Towards accessible human-computer interaction." In J. Nielsen (ed.), **Human-Computer Interaction**, Vol. 5. http://research.sun.com, accessed in November 2002.

Bhatt, S. (No date.) **IDRC's Environment and Natural Resources Management (ENRM) Programming in South Asia**. IDRC Discussion Paper for Regional Workshop. www.dgroups.org/groups/saro/enrm/docs/ENRM%20discussion%20paper.rtf, accessed in April 2003.

Bouguettaya, A., O. Mourad, M. Brahim, and A.K. Elmagarmid. 2002. "Supporting data and services access in digital government environments." In W. McIver, Jr., and A.K. Elmagarmid (eds.), **Advances in Digital Government: Technology, Human Factors, and Policy**. Kluwer, Boston.

Bouguettaya, A., M. Ouzzani, B. Medjahed and J. Cameron. 2001. "Helping citizens of Indiana: Ontological approach to managing state and local government databases." **IEEE Computer**, February.

Cabral, A. 1970. **National Liberation and Culture**. 1970 Eduardo Mondlane Memorial Lecture. Syracuse University, Syracuse, NY. Translated from the French by Maureen Webster.

Chatman, E.A. 1996. "The impoverished life-world of outsiders." **Journal of the American Society for Information Science**, Vol. 47, No. 3, pp. 193–206.

Connell, B.R., M. Jones, R. Mace, J. Mueller, A. Mullick, E. Ostroff, J. Sanford, E. Steinfield, M. Story and G. Vanderheiden. 1997. **The Principles of Universal Design, Version 2.0**. North Carolina State University, The Center for Universal Design, Raleigh.

Cook, M.E. 2000. **What Citizens Want From E-Government: Current Practice Research**. Center for Technology in Government, University at Albany/State University of New York. www.ctg.albany.edu, accessed in November 2001.

Dinkelacker, J., P.K. Garg, R. Miller and D. Nelson. 2002. **Progressive Open Source**. Proceedings of the 24th International Conference on Software Engineering. ACM Press, New York.

Driscoll, L. 2001. **HIV/AIDS and Information and Communication Technologies**. Final draft report. International Development Research Centre, Ottawa. www.idrc.ca/acacia/docHIV_AIDSfinaldraft.html, accessed in April 2003.

Finquelievich, S. 1999. **Community Informatics: The Slow Argentinean Way**. www.scn.org/tech/the_network/Proj/ws99, accessed in November 2002.

Garrett, L. 2000. **Betrayal of Trust: The Collapse of Global Public Health**. Hyperion, New York.

Gillespie, A. and K. Robins. 1989. "Geographical inequalities: The spatial bias of the new communications technologies." **Journal of Communication**, Vol. 39, No. 3, Summer.

Glinert, E.P. and B.W. York. 1992. "Computers and people with disabilities." **Communications of the ACM**, Vol. 35, No. 5, May, pp. 32–35.

Greenbaum, J. 1995. **Windows on the Workplace: Computers, Jobs and the Organization of Office Work in the Late Twentieth Century**. Monthly Review Press, New York.

Gurstein, M. 2002. "Community informatics: Current status and future prospects." **Community Technology Review**, Winter-Spring. www.comtechreview.org, accessed in May 2002.

————. 2000. "E-commerce and community economic development: Enemy or ally?" **SD Dimensions**. FAO, Rome. www.fao.org/sd/CDdirect/CDre0055i.htm, accessed in November 2002.

Hamelink, C. 1999. **ICTs and Social Development: The Global Policy Context**. Discussion Paper No. 116. UNRISD, Geneva. www.unrisd.org, accessed in November 2002.

Hausen, H.L. and M. Mollerburg. 1981. **Conspectus of Software Engineering Environments**. Proceedings of the Fifth International Conference on Software Engineering (San Diego, CA, 9–12 March). IEEE Computer Society, Los Alamitos, CA.

Innis, H. 1964. **The Bias of Communication**. University of Toronto Press, Toronto.

International Organization for Standardization/International Electrotechnical Commission (ISO/IEC). 1995. **Information Technology—Software Life Cycle Processes**. Document Number ISO/IEC 12207. ISO/IEC, Geneva.

Jansen, S.C. 1989. "Gender and the information society: A socially structured silence." **Journal of Communication**, Vol. 39, No. 3, Summer, pp. 196–215.

Johnson-Eilola, J. 2002. **Open Source Basics: Definitions, Models, and Questions**. Proceedings of the 20th Annual International Conference on Computer Documentation. ACM Press, New York.

Keniston, K. 2002. **IT for the Masses: Hope or Hype?** Massachusetts Institute of Technology (MIT), Cambridge, MA. www.mit.edu/people/kken/PAPERS/ EPW_paper.html, accessed in May 2003.

Kitchin, R.M. 1998. "Towards geographies of cyberspace." **Progress in Human Geography**, Vol. 22, No. 3, pp. 385–406.

Kling, R. 1999. "What is social informatics and why does it matter?" **D-Lib Magazine**, Vol. 5, No. 1, January. www.dlib.org, accessed in May 2002.

————. 1996. **Computerization and Controversy: Value Conflicts and Social Choices** (second edition). Morgan Kaufmann, New York.

Landauer, T.K. 1995. **The Trouble with Computers**. MIT Press, Cambridge, MA.

Margonelli, L. 2002. "The Rainmaker: How a low-cost, lightweight pump is changing the economy of a nation." **Wired**, No. 10.04, April. www.wired.com, accessed in August 2002.

Marx, G. 2002. "The new surveillance." In Joy James (ed.), **States of Confinement: Policing, Detention, and Prisons**. Palgrave Macmillan, New York.

Metoyer-Duran, C. 1991. "Gatekeepers in ethnolinguistic communities: Methodological considerations." **Public Libraries**, Vol. 30, No. 32, pp. 18–25.

McIver, W.J., Jr., and A.K. Elmagarmid (eds.). 2002. **Advances in Digital Government: Technology, Human Factors, and Policy**. Kluwer, Boston.

Moore, J. 1998. **ISO 12207 and Related Software Life-Cycle Standards**. Association for Computing Machinery (ACM), Technical Standards Committee, New York. www.acm.org/tsc/lifecycle.html, accessed in April 2003.

Mueller, M. 1999. "ICANN and Internet governance: Sorting through the debris of 'self-regulation'." **Info**, Vol. 1, no. 6, December, pp. 497–520. www.icannwatch.org, accessed in November 2002.

Muller, M., C. Wharton, W.J. McIver, Jr., and L. Laux. 1997. **Toward a Future of HCI Research and Practice Agenda Based on Human Needs and Social Responsibility**. CHI 97 Conference Proceedings (Atlanta, GA, 22–27 March).

Mumford, L. 1934. **Technics and Civilization**. Harcourt, Brace and World, Inc., New York.

Munya, H. 2000. "Information and communication technologies for rural development and food security: Lessons from field experiences in developing countries." **SD Dimensions**. FAO, Rome. www.fao.org/sd/CDdirect/ CDre0055b.htm, accessed in November 2002.

Myers, B., J. Hollan, and I. Cruz. 1996. "Strategic directions in human-computer interaction." **ACM Computing Surveys**, Vol. 28, No. 4, December.

Nielsen, J. and T.K. Landauer. 1993. **A Mathematical Model of the Finding of Usability Problems**. Proceedings of INTERCHI 93. ACM, New York, pp. 206–213.

Norman, D. 1998. **The Invisible Computer**. MIT Press, Cambridge, MA.

Noronha, F. (No date.) **Bringing Back "Baatchit" into the Villages; Getting the Info-Flow Going Again**. www.bytesforall.org/9th/html/batchit.htm, accessed in April 2003.

New York Network Exchange (NYNEX). (No date.) **NYNEX Accessibility and Universal Design Principles**. Trace Research and Development Center, Madison, WI. http://trace.wisc.edu, accessed in November 2001.

Pacific Bell Advisory Group for People with Disabilities. 1996. **Universal Design Policy: The Advisory Group's Recommendations and Pacific Bell's Response**. Trace Research and Development Center, Madison, WI. http://trace.wisc.edu, accessed in November 2001.

PicoPeta Simputers. (No date.) **About PicoPeta Simputers**. www.picopeta.com, accessed in December 2002.

Powell, M. 2001. "Knowledge, culture and the Internet in Africa: A challenge for political economists." **Review of African Political Economy**, No. 88, pp. 241–266.

Postman, N. 1992. **Technopoly: The Surrender of Culture to Technology**. Knopf, New York.

Richstad, Jim. 2003. "Right to communicate in the Internet age." In Claude-Jean Bertrand (ed.), **An Arsenal for Democracy: Media Accountability Systems**. Hampton Press, Cresskill, NJ.

Rodney, W. 1981. **How Europe Underdeveloped Africa** (revised edition). Howard University Press, Washington, DC.

Rudolph, S. 2002. **Digital Ecologies**. Jiva Institute, Faridabad, India. www.jiva.org/report_details.asp?report_id=49, accessed in December 2002.

Spink, Amanda, Martin Jaeckel and Greg Sidberry. 1997. **Information Seeking and Information Needs of Low Income African American Households: Wynnewood Healthy Neighborhood Project**. Proceedings of the 60th ASIS Annual Meeting (Washington, DC, 1–6 November).

Totaro, Donato. 2001. **Family Viewing and the Spatialization of Time Off Screen**. www.offscreen.com, accessed in March 2003.

Trace Research and Development Center. 1991. **A Brief Introduction to Disabilities**. University of Wisconsin-Madison, Madison, WI. www.tracecenter.org/ docs/population/populat.htm, accessed in August 2001.

United Nations. 1993. **Human Rights: The International Bill of Human Rights: Universal Declaration of Human Rights; International Covenant on Economic, Social and Cultural Rights; and International Covenant on Civil and Political Rights and Optional Protocols.** UN, New York.

United Nations. 2000. **United Nations Millennium Declaration.** Draft Resolution referred by the General Assembly at its 54th session, Item 61(b) of the provisional agenda. www.un.org, accessed in January 2001.

United Nations Development Programme. 2002. **Human Development Report 2002: Deepening Democracy in a Fragmented World.** New York. www.undp.org, accessed in November 2002.

World Wide Web Consortium (W3C). 2001. **Web Content Accessibility Guidelines 2.0.** Working draft. www.w3.org, accessed in November 2001.

Yajnik, N.M. 2002. **Challenges in the Design and Implementation of Sustainable Innovations in Developing Nations.** Second International Conference on Open Collaborative Design of Sustainable Innovation (Bangalore, India, 1–2 December). http://thinkcycle.media.mit.edu, accessed in January 2003.

The Other Information Revolution: Media and Empowerment in Developing Countries[1]

James Deane with Kunda Dixit, Njonjo Mue, Fackson Banda and Silvio Waisbord

Abstract

Too often, debate on the information society narrows quickly to information and communication technologies (ICTs), the potential of the Internet and worries about the digital divide. But another information revolution has been under way, especially in the South, less debated but equally dynamic, more pervasive and potentially even more far reaching. It concerns the "other" ICTs of radio, television and the press that determine, far more than the Internet, the type of information people get and the raw material they bring to bear in constructing and reconstructing our world. This chapter makes three claims.

First, a thoroughgoing liberalization and commercialization of media over the last decade in many parts of the world has led to a much more democratic, dynamic, crowded and complex media landscape. This is opening up new spaces for public debate and civic engagement, particularly in the field of radio; and to a more commercial, advertising-driven media where information and power divides within developing countries between rich and poor, urban and rural are growing.

Second, growing concentration of media ownership—at the global, regional and national levels—is squeezing out independent media players and threatening to replace government-controlled concentration of media power with a commercial and political one.

Third, developing countries are increasingly, not decreasingly, reliant on powerful Northern news providers, such as the British Broadcasting Corporation (BBC), Reuters and Cable News Network (CNN), for their international news and information, particularly on stories of globalization, trade and international politics; and in newly democratic countries in the South, and particularly within civil society, there is a renewed and growing frustration at the Southern media's dependence on what are perceived to be partial, biased or at least

---

[1] This chapter is an extended and amended, but not substantially updated, version of a chapter that appeared first in the *Global Civil Society Yearbook 2002*, a joint project of the Centre for Civil Society and the Centre for the Study of Global Governance, and the flagship publication of the Global Civil Society Programme of the London School of Economics (LSE). We are most grateful to the *Yearbook* editor and its authors for permission to use the original. Two new contributors, Kunda Dixit and Silvio Waisbord, have supplemented the original text.

fundamentally Northern-centric news organizations for international coverage and the setting of news agendas.

These trends play out differently within and between different regions, but their mark is everywhere. Furthermore, they are taking place largely in the absence of informed and widespread debate, and in a regulatory environment that in many cases can be described as rudimentary.

At risk here is the media's critical public interest role, and the danger of compromise by private interests. Suspicion, often understandable, of strong government action in the area of media places a heavier burden on civil society, including the emerging transnational civil society, to put pressure both on media and on government with the goal of supporting the public interest, and indeed with the goal of taking part itself in non-commercial media forms.

Introduction

The emergence, health and diversity of civil society depend on access to information on key issues that affect people's lives, and the capacity of people and organizations to have their voices heard in the public and political arena. No matter how one defines the emerging information society, this must surely be a central aspect of it.

The role of the information technology revolution and its implications for global civil society have been well documented in this respect (Castells 1998; Naughton 2001). The potential of the Internet, and mobile telephony in particular, to provide unprecedented access to information and knowledge, and their record in providing new ways for geographically disparate people to form communities of common interest, to communicate, to organize and to make their voices heard, is widely acknowledged. This information revolution—complex, unevenly distributed, creating new divides while narrowing others, but undoubtedly transformative—has overshadowed a broader, more pervasive information revolution that is less understood and certainly less documented.

For much of humanity, particularly the almost 3 billion people earning less than two dollars a day, access to information through information and communication technologies (ICTs), such as the Internet, remains a distant (though not impossible) prospect. For most people in most developing countries, it is the rapidly changing media that provide the information, perspective and analysis that enable them to make sense of their world and to engage as citizens in their society; provide an increasingly important means of making their voices heard; increasingly facilitate horizontal and interpersonal communication and debate; and provide mechanisms for the formulation of identity and the creation of community spaces. Conversely, it is the media that are often most instrumental in creating new forms of social and political division in society, depoliticizing public debate, and fostering tension and conflict between countries and communities.

Over the last decade, and the last five years in particular, the media in most developing countries have undergone a revolution in their structure, dynamism, interactivity, reach and accessibility. This has had a profound impact on and for civil society in these countries, and very mixed implications for the inclusiveness and character of public debate, particularly in relation to the exposure of public and political debate to the voices, concerns and perspectives of the poor and marginalized in these societies. Independence, plurality and accessibility of the media constitute fundamental constituents of an environment that facilitates social change. The role of the media in fostering democratic inclusion, underpinning social and political change, economic development and empowering marginalized communities is well documented.[2]

The vibrancy, intensity and effectiveness of civil society, particularly in developing countries, are intimately related to the freedom and pluralism of the media. Civil society depends heavily on people having access to information and having channels to voice issues of concern in the public arena. If civil society organizations are to effect positive change, they need to articulate their arguments in the public arena and subject their arguments to public debate. While there are plenty of examples of civil society organizations exerting influence in closed and oppressive regimes where the media are tightly controlled, free and genuinely plural media clearly provide the opportunity and foundation for the kind of inclusive public debate where civil society perspectives can be aired, heard and tested. Freedom and pluralism of the media are both a product and an engine for an inclusive, genuinely civil society.

This chapter examines some of the changes in the media over the last decade, particularly in developing countries, and provides a broad examination of some of the implications for public debate, free expression and civil society, at both the national and international levels. It argues that, in terms of how most people on the planet access information and knowledge on issues that affect their lives, and how most people articulate and make their feelings heard in national and international public debates, the changes in structure, content, ownership and access within the "traditional" media in the last five years have been equally, if not more, profound than those occurring in the new technologies. While changes in the global media and the increased concentration of the media internationally have been the subject of substantial comment,[3] changes

---

[2]   Sen 1999; Besley and Burgess 2000; Hamelink 1994; Lush 1997; Westoff and Bankole 1999; Dreze and Sen 1989.

[3]   For example, McChesney and Herman (1997); and Gerbner et al. (1996). Also see the Mediachannel Web site, www.mediachannel.org.

in the media within developing countries have received substantially less attention. The chapter argues that the implications of these changes for civil society are extremely contradictory.

Out with the Old: The Former Status Quo

Little more than a decade ago, most people on the planet accessed information from beyond their immediate communities, mainly via state-owned and state-controlled monopoly media. Throughout the Soviet Union and most of its sphere, government control of media was total. In China, the same situation applied. Throughout much of Africa and much of the rest of Asia, post-independence governments invested heavily in their radio broadcasting and press infrastructures as key tools of nation building. In these countries, governments were keen to assert strong control and monopoly ownership of the media, partly to guard against fragmentation of the media along ethnic, tribal or political lines, and partly to maximize political control over their peoples. In many countries, media systems were inherited from the former colonial powers, and in several cases, media infrastructure was non-existent, either because it had not been established or because radio stations, for example, had suffered wholesale demolition by the outgoing colonial governments.

In many cases, aspirant presidents sought to take power by making their first coup objective the commandeering of their nation's broadcasting station, and governments protective of their power have since kept jealous control of "their" media systems. The degree of control exerted over the media was generally closely linked to the autocracy of the government in power but, even in democracies such as India, governments insisted on monopoly control of the broadcast media. The print media, generally with a much smaller reach and limited principally to urban populations, were less controlled. In Latin America, tight control of the media was less often exercised through direct government ownership and more often by privately owned media whose owners' interests were closely allied to those in power or, at a minimum, served the interests of a small and wealthy elite.

Much of this control took place in the context of the Cold War when superpowers and their client states exercised definitive influence on who was in government and how long they remained in power. Much of the information available to people through the media was similarly defined by that context. This chapter is not designed to provide a detailed analysis of the history of the media over the last 50 years, and there are many examples of developing countries that have a long tradition of free and open media, as well as cases of industrialized countries seeking to keep a tight a rein on freedom of the media. But its starting point is that, for much of the post-Second World War period, the vast majority of people on the planet had access only to information from the media to which their governments allowed them access. Although the complexity and penetration of social, community, and other informal and non-media information networks should not be underestimated, state control and influence over the media in most countries defined political and social discourse, and fundamentally constrained the emergence of non-governmental and civil society actors.

In many countries, state control of the media remains extremely powerful. While China, for example, is witnessing increasing diversity and energy within its media, they continue to operate under a tight regimen controlled by government (Sun 2001).

And, as this chapter argues, where state control of the media has declined, commercial and corporate control has taken its place. However, for most developing countries the end of the Cold War prompted an information revolution every bit as important as the digital information revolution.

Freedom, Choice . . . and Money

Since the fall of the Berlin wall and the end of the Cold War, in tandem with other processes, there has been a rapid, widespread liberalization of media in general and of broadcast media in particular.

Pressures on governments to liberalize the media take a number of forms. The fall of many one-party systems of government in the 1980s across Africa, parts of Asia, in Eastern Europe, the former Soviet Union and elsewhere led to the coming to power of many governments committed to ending state media control. They embarked on rapid liberalization, some of them from a genuine belief in the importance of free and plural media in ensuring democratic, inclusive societies, often combined with the belief in the importance of a free flow of information as a prerequisite for the effective functioning of a free market economy.

Most governments have also understood that maintaining a monopoly over their citizens' access to information in the wake of satellite, Internet and mobile telephony is no longer possible. An increasingly well-informed, powerful and pervasive civil society has reinforced that reality. This has been combined with huge international information flows that underpin the global economy and the importance for most governments of being part of that economy. For poorer countries, these factors are reinforced by pressure from donors and other international actors, and countries that refuse to liberalize media and guarantee media freedoms find donor funding and loans withdrawn.

The net result has been that in areas formerly dominated by state-controlled media systems, particularly in much of Africa and Asia, full state control over the media remains in only a few countries.

Liberalization, particularly of broadcast media, has often been partial, haphazard and evolutionary rather than revolutionary, but it has nevertheless been transformative. In other regions, such as in large parts of Latin America, which has a long tradition of community media and where government control of the media has tended to be more complex, the transformation has tended to be less dramatic.

The most immediate consequence of these changes has been far greater freedom of information and expression. Liberalization and diversification, particularly in Africa and Asia, have transformed both print and broadcast media from a largely government-owned, monopolistic and uncreative environment to a more dynamic, popular, democratic, creative, commercial and complex one.

Print media

The print media have, despite their sometimes limited readership, played a critical role in providing internal scrutiny of governments, and a free press has become increasingly regarded as both a precondition for and major indicator of democracy, effective and sustainable development, and good governance (Roth 2001). Media freedom remains under constant pressure and attack, but the general trend is of an increasing number of print titles in many countries, and while numbers rise and fall rapidly, particularly during election periods, many have been able to sustain themselves financially and have retained a genuine political independence from government.

The international image of the print media in developing countries has tended to be shaped by fiercely independent, courageous journalists exposing corruption and wrongdoing, and battling to retain their professional integrity in the face of an often brutal state. There are many astonishing and inspirational examples of this, ranging from the bombed *Daily News* in Zimbabwe continuing to publish independently of the government despite sustained and violent intimidation, to journalists such as P. Sainath (author of *Everyone Loves a Good Drought*) who spends several months of each year travelling in and reporting from India's rural villages for the *Times of India* (Sainath 1996). Throughout much of Africa, independent newspapers have played central roles in guaranteeing and nourishing new democratic systems.

These courageous examples and individuals are, however, just one side of a coin, the flip side of which is a print media sector that sees itself as increasingly serving a metropolitan business and political elite augmented by a lifestyle agenda catering for a burgeoning middle class. Journalists who want to invest time in investigative stories, stories concerning the poor, or serious and more objective analysis underlying conflict find themselves in a minority and have to struggle for the attention and respect of their editors and newspaper proprietors.

Increasingly, the media are interested only in those who have something to sell or seek something to buy. The evolution of the media is characterized by a generalized lack of interest in the fate of those who can neither buy nor sell the products the media are advertising, even though these constitute the large majority of the populations of their countries.

Proprietors are in turn becoming more and more remote and impersonal as print media, even in the poorest countries, become more concentrated in the hands of either international (global and regional) media conglomerates or narrow party political interests. India, for example, has seen a major shift in the attitude of press proprietors. Once greatly respected for their commitment to journalistic integrity, democratic principles and professional ethics, newspapers are, according to a recent report by the UK Department for International Development, "increasingly treated as commercial brands, their independence made suspect by collaborative ties with the state-owned media" (Roth 2001:13).

Print media in most developing countries are also becoming more parochial in their views. Twenty-five years ago, media in developing countries were engaged in a fierce debate and attempt to create a New World Information and Communication Order (NWICO), where they could free themselves from dependence on Northern news sources and create their own common news-gathering and exchange systems. They would source their news increasingly from other developing countries through information exchange, news agencies and other mechanisms designed to improve South-South communication.

While the credibility of the NWICO perished many years ago, largely because its ideals were undermined by government attempts to use the new initiative to control rather than facilitate new information flows, the extent to which these ideals have been abandoned is striking.

In an increasingly globalized world, editors find it increasingly difficult to interest their readers in stories that are not explicitly locally, nationally or regionally relevant, or are not following a global news agenda (generally set in the North). Reporting of stories from Africa in the Asian print media, for example, is rare, despite the many shared issues of trade, debt and other globally relevant issues. Meanwhile the major international agencies, such as Reuters, are increasingly focusing their reporting on the lucrative business and economic reporting markets, while their news reporting (like those of other major international agencies such as Associated Press and Agence France Presse) continues to follow a heavily Northern-focused agenda. Developing country news services, meanwhile, such as the Inter Press Service and Gemini News Service, are struggling partly because of falls in donor funding that helped subsidize them, and particularly because major developing country media are increasingly being bought up by international conglomerates, many of whom have their own—again, Northern-focused—features services.

Many optimists in the 1980s foresaw a flowering of a new age of media pluralism and public debate as new media began to flourish in the new political dispensation of the end of the Cold War. Media freedom has increased, but while a political environment exists that enables more open public debate in the media, the liberalized commercial media are often unwilling to facilitate or contribute to such debate. As the World Bank points out, in Hungary before 1989, the relatively relaxed regime allowed many dissident writers to have their work published in ways that could stimulate public debate, but these same writers are now finding it increasingly difficult to get their work published in a profit-oriented free market (World Bank 2001). That situation pertains in many other former one-party states.

There are further trends toward sensationalism and media-fostered divides along ethnic or religious lines. Senegal, for example, has recently witnessed the emergence of a generation of highly populist and salacious print titles clearly modelled on the British tabloid papers (Diop 2001). The titles of these newspapers leave little doubt of their content: *Le Populaire, Le Tract* and *Le Scoop* deal with sex, crime, the freakish and gossip. In Nigeria, a country with a very rich tradition of public interest journalism and where journalists are often held in high public esteem for their role in restoring democracy to the country, increasing concern is being expressed at the emergence of "ethnic journalism" with media reporting and journalism increasingly fragmenting along Christian and Muslim faultlines.

The salaries and status of journalists in society have often increased substantially following liberalization, but in some of the poorest countries journalism continues to be a desperately difficult profession, both politically and economically. In Guinea Bissau, for example, journalists operate not only in a hostile political environment but also with poor equipment and even poorer salaries. The editor-in-chief of one (government) paper, *No Pintcha*, earns approximately 240 French francs per month in a country where a five-kilogram bag of rice costs between 1,250 and 1,400 FF (Diallo 2001).

Despite this, and although most media continue to serve a metropolitan elite, print media are the most important credible way of informing and stimulating public debate on key development issues, particularly the complex, contested and often technical issues of globalization. However, an ugly combination of increased concentration of ownership, a growing focus on business and lifestyle agendas, and editors' lack of interest in supporting investigative or specialist journalism on social or development issues is fatally undermining the extent to which the public in many developing countries have access to information about, and the means to sensibly interpret, issues of globalization or those facing the poor in their countries. Even for those editors who want to cover these issues in more detail, there is a growing shortage of credible, independent, developing-country-focused news and analysis of global issues.

The print media more than any other outlet have the capacity to provide explanation, reporting, analysis and opinion on complex issues that affect their readers' lives. Print provides a medium that can deal with complexity unlike any other. But, although literacy rates have increased substantially over the last three decades even in some of the poorest countries, access to newspapers continues to be constrained by relatively low literacy rates. Even in India, which has one of the richest newspaper publishing industries in the world, national literacy levels are still as low as 51 per cent.

The print media in most developing countries are more free and more diverse than a decade ago, and have played a central role in the political evolution of many countries. But there are major questions as to whether, given their increasing obsession with commercial advantage, they are becoming more plural or are able to inform public and political debate to the extent that democratic societies require.

The rebirth of radio and a new oral tradition?

Changes in the print media, which have a long tradition of providing independent journalism including in several one-party states, are less pronounced than those in the broadcast sector. It is the broadcast media, particularly radio, that have undergone the greatest transformation in many countries, with competition ushering in a new environment of choice and creativity in programming, with many new private and (to a much lesser extent) community-owned radio and television stations rapidly establishing audience dominance over old state-run broadcasting systems. In the radio sector, liberalization has led to three main trends. The first of these is the flourishing of a new generation of commercial, generally independent FM radio stations. From Uganda to Zambia, Sri Lanka to Nepal, and in the large majority of countries formerly controlled by one-party states, a plethora of new mostly privately run and heavily commercially oriented stations has emerged. These stations, which emerged mainly in the 1990s, were dependent entirely on advertising for their funding and have often been criticized by civil society organizations for their general avoidance of public debate and political discussion. Many commercial FM stations carry little or no news, or relay brief news from an international news provider such as the BBC (thus providing little or no local analysis or news). Programming, at least in the early stages of liberalization, typically consists of music programming often originating in the North. Some early FM stations in Africa, such as Capital Radio in Uganda, won praise from civil society organizations for their range of programmes and particularly, in the case of Capital Radio, for the development of innovative health and sex education programming, such as Capital Doctor, which was a global pioneer in addressing the issue of HIV/AIDS, and stimulating public discussion and dialogue on the issue.

However, the apolitical, non-news and music-based content of many radio stations led civil society organizations to complain increasingly that liberalization was leading to commercialization and privatization of the airwaves, with content being defined entirely by a consumer-oriented, advertising-dependent, urban-focused and generally youth lifestyle agenda. There was little or no investment in news or analysis of global or national political developments, and very little exposure or reference to the rural, marginalized majorities in these countries. While the FM stations were successful in rapidly gaining an often eager audience through more dynamic, engaging and popular programming, they had a very poor early record in addressing issues of public concern.

This trend toward an urban, consumer-oriented agenda was further reinforced by the second key trend in this sector, with state broadcasting systems plunging into crisis. The loss of monopoly effectively involved a loss of incentive by governments to invest in state broadcasting systems. These have mostly tended to try to reinvent themselves as commercial broadcasters, supplementing dwindling government subsidy with advertising income. In doing so they have followed the same content agenda as the commercial sector. They have tended to cut back on both content and infrastructure, with the most common and critical consequence being the reduction of transmitting capacity to rural areas, a shift to mainstream language programming (at the expense of minority languages), a decrease in programming aimed, for example, at education, health, environmental or agricultural support, and, with some exceptions, an unwillingness to invest in programming that provides a voice for rural communities in national debate. There are very few examples of former state broadcasting monopolies successfully transforming themselves into genuinely public service broadcasters.

A third, more positive, trend is the increasing investment in and flourishing of community radio. Originally strongest in Latin America, community radio is growing very rapidly in much of Africa and some parts of Asia. West Africa has 450 radio stations, the vast majority of which have been formed in the last decade, and South Africa has more than 100. Community radio is by most definitions taken to mean radio that is substantially owned and/or formally controlled by a community and is not run for private profit. The flourishing of community radio, although facilitated by and generally dependent on government liberalization of the airwaves, is also being driven by much lower start-up costs, as the price of transmitters and other radio equipment falls. All the equipment required to establish a community radio station can be acquired for less than $20,000 (and a very basic set-up could be established for a tenth of that amount). Although facing problems of sustainability, with several examples of donor-funded community radio stations being initiated and then collapsing after initial investment, organizations such as the World Association of Community Broadcasters (AMARC) are facilitating growth in this area. Community stations, such as Radio Sagarmatha in Nepal, have become increasingly professional, national and commercial entities, blending their original commitment to community issues and public debate with a commercial business plan. In some cases, original community radio organizations have abandoned their roots and transformed themselves entirely into commercial, advertising-driven organizations.

These trends, which were set in motion in the 1990s, reflect a complex picture of privatization and commercialization of the airwaves with a small window also being opened to the community sector. More recently, however, a new, largely unpredicted trend has emerged, offering major new opportunities for public debate: the rise of the talk show. Talk-based radio, involving free-ranging studio discussions, phone-ins, political interviews, interviews with celebrities and music, are becoming some of the most popular programming for FM broadcasters. Although few FM radio stations have the resources to invest in significant independent news-gathering operations, talk shows are opening up new spaces for political and public debate, and through debate to public engagement. They are, according to Muthoni Wanyeki, director general of the African Women's Development and Communication Network (FEMNET) in Africa, leading to "reinvention of the African oral tradition" (Wanyeki 2000). New radio stations specifically devoted to talk-based radio, such as Monitor FM in Kampala, are emerging. Although still heavily urban-based and urban-oriented, and with very limited access to and reporting from non-urban areas, these are creating new channels and opportunities for public debate in general and for civil society organizations in particular to have their voices heard in the public arena. The complexity and potential of radio as a reborn medium in many developing countries is further augmented by other technological developments, particularly the potential of the Internet to enable resource-poor radio stations to access and exchange content, and the telephone which, through phone-ins, is making radio a much more horizontal and interactive medium. Audio files are easily digitized and, although there are major constraints caused by poor levels of connectivity and capacity to take advantage of these technologies, there are several projects that are seeking to use the technology to improve coverage of development issues by FM and community radio stations.

Despite this, the gaps between rich and poor, rural and urban remain. While the community radio movement is providing empowering new forms of information and communication, the movement is patchy and many governments (in Zimbabwe, for example) are refusing to grant licences to community media. More broadly, governments in much of the developing world appear content to allow a burgeoning of the FM radio sector, provided that the limited geographical reach of FM radio transmitters makes them a principally urban phenomenon. Walk more than a few miles outside of the urban centres in most countries, and this radio revolution might never have existed. While liberalization in the radio sector is a dominant trend globally, it is far from a universal one.

Governments generally are much less willing to grant licences to short- or medium-wave radio stations, which have the capacity to reach rural areas and are proving fiercely—and effectively—protective of their broadcasting monopoly in rural areas where, for many, their political power base rests. The decline in investment in state-run broadcasting systems, including the closing or breaking down of transmitters, the cutting of minority language services and lack of investment in appropriate content, means that rural areas are becoming increasingly, rather than decreasingly, marginalized from public and political debate. The urban-rural divide is intensifying in media, and in doing so reflects a similar divide in civil society, with most civil society organizations also being very heavily an urban phenomenon. Together with other more conventionally understood characteristics of the "digital divide", such as the lack of access to telephony and Internet by rural populations and the poor, this marginalization is becoming increasingly stark.

Religious organizations have also responded to broadcast liberalization with alacrity. Mostly US-based or US-funded fundamentalist religious organizations broadcast to large parts of the developing world. Religious organizations have also been quick to take advantage of new broadcast licences, sometimes with the help of strongly religious governments or government leaders. In Zambia, the first independent radio station was a Christian one; and, of six supposedly independent community radio stations recently granted radio licences, four are owned and controlled by the Catholic Church.

Liberalization is also leading to a strengthening and increasing dependence on international news networks, particularly the BBC. The BBC has always been a valued and respected news source in much of the developing world, and its value has generally risen in inverse relationship with the credibility of local news sources. The less plural, the more controlled the national media, the more people turn to sources such as the BBC for their news and information. It is perhaps curious that, at a time of increased freedom, the BBC is on the whole thriving, reporting steadily increasing audiences for its radio output on the BBC World Service and through its strategy of becoming, in effect, a national broadcaster by securing national FM licences for its broadcasts. The BBC's growing audiences at the national level no longer reflect principally a lack of freedom in most of the countries it works in, but the inability or unwillingness of local broadcasters to access and provide news and information to their audiences in a detailed way. Although the picture is complex, and in some countries the BBC is suffering significant audience losses while in others achieving major gains, countries where the BBC's audience share tends to be low, such as in Uganda, tend to be those where domestic news sources and the domestic broadcast environment do provide sufficient, locally relevant news and information. The key to addressing the challenges of providing public interest radio in a liberalized and commercialized environment lies in creating intelligent, flexible and creative regulatory environments that encourage diversity and genuine pluralism. There are, however, very few examples where such regulation has been successfully developed and applied.

Television: Consumerism, conflict and an end to boredom

The transformation in media content following liberalization is seen nowhere more graphically than in television. Although Malawi opened its first television station only in 2000, and television signals are available to just 70 per cent of Kenyans, global access to television has grown massively in the last decade. It remains, however, a minority medium, particularly when compared with radio, and, for rural areas in Africa and Asia (but to a lesser extent in much of Latin America), television penetration remains very limited. In terms of where its content is principally targeted and for whom it is produced, rural populations in general could be on another planet.

An increasingly competitive, commercial and ratings-hungry television industry is clearly not restricted to the developing world, but the rate and scale of change in the television industry and consequent implications for public debate and social change are particularly intense in much of the South. As with radio, a little over a decade ago most governments monopolized television. State ownership and control of the media was (and in several countries still is) a fundamental pillar of oppression, disenfranchisement and control. But this has changed, and for many people its passing is celebrated almost as much for an end to boredom as an end to state control of their lives. Commercialization of this sector has, if nothing else, created television that is more dynamic, entertaining and far more popular than the state-controlled fodder that preceded it.

Perhaps the most dramatic change in the television industry anywhere on the planet has occurred in South Asia, with the introduction of mostly Indian-based satellite television (as discussed below). South Asian governments have proved very reluctant to surrender control of the broadcast media, even in India, where the birth of the satellite revolution has been rooted. But satellite television has been licensed and in a decade has transformed television, has had major repercussions for culture, regional political relations, economic development and political debate, and has impinged on almost all other aspects of life on the subcontinent. The Zee TV and Rupert Murdoch-owned Star TV networks first started broadcasting in the early 1990s. These channels, and others such as Sony TV, Gemini and Sun, are based in India but have a footprint across the South Asian region and beyond. They have revitalized media in much of the region, throwing down a gauntlet to traditional, staid programming of the monopoly broadcaster Doordarshan through a dynamic, energetic and massively popular mix of lifestyle, music, movies and news. Zee TV in particular has met with huge success through its adaptation of a general entertainment formula to the Hindi language, a process which has become known as "Hindigenization".

However, both the popularity and the content of these new Hindi language entertainment channels are, according to David Page and William Crawley (2000a), giving rise "to apprehensions that the culture of Bollywood is swamping other national cultures and even destroying the ideological boundaries of the nation state". It is also creating a new "lingua franca" for the region, a hybrid of English and Hindi developed particularly by Zee TV.

At a time of increased international tensions in the region, satellite television is leading to markedly increased suspicion and resentment of India among other populations in the region. The dominance of Hindi channels such as Zee and Star is having increasingly significant political as well as cultural repercussions, particularly feeding tensions and public resentment of India in Pakistan. Reporting and analysis by Indian-based satellite news organizations of Kashmir and the Kargil crisis are widely perceived as being biased, nationalistic and often inflammatory. Reporting on the satellite channels, which are widely accessed in Pakistan, is pushing a heavily patriotic and nationalistic Indian line on what is a regional medium. This has substantially exacerbated public suspicion in Pakistan, and satellite broadcasts were prohibited recently by the Pakistan government from being relayed on cable channels. The names given to programmes on the conflict, such as *The Big Fight,* further contribute to this feeling. The role of the satellite television media in fuelling conflict between these nuclear powers, and their unwillingness to provide a space and a voice to independent, peace-oriented views, are a source of increasing alarm within civil society in the region. While there are some attempts by satellite television to address these issues (Star TV started but has since discontinued a regular letter from Pakistan), the overwhelming sense is of a regional media giant acting as a national and narrowly patriotic broadcaster. Nor is this confined to relations between India and Pakistan. Nepal and Bangladesh are barely featured in this South Asian regional medium, and claims have been made that Zee TV has significantly affected relations between the people of Nepal and India (Page and Crawley 2000b:386–388).

Liberalization of television is, as with radio and print, a principally urban-focused phenomenon. Sixty per cent of South Asians live in rural areas, where access to television, while beginning to spread rapidly, nevertheless continues to be limited. The social and political reverberations caused by satellite television have perhaps been felt even more strongly in the extraordinary global and regional prominence achieved by Al Jazeera television in the wake of 11 September 2001. Al Jazeera ("The Peninsula") was launched in 1996 with $137 million of funding provided by the Qatari emirate with the express purpose of modernizing and democratizing Qatar. It rapidly developed a reputation for outspoken, independent reporting, and equally quickly became the most popular television news station throughout the Middle East and beyond. It claims 35 million viewers.

Al Jazeera has become famous through its coverage of Afghanistan and its exclusive broadcasts of tapes provided by Osama bin Laden and latterly in the invasion of Iraq and its bombing by United States forces. However, it is not just the quality and independence of its journalism that has marked it out, but also its free-ranging studio discussions and phone-ins, some of them resulting in loud shouting arguments with often extremist positions. It has upset not only the United States but also many political leaders in the Arab world and has been banned from Saudi Arabia. Tunisia, Morocco and Libya recalled their ambassadors to Qatar, and Jordan closed the station's bureau after a programme critical of the government. Popular it may be, but a lucrative business proposition it was not. Advertisers were wary of being associated with controversy, and Al Jazeera generated only $15 million in advertising revenue in 2000, compared to $93 million by the Lebanese Broadcasting Corporation (LBC), Lebanon's entertainment network (Zednick 2002). It was creeping slowly toward commercial sustainability before 11 September 2001 and is still reliant on Qatari funding, but since then its revenues have escalated rapidly. Nevertheless, it is difficult to imagine it establishing the kind of reputation it has if it had been established with principally commercial objectives. For all that, there is little evidence that it might emerge as a model for a new generation of non-Northern, Southern-based regional media capable of establishing a credible, independent, professional—if sometimes contentious—news source reflecting the priorities of their publics.

Television remains the least plural and least democratic of all media, with ownership continuing to be concentrated in the hands of the few. In Latin America, television has long been a far more pervasive medium than in much of the rest of the developing world, with even some of the poorest communities having access, and ownership has long been tightly controlled by extremely powerful private companies generally with strong links to government. In this sense, the changes in Latin America have been less dramatic than elsewhere. In Brazil, 80 per cent of the population, amounting to 90 million people, have access to television, and glamorous soap operas have been credited with helping to reduce fertility rates as poor families aspire to the exclusive lifestyles they see on television and have smaller families as a result.

Latin America is also the home and international inspiration of a host of community and participatory communication initiatives, many of which use television to give voice and expression to people otherwise marginalized, but these are principally found outside the mainstream television infrastructure. The Brazilian initiative, TV Maxambomba, for example, uses video to record the experiences of local people, appraises what is done by grassroots or community organizations and brings information necessary to the understanding of people's rights. It also produces videos on local culture and programmes for children, with more than 100 videos being produced since its inception in 1986 (Gumucio-Dagron 2000).

There are also increasing numbers of cases where television has proved itself to be the most effective way of stimulating social change. In South Africa, the most popular television soap opera is *Soul City*, a high-quality drama series which also has a very explicit social remit. Dealing with issues of domestic violence, HIV/AIDS, diarrhoeal diseases and urban violence, it has become one of the most respected examples in the world of a communication initiative which can inform, engage and entertain while having a demonstrable and proven impact in achieving change. Every three out of four television viewers watched the most recent series of *Soul City*.

Media's Cultural Dimension

The effect of media on cultures, values and consumption patterns has been the subject of vigorous debate. Many studies have sought a correlation between what people, especially young people, watch on television, and how they dress and speak, and what they buy. Studies have found strong correlations between television viewing and how this affects traditional habits among, for instance, the Caboclo in Brazil.

Similar studies in Venezuela and other parts of Asia have shown that families change their eating, socialization and time management when television is "embedded" in the home.

But there have been also studies that show a positive impact of television, which has created greater awareness of the outside world, a healthy scepticism of politicians, and in some closed Islamic societies, it has given women a glimpse of a world where women have more independence. In many other studies of media impact, it has been found that viewers take what is familiar to them from a programme, and this may not necessarily be what was anticipated by the producer.

As we have seen with news, the media tends to have an exaggerated sense of its own importance. Media is an important purveyor of news and information, and if this is selective or biased it does change perceptions. But the causal factors linking information to awareness to behaviour change, or people being swayed by a slant in information via media, is not as direct or logical as it sounds.

In fact, the absence of proportionate impact after massive advertisement campaigns about HIV/AIDS in many developing countries is evidence that the media may be able to present and disseminate information and seek to raise awareness, but there is a big gap between that and change in individual conduct. In Nepal, awareness of condoms has risen exponentially to 85 percent in the past five years, but actual use of protection (except among vulnerable groups like sex workers) has not shown a similar increase. Similarly, a pro-US slant in news and current affairs reporting on the Iraq war did not necessarily turn world public opinion in favour of America. In fact, in the Arab world, the images of the toppling of the Saddam statue appears to have had the opposite effect.

Much of the scientific research into media impact on behavioural change has demonstrated only one certainty: the uncertainty of gauging impact. In local focus group studies on the Indian subcontinent three years ago, respondents gave widely disparate answers about how media, especially television, affected their behaviour. Most tended to underestimate the impact on themselves, for instance, on the way they dressed, while exaggerating the impact on peers. But even when asked about the general effect on societal mores, there were diametrically opposed perceptions.

The presumption that soaps like *Dallas*, or *The Bold and the Beautiful* bring about irreversible and long-term changes in developing country societies is therefore not as clear-cut as some academics from the developing world itself predicted not so long ago. Many variables interact: the level of development of the society, familiarity of a particular community with Western programming, how intricately the country is integrated into the global economy, the local cultural coherence and more. In many countries, surveys have shown that Western programming has greater viewership, and perhaps greater impact, in the beginning, but that this tails off as the novelty wears off. When pure Western content is replaced by local programming, it is always much more popular and tends to capture prime time slots. In many cases, for instance India, Egypt and East Asia, Western soaps have been progressively replaced by local soaps, and there are Hindi or Mandarin clones of the originals. In Pakistan and Nepal, domestically produced local language dramas achieve the highest rations. Given an alternative of interesting, funny, professionally produced drama about issues relevant to their lives, people in most developing countries will switch away from foreign programming.

It is not just Western entertainment content that has made inroads into the South. Among the most popular programmes in the Philippines is a Mexican soap opera. Indian musicals are popular wherever the diaspora is located, but also in Central Asia and Indonesia. In Nepal, Pakistani drama series are exceptionally popular and carry the highest ratings.

The trend toward "localizing the global" has happened also in talk shows, in news and current affairs (Al Jazeera in the Gulf, the local-language Murdoch-controlled news channels in the rest of Asia) as well as the dubbing of nature programmes into local languages (National Geographic, Discovery, and even some local productions on these channels), and of course the 24-hour movie channels showing archival Bollywood or Chinese feature films.

But measuring the impact of all this on the behaviour and attitude of viewers is less charted territory. Many opposed to the cultural media exports target multinational media conglomerates. Five to 10 years ago there may have been substance to this, as content was indeed Western-dominated, but this has since changed to comprise much more local programming. Yet the value system of the latter still projects the underlying message of escapism and consumerism. In fact, some researchers have argued that having the message in a local language is actually more dangerous because it is easier to assimilate.

Producers of entertainment content often tailor their plots, wardrobes and conduct on screen to define lifestyles that will be conducive to advertising. There is thus a natural drift toward escapism, opulence and luxury well beyond the reach of the majority of viewers. There are reports that advertisers may be permitted to screen and censor content on entertainment material, and in some cases advertising agencies hired by sponsoring companies will insist on onscreen "plugs" for their products. The media therefore prioritizes the segments of society with the purchasing power to be able to afford (or at least aspire to) some of these goods. In many developing countries, local media is therefore urban-targeted, and advertising, entertainment and news content are aimed at the preoccupations of the urban middle class. Many channels in India, for instance, carry programmes on aerobics and weight loss. The irony of such content being broadcast in a country where more than half the children are undernourished is probably lost on the owners of the station and the sponsors. But with increasing penetration of television in rural India, weight-loss exercising is being watched in rural homes where inhabitants already get more exercise than they need.

There may be no direct partnership between manufacturers of consumer goods and of television stations, but this is not needed where a close symbiotic relationship develops between the two. The casualty in all this, of course, are the public broadcasting values that should ideally guide the medium. Public channels like Australian ABC, Canadian CBC and the BBC are mandated to provide a wholesome mix of information, entertainment and education. In many countries where the laws are either lax (United States) or non-existent (much of the developing world) over-commercialization of television has turned the medium into a carrier of lifestyle values aimed at consumers.

The advertising industry, with its psychographic research and focus group testing will find the best way to bring about not just awareness of products, but also behaviour change to incite consumers to buy their products. The cause-effect here is much more direct than with cultural products, and can be measured.

Much of the blame for this can rightly be set at the door of multinational corporations, which own the manufacturing base as well as the channels of communications. However, domestic media also depends on local big business for sponsorship of television entertainment, advertising fast-moving consumer goods, snacks, detergents and beauty products. Many of these are in fact products manufactured by affiliates of multinational companies. Though advertisers may be local, the product range broadcast during the commercial break is the same.

Why This Matters

All of the above amounts to a series of complex, contradictory trends that have major implications for social inclusion and public debate. First of all, they raise major issues of access to information which enables people, particularly poor and marginalized people, to make sense of their lives, especially in the context of an increasingly complex and globalized society; and second, they raise issues of voice, the role and potential of the media to provide a channel and space for the voices and perspectives of those most affected by these issues, in terms both of reporting from the poor and of providing a voice or space for civil society. Access to information is being transformed. There is a major and growing gulf between information accessible and relevant to the rich and the poor, the urban and the rural. Despite new media freedoms, the liberalized environment has led to a decline in both the inclination and the capacity of media to cover complex, contentious and technical issues such as those relating to globalization and poverty. The media are becoming increasingly fragmented and politically partial, and the decline of state-run media infrastructures is, along with a welcome loss of control over information, leading to the emergence of an information vacuum for an increasing number of communities. Despite this, the traditional media remain the principal source of information for much of humanity on issues outside their community and are likely to continue to do so for decades to come. Taken as an average, every African household has a radio, whereas fewer than 1 per cent have access to the Internet. Internet access, while growing rapidly, is still available to only 3 per cent of Brazilians.

The potential of media to act as a conduit for perspectives and a voice for the poor is growing, both through the emergence of community radio and through other forms of broadcasting. Discussion programmes on new FM radio stations are creating new and unprecedented spaces for public debate and an increased political vibrancy, and these provide major new opportunities to place issues of public concern onto public agendas. However, this goes hand-in-hand with a lack of resources and the emergence of a new journalism culture that is uninterested in providing in-depth reports and analysis of major development, inter-national or social issues, and where journalists rarely venture out of the major cities. There are many journalists who remain committed to covering public interest issues, but they increasingly operate within a media culture that neither encourages nor values their work.

In the context of globalization, these trends are particularly acute. The challenge of global inclusion is to ensure that decisions that affect peoples' lives are subject to debate by those whose lives they affect. That means a much stronger, not weaker, public understanding and engage-ment on issues of globalization. The media in most developing countries, despite the early promises and optimism of liberalization and the growth of new media freedoms, appear decreasingly, rather than increasingly, equipped to play this role.

These issues also raise significant questions on the sustainability and health of democracy and democratic culture, and the capacity of people to hold their governments to account; but they go deeper than this. Arguably there has never been a greater opportunity or a more critical time for open public debate. This is true for issues of globalization, but also encompasses wider development processes and strategies, which are increasingly premised on issues of popular consultation, ownership and debate. Much current mainstream development thinking (especially from the World Bank and donors committed to new sets of international development targets aimed at halving poverty by the year 2015) stresses the importance of ownership, holding that countries should shape and drive their own development agendas and that these agendas should be informed by the "voices of the poor". Poverty reduction strategy papers (PRSPs) that form the centre-piece of much current development thinking and strategic planning are founded on this premise. This cannot happen in an environment where the public, and particularly the poor, have so little information on the issues that affect them.

Nor has liberalization yet led to a true diversity in media ownership. The globalization, concentration of ownership and increasingly profit-oriented nature of the international media have been well documented. However, patterns of media power at the national level have been less documented. The ceding of state control of media has been far from universal, and even in more liberalized media environments, state ownership and influence often remain pervasive. According to a World Bank study of 97 mostly developing countries, the largest media firms were owned either by governments or by private families, with government ownership being more widespread in broadcasting than in the print media. The study's authors argued that "government ownership of the media is generally associated with less press freedom, fewer political and economic rights and, most conspicuously, inferior social outcomes in the areas of education and health" (Djankov et al. 2001:1).

Media freedom and media liberalization have only rarely resulted in media pluralism. This is a global trend, but one which is particularly acute in poorer countries where those with most to win or lose from political and public debate—the poor and marginalized—have least access and least representation in mainstream media.

Freedom of expression is just one essential component of a plural media. Genuine media pluralism also implies a diversity of ownership, including media that explicitly serve a public or community interest, media that are accessible by and intelligible to (particularly in relation to issues of literacy and language) all citizens, media that reflect diversity of public opinion, and particularly that give voice to and reflect the expression of the marginalized (often a majority in many developing countries) in society. According to these criteria, the global trend is moving away from, not toward, real media pluralism.

What Is To Be Done?

Analysing a communication environment as complex and fast-moving as the one outlined above is a great deal easier than identifying clear-cut policy responses to it. At the least, in the context of this book, the issue of public access to information in developing countries should preoccupy civil society organizations a good deal more than it does. Freedom of information and expression remains the primary concern for journalists around the world, and most governments on the planet still have much to do to guarantee such freedom.

Beyond that, however, while much attention is rightly focused on the concentration of media ownership in the North, genuine global inclusion depends also on the emergence from within the fascinating media liberalization maelstrom of a stronger public interest media in the South. The most obvious solution to this—the creation of intelligent, flexible regulatory frameworks for media—is a highly sensitive issue among journalists who have fought for years to escape the clutches of government control. It is clear that a range of policy responses is required, of which regulation is just one.

The rapidity and scale of the transformation of media internationally, particularly within developing countries, over the last decade demonstrates the power and influence of the mostly economic pressures shaping the new media environment. There are many within the media who are struggling in the teeth of these pressures to retain the media's critical public interest role, but the evidence is that they are losing. While governments clearly have a major role to play in creating the legal and policy environment for free and plural media, the media generally remain distrustful and cautious about strong government action in this area. In this context, civil society has a major role to play in putting pressure on both media and government to create and support more public-interest-oriented media. It also has much to lose if media continue to develop in ways that serve the private interest and ignore the public interest. With 2 billion people in the world still living in absolute poverty, the public interest and the role of the media in serving the public interest, have never been so important.

Women and the media

Women continue to suffer marginalization in and from communication networks, and evidence of the scale of sexual harassment and discrimination within the media itself in Africa (and elsewhere) is growing. When in 1995 the United Nations Educational, Scientific and Cultural Organization (UNESCO) sponsored a global media monitoring project to explore the representation of women in 71 countries, it found that women made up just 17 per cent of all interviewees in the news worldwide. Women interviewees were much more likely to be lay voices, even on topics which were specifically focused on women. Male interviewees were more typically interviewed as voices of authority. Twenty-nine per cent of all female interviewees were portrayed as victims of crime or accidents, compared with just 10 per cent of male interviewees. A follow-up worldwide study in 2000 found similar results, and these are relatively consistent across regions (Spears and Seydegart 2001). Similar findings have been repeated in many national studies. A further twist in the story is the split in news coverage between urban and rural concerns, the latter receiving comparatively little attention. In one Kenyan study, rural women featured in a tiny fraction of news coverage and a striking 76 per cent of rural women who appeared in the media were portrayed as criminals or victims. Liberalization of radio and television has also prompted major concerns about the increasing objectification of women in society through advertising and highly sexualized content. Counterbalancing some of these trends is the prominent role played by the women in the new media environment, including in societies, such as in Pakistan and elsewhere in South Asia, where women are particularly prominent as editors and owners of news organizations.

Regional Trends

This section looks at some regional trends in Southern and Eastern Africa, Asia and Latin America.

Media trends and dynamics in Southern Africa[4]

The last 10 years have seen unprecedented changes on the media landscape across Southern Africa. These changes have been occurring at two interconnected levels: the global and the local. In part, these have been a function of greater political pluralism across various nation-states. Also, foreign media giants, such as CNN, BBC and others have taken advantage of this situation to export international capital to finance many of the local-foreign media ventures that the subregion has begun to witness. Locally, there have been organic media formations, such as community or alternative radio, private FM radio stations and other initiatives which, nevertheless, have ended up looking to foreign financiers for their sustainability. For instance, UNESCO has been in the forefront of supporting community radio initiatives across Southern Africa, from Malawi's Dzimwe Community Radio, through Namibia's

---

[4]   This section has been prepared by Fackson Banda.

Katutura Community Radio Station, to Zambia's Mazabuka Community Radio Station. For all its efforts, UNESCO has been accused of failing to sustain such radio stations, with the result that most of them end up operating as though they were private, commercial stations.

The global level

The liberalization of the media industry and the attendant commercialization and privatization of hitherto state media have had a profound effect in local media spaces. The 1990s have seen the transnationalization of major world media (CNN, BBC, Bloomberg and others) as a consequence of such satellite broadcasting services as Multichoice Kaleidoscope in South Africa. Multichoice has set up agents throughout the African continent, with thousands of subscribers shifting to this multichannel television and radio broadcasting service.

The print media, such as *The Mail* and *Guardian* and *Mmegi*, are also beginning to regionalize, reaching out to such countries as Zambia, Zimbabwe and Kenya, cultivating in the process a regional media entertainment consumer network. As a consequence, many people in different countries—apparently those who can afford such continent-wide satellite broadcasting and regional newspapers—are now exposed to a lot of foreign content across different genres. This seems to be a common or homogenizing factor. It is not far-fetched to argue that an elite is emerging that may well be "delocalized" from its local cultural roots, basically united in common, cosmopolitan lifestyles, values and worldviews.

But this has raised questions about the importance of local content as a counter to any possible undesirable influences on the local cultures of the consumers of such media products.

Perhaps, given the rate at which South Africa's Multichoice Kaleidoscope is developing on the continent, there is growing concern that this economic powerhouse might, in fact, be on the verge of becoming one of the main exporters of media products to the rest of Africa. M-NET, South African Broadcasting Corporation (SABC) Africa, e-TV, Africa-to-Africa, and other South African channels are beginning to make great inroads into several countries. In fact, SABC Africa prides itself on being "the pulse of Africa", almost as though it were promoting itself as the essence of African broadcasting.

Furthermore, this trend has resulted in a realignment of the local media landscape. There appear to be emerging state-private media business alliances. For instance, the Zambia National Broadcasting Corporation (ZNBC) has entered into strategic partnerships with M-NET, African Broadcasting Network (ABN), TV Africa and Sandon Television to bring entertainment-based television programming to Zambian audiences of the ZNBC TV. The same trend is true of Malawi, which has just introduced locally produced television services, as well as Mozambique, Botswana, Zimbabwe, Lesotho, Namibia and Swaziland.

The local level

As noted above, Southern Africa has experienced a process of deregulation in which the media industry has essentially been opened up to private capital. Thus, state media have begun to face stiff competition from their private counterparts for audiences.

However, purely private commercial media are themselves coming into competition with so-called community or alternative media. With more defined audiences, community or alternative media are becoming more pronounced as agents of social and political change across the continent, although most of them are turning out to be purveyors of popular entertainment rather than serious political analysis. Over 80 community radio stations have been given licences by the Independent Communications Authority of South Africa (ICASA). The Ministry of Information and Broadcasting Services in Zambia has given out over 10 licences to private FM radio stations, some of which, although not necessarily owned or controlled by communities, claim to be *community* stations.

Even with all these unprecedented changes on the ground, however, little has happened in terms of consistent, coherent and comprehensive policy frameworks to deal with the ever-evolving media scenario. This policy laxity has extended to the so-called new media, such as the Internet and email services.

On the contrary, new laws and policies seem to be an attempt at *re-regulating* the media industry with a heavier hand. In Zambia, efforts to set up an independent broadcasting authority have not succeeded, with both the state and private broadcasting arenas largely filled on the basis of political caprice. In Zimbabwe, though the Broadcasting Authority of Zimbabwe (BAZ) has been established under the Broadcasting Services Act 2001, there is suspicion that the state's purported desire to finalize the drafting of the frequency map, which will allow more private broadcasters to obtain frequencies, is not likely to open up the airwaves in ways that will promote independent broadcast journalism.

Indeed, the process of re-regulation is taking place in other, more subtle ways, such as harassment of journalists, toleration of policy gaps and removal of advertising from private media.

Conclusion

The future of free media is bleak in most countries in Southern Africa, with the exception of South Africa. And even there, the highly commercialized nature of the mostly urban-based media seems to be working against poor people's access, although this is somewhat mitigated by the mushrooming of community media initiatives. The entertainment media industry, on the other hand, seems to have a bright future. The "liberalization" of the media industry has worked to promote largely foreign music and-movie media outlets. Local news, especially that which focuses on political issues and events, on community or private FM radio stations, has met with state censure.

Media trends in Eastern Africa[6]

Recent developments in Eastern Africa reflect the complex and contradictory character of political and social trends that have affected many other parts of the continent. Since 1990, most countries in the subregion have undergone a far-reaching political transformation, mostly by replacing former one-party regimes with nominal multiparty democracies. Freedom of expression, press freedom and media diversity have become critical indicators of the health or otherwise of democratic transition in the subregion.

On the whole, the transformation of the media landscape over the last decade has been impressive. The political transitions from monolithic one-party rule, as well as external and internal pressures on governments of Eastern African countries for constitutional and legal reforms—including calls to "free the airwaves"—have substantially changed radio and television broadcasting regulation and ownership in the subregion. Where governments previously retained broadcasting as the preserve of the state and the ruling party, now most have accepted the establishment of independent, private broadcasters and in some cases community radio stations.

Most countries in the region now have a nascent private broadcast sector, and citizens have access to alternative voices. But as a publication from Panos Eastern Africa points out, "While it is easy to track quantitatively the number of new broadcasters, it is less easy to assess qualitatively their ownership, content and meaning to their audiences. The real impact of independent, private broadcasters on access to and dissemination of information in the subregion is as yet unknown, as is the potential role of regulation in directing the development of broadcasting so that it brings real and widespread benefits" (Wanyeki 2000).

Thus, while media freedom has undoubtedly advanced, the record of the media in contributing to more informed, inclusive and democratic societies in the subregion is much more mixed. New FM radio stations are beginning to emerge, creating a highly populist, music-based programming while, at least in some cases, also providing new ways for

---

[6]   This section has been prepared by Njonjo Mue.

people rarely heard in public domains to have their say through live debates and phone-in discussions. But many more of the media emerging in the region are heavily advertising dependent and consumer oriented, and have limited interest in highlighting issues of concern to people in the rural areas. Indeed, one of the greatest challenges emerging from the way media are developing in the region is the dichotomy between metropolitan areas—with a diversity of print, electronic and new media—and the rural areas, which have largely remained neglected and where government propaganda remains the only source of news and information.

Governments in the subregion have also been reluctant to loosen their grip over state broadcasters. In spite of campaigns by civil society groups to have these transformed into public broadcasters representing all the viewpoints in society, all state broadcasters in the subregion have remained mouthpieces for the ruling party. The distinction between public and government broadcasting is not widely recognized, and there is little clear policy articulation of the necessity for retained public service broadcasting and of a revised role in this respect for the public broadcaster.

New information and communication technologies, and trans-national satellite broadcasting, are so far available only to those with disposable income in urban areas. The implications of technological convergence are as yet unknown. But the likely impact on the region of the international trend toward the consolidation of media ownership can be inferred from the case of the Nation Media Group, which owns the largest circulation daily in East and Central Africa, the only regional weekly newspaper, and radio and TV stations in Kenya and Uganda, and which has plans to rapidly expand its dominance. This highlights issues of regulation of cross-media ownership, which has not been regarded as a priority by regulators in the subregion.

Print media continue to play an important part in creating democratic space in the subregion, but are hampered by draconian legislation, some dating to colonial rule, which severely restricts media freedom and exposes journalists to harsh punishments for transgression and therefore promotes self-censorship.

As the media landscape in Eastern Africa changes rapidly, the key challenges remain those of providing regulatory frameworks that can cope with the rapid developments; providing content that is relevant to the context and developmental challenges of the subregion; and enhancing the capacity of journalists to provide professional and quality services in one of the fastest-growing sectors in the subregion, to enable it to play its historic role in the promotion and entrenchment of democracy, good governance and development in this part of the world.

Media in Asia[6]

Only a fluke of history lumped Asia together as one continent. There are at least six Asias: the Middle East, Central Asia, South Asia, Southeast Asia, East Asia and the Pacific. Media trends and dynamics in these regions vary widely. But two threads run through them all: the links between technological leaps brought about by convergence, and media globalization and ownership.

As leaders in hardware production for the information revolution, the East Asian tigers have been at the forefront of a great leap forward in the advancement of computers and telecommunications, and the media rode the crest of this wave. Paradoxically, information content in some of these countries has not kept pace with hardware development. Countries that have hitched their wagons to the IT revolution, like China, Malaysia and Singapore, keep tight restrictions on access to information by their citizens and on political freedoms. Two of these East Asian tigers (Taiwan Province of China and the Republic of Korea) have in the past decade made the full transition from authoritarianism to democracy and a free press. Partly, the push for reforms has been a result of the nature of the development of new media. These two countries have been able to play catch-up with Japan (the Republic of Korea, in fact, has overtaken Japan in broadband access and is much further ahead than the United States), and both have a vibrant and creative media sector (Patelis 2000).

We see that the role played by the media is determined not just by the technology, but also by the freedom to use new media (as Marshall McLuhan said in the 1960s, "the medium is the message"). Singaporeans may have broadband access through their home computers simultaneously to cable movies, Internet and streaming television news, but the content of that information has not changed all that much from pre-Internet days. Curbs on Internet use, surveillance, severe penalties for accessing restricted sites and crackdowns on independent news portals carrying non-official sources of information have dampened the initial euphoria in East and Southeast Asia over the Internet playing a leading role in "democratizing information" (Keniston 1998).

The other hope was that information technology would level the playing field and bridge the digital divide. Nowhere is this digital divide more glaring today than between South Asia and East Asia. Despite India's entry into the IT age with the emergence of Bangalore's "silicon plateau", the region lags behind in phones per capita and Internet connections. The joke used to be that 95 percent of Indians are waiting for phone lines, and five percent are waiting for dial tones (Cherribi 2003).

---

[6]   This section has been prepared by Kunda Dixit.

But, as Bill Gates himself admits, the world does not just have a digital divide between rich and poor. There is also a school divide, a hospital divide and a literacy divide. We do not need just to leap-frog technology, we need to see how media can help societies leap-frog in social and political reform. But the corporate values that drive the information revolution are the same ones that drove the industrial revolution, and technology by itself is not going to provide answers to deep-seated structural problems of governance, social justice and equity. This can be best seen in the spread of the supranational media conglomerates and their reach in Asia. Rupert Murdoch's News Corporation, for instance, is now aiming to capture the gigantic 2.3 billion-strong Indian and Chinese markets. When Beijing found a BBC news broadcast objectionable seven years ago, Murdoch's Star News channel dumped it from its Northern feed. On the subcontinent, Star takes an Indian-centric line on news and current affairs even though its footprint extends across several regions. Star's entertainment channels now reach up to 50 million households in East Asia, South Asia and the Middle East. Star's viewership is already half the population of India: it reaches 80 per cent of urban households and 40 per cent of rural ones. But it is East Asia that is the big prize. Star already reaches 65 per cent of homes in Taiwan Province of China, and through the Hong Kong-listed Phoenix TV, Murdoch reaches 45 million households in China alone. China's television viewership has grown from 18 million in 1975 to 1 billion in 1995, and state-owned CCTV has 900 million viewers. News Corporation is getting greater access to the cash-rich Guangdong province in exchange for beaming CCTV to the US market. In Japan, News Corporation has partnered with Japan Sky Broadcasting Company (Herman and McChesney 1998; Thomas 2003).

The international and regional patterns of big business owning media is repeated within countries. There has been a boom in television channels in South India, especially Tamil Nadu, with a dozen new channels going satellite. This is television without borders, as Tamil and Malayali channels reach the diaspora in Sri Lanka, Malaysia and the Middle East. Similar trends can be seen with Bengali channels with regional footprints, and new Nepali channels beaming via satellite from India to Nepal, and vice versa, to Nepali-speaking populations.

Satellite television is essentially an entertainment medium. News and current affairs do not normally even appear among the top 10 rated programmes in India. But in times of crisis, such as border clashes with Pakistan, or hijackings and terrorist attacks, 24-hour news channels attract large transboundary viewership. Internationally owned channels with regional footprints, however, can be as nationalistic as a 100 per cent national television because the owners prioritize the main market that they target.

Yet all is not gloom. When cable television and the music channels first started broadcasting in East Asia, most analysts wrote obituaries to local cultures and said they would soon be devoured by the "global industrial monoculture" of Hollywood and American pop music. Yet, 10 years down the road, we can see that the opposite has happened. Across China, India, Nepal, Pakistan, Taiwan Province of China and Thailand, there has been a phenomenal increase in local content. Instead of stifling local music, dance and drama, television has done the opposite.

In news and current affairs, however, the power of television has turned the tables. It used to be that daily newspapers set the news agenda; now television increasingly calls the shots. Newspapers and magazines compete not with each other so much as with television, and across the region we see them becoming less text-heavy, more visual and graphics-rich. This "tabloidization" of the print media can be seen even in the established papers in New Delhi, Bangkok, Manila and the Middle East.

The greatest opportunities, perhaps, have been missed in radio, especially in the poorer parts of Asia. Nothing competes with radio for access and affordability, yet probably because of this, information on radio has been tightly controlled, even in that bastion of democracy, India. Especially on the subcontinent, radio has been used as a public address system for government propaganda, and its potential for development communication has been squandered.

The paradox is that officialdom in these countries does not regulate the newest communication technologies (private ownership of satellite television is allowed in India, for example). No one controls private cable operators, there is competition among mobile phone operators and there is a choice of Internet service providers. And yet radio, the one medium that can reach the maximum number of people, is still under the grip of most governments. States have become more sophisticated in controlling information, and they do this through private monopolies as well as pressuring the business owners of media. Political leaders in many countries have spawned mini-Berlusconis. Both the show-biz nature of television and the power of its new programmes have proved irresistible to politicians, who either own media through intermediaries, or, as media personalities, have propelled themselves into politics using their broadcast personas as launch pads. Thailand's prime minister, Thaksin Shinawatra, owns one of his country's largest telecommunication companies and has exhibited intolerance of media criticism of him in the mainstream press.

But there are signs of local resistance. Media activists in Nepal lobbied for five years for the government to deregulate FM licenses. Nepal became the first country in South Asia to have a public radio service, and today has a network of community radio all over the country.

India is finally allowing private companies to start commercial urban-based FM, and Sri Lanka has also allowed private FM.

Despite the seemingly unstoppable juggernaut of the concentration of media ownership and multinational control over content of media, there are pockets of resistance across Asia. More encouraging, examples of local cultures and voices are asserting themselves, using the very technologies that people thought would dominate them.

Media trends in Latin America[7]

One of the most telling ironies of contemporary Latin America is the presence of a media-rich environment amid alarming levels of poverty. While social inequalities widened in the past two decades, the media landscape experienced formidable transformations. Video, cable and satellite technologies have increased the number of television hours. National television and radio networks have been consolidated. Internet kiosks have boomed in metropolitan and urban areas. Although print media is scarce in rural areas, low-budget tabloids and other publications proliferate in urban centres. The number of movie theatres has declined dramatically, but commercial and non-profit video clubs have mushroomed.

By all accounts, there are more places for citizens to get information than in the past. Even a significant number of poor citizens own radio and television sets, or have access to them in common public spaces (bars, community centres, streets and buses). However, cable and Internet fees (let alone access to computers and telephone connections) are out of reach for the immense majority. Likewise, the downward trend of newspaper and magazines sales confirms that income strongly limits access to any "pay-per-view" medium. For example, every time a financial crisis and subsequent economic collapse hits the region, the consumption of print media and cable television remarkably declines.

Shadows and lights in audiovisual industries

This technological explosion went hand-in-hand with the implementation of market policies, which contributed to a consolidation of the power of private owners. The structure of the Latin American media has historically been a mix of state and private ownership (Fox and Waisbord 2002). Public institutions have never been the backbone of media systems. Threatened by the political ambitions of government officials and the greed of captains of industry, public service media has been weak. Public broadcasting has been notoriously underfunded, and operated according to a mix of commercial and political expectations.

---

[7] This section was prepared by Silvio Waisbord.

Recent privatization and the removal of cross-ownership regulations have strengthened the position of private groups and accelerated the formation of vast multimedia conglomerates.

Most Latin American media markets are imperfect duopolies in which two conglomerates control the lion's share of media properties, advertising and audiences (Waisbord 2000a). Some of the biggest global media groups, such as Brazil's Globo, Mexico's Televisa and Venezuela's Venevisión, are based in the region. Historically, they used their quasi-monopolistic control of the domestic market to launch regional and international business. Globo, for example, has an estimated 80 per cent of the television audience and 60 per cent of annual media advertising in Brazil, as well as a wide diversity of interests in media (newspaper, cable, satellite television, publishing, film, music) and other industries. Likewise, Televisa has had a choke-hold on Mexican media for several decades through the virtual monopoly of television, radio, music and film.

The affirmation of private media has not made governments irrelevant, however. The latter are still in control of substantial resources that affect media dynamics and content. Quid pro quo dealings between officials and business are customary.[8] The intertwined relationships between political and economic powers underlie media policy making and daily news management. When governments control decisions that affect media economics (for example, the allocation of broadcasting licenses, advertising budgets, import permits and state-owned bank loans), business courts officials and cozies up to them. If big media interests and governments maintain a close proximity at the national level, there is virtually no separation between government and the media in local politics. Typically, political bosses control the media directly (as owners) or indirectly (through nepotism and family ties).

Such dealings are expressed in the overall treatment of news and information. At times, media organizations reward favours by keeping silent on thorny issues involving government officials; at other times, they punish or put pressure on officials by bringing out damaging information. During military dictatorships, the big media generally ignored human rights abuses and corruption, and actively collaborated in the regimes' media propaganda. During the tenure of elected governments, the patterns are more complex. There is rarely a unified media bloc that takes a single position vis-à-vis governments. More frequently, media organizations are divided according to political and economic interests. In some cases, the largest media groups mobilized the population to overthrow the government as happened to Hugo Chavez in Venezuela. In other cases, such as that of the Alberto Fujimori government in Peru in the 1990s, the government assiduously cultivated

---

[8] See Fox and Waisbord (2002); Rockwell and Janus (2003).

relations with media owners, and gave bribes and favours to secure a propaganda machine. In yet other cases, newspaper and television stations owned by rival business groups adopted diametrically different positions vis-à-vis the government, for example, during the Alfonso Portillo administration in Guatemala.

Community media and other "small" media outlets provide opportunities for the expression of voices and ideas that are largely absent in the big media. Latin America has a rich tradition of alternative media that, despite continuous problems to stay afloat given economic and legal difficulties, still manage to survive. Some are government-funded projects such as indigenous radio stations in Mexico; others are community-based efforts operated on a shoestring by youth groups, religious organizations and non-governmental organizations (see Gumucio-Dragón 2001).

While some audiovisual industries produce a considerable amount of content, particularly in large countries (such as Argentina, Brazil, Mexico and Venezuela), others have limited production capacity and largely rely on foreign (both regional and US) content. There has been a boom in domestic television production in the past decades, and many companies have successfully exported programming. Latin American *telenovelas*, particularly from Brazil, Mexico and Venezuela, are ubiquitous in television markets worldwide. The number of productions is strongly dependent on the situation of the economy. In times of recession and crisis, fewer programmes are produced and production is limited to low-cost programming (such as news, talk shows and game shows).

Press and journalism

Journalistic practice differs across the region as a result of editorial policies, economic conditions, political environment and professional culture. There are journalists who, against all obstacles, report on powerful actors involved in wrongdoing and produce in-depth and well-researched stories. Investigative journalism showed remarkable vigour and played an important role in holding government accountable during the last two decades (Waisbord 2000b).

The achievements of watchdog journalism in holding authorities accountable, however, are only one side of the reality of the press in the region. Most reporting is superficial, timid and formulaic. Working conditions in most newsrooms are not conducive to hard-hitting, high-quality reporting. With a few exceptions, reporters are notoriously underpaid and have scarce resources to produce stories. Unwritten rules about subjects and sources limit what is news.

While journalists in metropolitan newsrooms are mostly expected to report news, their colleagues in the interior generally moonlight as advertising salesmen for their employers. While some practice fair and responsible reporting, others favour sensationalistic information and use reckless news-gathering techniques. While some reporters enjoy a considerable degree of autonomy, others act basically as stenographers to owners.

In terms of freedom of expression, the present situation is better than when authoritarian governments ruled, but it falls short of being ideal. Many press laws grant substantial power to authorities to prosecute critical reporting. The overall legal framework promotes the formation of large media conglomerates rather than nurturing media diversity. Anti-press violence continues, particularly in Colombia. Journalists reporting on human rights violations, police brutality and drug-trafficking, mostly working for news media in the provinces, are generally the victims of the attacks (Waisbord 2002).

Conclusion

No broad-brush conclusion accurately describes the complexities of media systems in the region. Whether in terms of access, production capacity, and quality and practice, important disparities remain in media organizations across rich and poor countries, and metropolitan and rural areas. The media are largely oriented to the interests of powerful officials, advertisers and elites. However, there are pockets of news and entertainment in both commercial and community media, which push the boundaries to present a diversity of ideas and voices. This is remarkable considering they subsist in an environment that favours submission over criticism of well-entrenched political and economic powers.

References

Besley, R. and Burgess, R. 2000. **Does Media Make Government More Responsive? Theory and Evidence from Indian Famine Relief Policy**. Mimeo, LSE working paper. http://econ.lse.ac.uk/staff/rburgess/wp/mediaf.pdf, accessed in December 2001.

Castells, Manuel. 1998. **The Information Age: Economy, Society, and Culture**. Blackwell, Oxford.

Cherribi, Oussama. 2003. "Global aspects of Internet." In Donald H. Johnston (ed.), **Volume 2: Encyclopaedia of International Media and Communications**. Academic Press Elsevier Science, St. Louis, MO.

Diallo, M. A. 2001. "When a journalist is 'worth' less than a bag of rice." **Media Actions**, No. 26, April-June. www.panos.sn/mediaction/archives/bissau.htm, accessed in October 2003.

Djankov, S., C. McLiesh, T. Nenova, and A. Shleifer. 2001. **Who Owns the Media?** Working Paper No. 2620. World Bank, Washington, DC.

Diop, Jean Meissa. 2001. "Senegal: Sex, blood and gossip on the front page". **Media Actions**, No. 26 April-June. www.panos.sn/mediaction/ archives/senegal.htm, accessed in October 2003.

Dreze, J. and A. Sen. 1989. **Hunger and Public Action**. Clarendon Press, Oxford.

Fox, Elizabeth and Silvio Waisbord (eds.). 2002. **Latin Politics, Global Media**. University of Texas Press, Austin.

Gerbner, G., H. Mowlana and H. Schiller (eds.). 1996. **Invisible Crises: What Conglomerate Control of Media Means for America and the World**. Westview Press, Boulder, CO.

Gumucio-Dagron, A. 2000. **Making Waves: Stories of Participatory Communication for Social Change**. Rockefeller Foundation, New York.

Hamelink, C.J. 1994. **Trends in World Communication: On Disempowerment and Self-Empowerment**. Southbound and Third World Network, Penang.

Herman, Edward and Robert McChesney. 1998. **The Global Media, New Missionaries of Corporate Capitalism**. Cassell, London.

Keniston, Kenneth. 1998. "The political economy of software". **Himal South Asian**, Vol. 11, No. 4, April. www.himalmag.com/apr98/cover.htm, accessed in October 2003.

Lush, D. 1997. **The Role of African Media in the Promotion of Democracy and Human Rights**. Paper commissioned by the Swedish Ministry of Foreign Affairs for the Partnerships Africa Conference (Stockholm, 25–27 June).

McChesney, R.W. and E.S. Herman. 1997. **Global Media**. Continuum Publishing Group, New York.

Naughton, J. 2001. "Contested space: The Internet and global civil society." In Helmut Anheier, Marlies Glasius and Mary Kaldor (eds.), **Global Civil Society 2001**. Oxford University Press, Oxford.

Page, D. and Crawley, W. 2000a. "Satellites and South Asia." **Himal South Asian**, Vol. 13, No. 12, December. www.himalmag.com/dec2000/coverfile.html, accessed in December 2001.

————. 2000b. **Satellites over South Asia: Broadcasting, Culture and the Public Interest**. Sage Publications India, New Delhi.

Patelis, Korinna. 2000. "The political economy of the Internet." In James Curran (ed.). **Media Organisations in Society**. Edward Arnold, London.

Rockwell, Rick and Noreene Janus. 2003. **Media Power in Central America**. University of Illinois Press, Urbana, IL.

Roth, C. 2001. **The Media and Good Governance: Developing Free and Effective Media to Serve the Interests of the Poor**. Department for International Development, London.

Sainath, P. 1996. **Everyone Loves a Good Drought**. Penguin India, New Delhi.

Sen, A. 1999. **Development as Freedom**. Random House, New York.

Spears, George and Kasia Seydegart. 2001. **Who Makes the News? Global Media Monitoring Project 2001**. World Association for Christian Communication, London.

Sun, Wanning. 2001. "The politics of compassion: Journalism, class formation and social change in China." **Media for Development**, No. 3. www.wacc.org.uk/publications/md/md2001-3/wanning_sun.html, accessed in December 2001.

Thomas, Bella. 2003. "What the poor watch on TV." **Prospect**, No. 82, January.

Waisbord, Silvio. 2000a. "Media in South America: Between the rock of the state and the hard place of the market." In James Curran and Myung-Jin Park (eds.), **De-Westernizing Media Studies**. Routledge, London.

————. 2000b. **Watchdog Journalism in South America**. Columbia University Press, New York.

————. 2002. "Anti-press violence and the crisis of the state." **Harvard International Journal of Press/Politics**, Vol. 7, No. 3, pp. 90–109.

Wanyeki, L. M. (ed.). 2000. **Up in the Air? The State of Broadcasting in Eastern Africa**. Panos Eastern Africa, Kampala.

Westoff, C. and A. Bankole. 1999. **Mass Media and Reproductive Behaviour in Pakistan, India, and Bangladesh**. Demographic Health Surveys Analytical Report No. 10. Macro International Inc., Calverton, MD.

Zednick, Rick. 2002. "Perspectives on war: Inside Al Jazeera." **Columbia Journalism Review**, March/April. www.cjr.org/year/02/2/zednik.asp, accessed in December 2001.

Media and Democratization in the Information Society

Marc Raboy

Abstract

Globalization and the technological and economic advances that have accompanied it have been marked by a number of tendencies with mixed implications for the media. This paper examines the impact of these changes on the role played by the media in the democratization of societies.

Privatization and liberalization carried the promise of more channels, but this has not resulted in a broader and more pluralistic media. The breakdown of state monopolies on broadcasting has had a positive impact in many developing countries, but in many others the state monopolies have merely been replaced by private ones with equally suspect aims. The decline of public broadcasting is a major concern even in the developed countries of Europe. Alternative or community media hold out great promise but are chronically under-resourced and otherwise marginalized. Consolidation of ownership and control, and the rise of massive global multimedia conglomerates with influence over practically all aspects of cultural and political life is another area of concern for its restrictive influence on pluralism and local content.

Given these characteristics of the global media environment in the information society, the paper focuses on issues of media governance and regulation, including:

- the effects of growing concentration of commercial media ownership;
- the place of mainstream public media;
- how to foster and promote independent, alternative media initiatives;
- how to promote freedom of expression and communication through the media; and
- the plethora of issues surrounding new technologies and new communication platforms such as the Internet.

Particular attention will be paid to newly emerging transnational sites of media governance and regulation and their role in the broader project of democratization of global governance. Access to global media policy making through civil society participation in processes such as the World Summit on the Information Society (WSIS) is crucial to this project, insofar as the fostering of a plurality and diversity of media can be seen as facilitating widespread participation in every aspect of public life.

Introduction

Changes in the way that information and entertainment media are produced and distributed have an enormous impact on their role in society, and yet these changes have attracted little attention in the debate on the information society. This paper will underscore some of the leading issues surrounding media from a perspective of democratization, and then suggest how some of these issues can be highlighted in the international policy arena through interventions in venues such as the World Summit on the Information Society (WSIS).

Some of the aspects of media organization and performance that need to be taken into account here include:

- the increasing concentration of ownership in the commercial media sector;
- the challenges to the traditional role of national public service media;
- the continued existence, in many parts of the world, of state (as opposed to independent public service) media;
- the limits and possibilities of so-called third sector (non-commercial, non-public) media—known variously as not-for-profit, alternative or community media; and
- encompassing all of the above, the changing nature of media regulation and other public policy interventions in light of globalization and the shifting sands of decision making with respect to media (Raboy 2002; Ó Siochrú and Girard 2002).

The Historical Context

Conventional thinking about mass media in the twentieth century focused on the capacity of media institutions to play a role in the democratization of societies, in creating a public sphere through which people could be empowered to take part in civic affairs, in enhancing national and cultural identity, in promoting creative expression and dialogue. In just about every setting in which the media were seen as essential to these values, some form of arm's-length government intervention was deemed necessary to enable and facilitate the role of the media. As soon as media production required a greater degree of organization and resources than could be provided on an artisanal basis, some form of structural regulation was deemed necessary to ensure that these media met a minimum standard of social responsibility. This would be ensured through various means: the awarding of broadcasting frequencies, creation of public service radio and television services, the funding of community-based not-for-profit media, various restrictions on ownership of commercial media (limiting the amount of outlets a particular firm could control, or excluding foreign nationals from ownership).

With the advent of new communication and information technologies, for a variety and combination of reasons—some technical, some political, some economic, some ideological—national policy makers have become less willing and less able to intervene in the sphere of media activity. At the same time, powerful formal and informal mechanisms (such as international trade agreements) have emerged at the international level, constraining the capacity of national governments to influence the media sector. The global media environment is a new frontier where rules are being made on the go; as in every frontier situation, the powerful are making the rules to suit their particular needs. This is, to say the least, a paradox, given the conventional vocation ascribed to the media in liberal democracies during the past century.

Each of the main mass media models referred to earlier (commercial, public service, state, alternative media) present different problems and possibilities; each is also fraught with paradox and contradiction.

Independent media arose in opposition to the state, and in favour of values of free expression. Early media were politically and ideologically driven, best exemplified by the pamphlets of Thomas Paine and other advocates of the French and American Revolutions (Keane 1991). In the early nineteenth century, more than 100 newspapers were published in the French-speaking portion of British North America (Quebec) alone, to take but one example. By the 1880s, the main function of the media was transformed as a commercial press emerged in all of the advancing capitalist societies—a phenomenon characterized, famously, by the German philosopher Jürgen Habermas (1989) as "the structural transformation of the public sphere". Paradoxically, one of the great driving forces in support of media commercialization (or commodification) was the emergence of a newly literate mass public, making possible the demographic success of a "penny press" and the accompanying development of advertising. By the 1920s, just as electronic media were making their appearance, the mainstream mass-audience commercial press had become the dominant media form. In the 1950s, the American critical sociologist C. Wright Mills (1956) was prompted to distinguish between a "public" and a "mass", based on media function.

In the United States and other countries (such as Australia, Canada and most of Latin America), radio and later, television, while regulated by a government authority responsible for awarding broadcast licenses, developed on the economic model of the press. Mills and other critics did not take account of the emergence of a new phenomenon, from the 1920s onward, primarily in Western Europe but also—at least for the elites concerned—in the colonial outposts: public service broadcasting (PSB). In some parts of the world, PSB coexisted with commercial media, but in most of Western Europe it enjoyed a monopoly status well into the 1980s (Raboy 1997). Based on a set of universal principles, PSB presented a new paradox: a state-sponsored medium conceived to present an alternative, or to undercut the dominant press model in broadcasting. Broadcasting in these countries would have a social, cultural and educational vocation, rather than a commercial one (or so the theory went). Crucial to this were provisions guaranteeing arm's-length independence of public broadcasting institutions from the states and governments that nurtured them through funding and protectionist policy measures. Public broadcasting underwent various fiscal and moral crises during the latter decades of the twentieth century, but is still recognized today as a key instrument of democracy, for example, in the so-called Amsterdam Protocol of the Treaty of the European Union (Council of the European Union 1997).[1] According to one recent study, public broadcasting constitutes the public policy instrument of choice for countries that choose to intervene in the media sphere (McKinsey and Company 2002).

Meanwhile, alternative and oppositional media, often tied to political movements, have continued to play a substantial role in situations of authoritarian or colonial government as well as in the Western liberal democracies, where pockets of third sector media began to emerge in parallel with the rise of youth and new social movements in the 1960s (Downing 2000). In the West, the alternative press and later, community radio and television flourished—often, paradoxically, with resources provided by the state. In Europe, radical pirate media arose to challenge the PSB monopolies. Liberalization permitting non-state media introduced in countries such as France and Italy in the 1980s had the unforeseen effect of legitimizing the pirate media and opening the floodgates for introduction of commercial media on the American model. Toward the turn of the century, alternative media were instrumental in bringing down the Soviet system, democratizing parts of Asia, Africa and Latin America, fostering alternatives for "another" globalization, promoting gay and lesbian rights, maintaining diasporic cultures and so

---

[1] The Amsterdam Protocol on the system of broadcasting in member states was signed in 1997. This and other relevant documents on public broadcasting can be found in a recent compilation by Price and Raboy (2001).

forth. In countries with well-developed commercial and public service media sectors, such as Canada and Germany, third sector media were recognized in legislation and regulation and enjoyed both legitimacy as well as a certain degree of state support.

This was roughly the portrait, then, in the early twenty-first century: increasing concentration of media ownership and loose minimal regulation regarding the most basic elements of social responsibility for commercial mass media, be they in press, radio or television; continued persistence of public broadcasting with a serious funding and legitimacy crisis in the wake of government fiscal policies and dropping audience shares vis-à-vis commercial media; recognized legal status and minimal regulatory and financial support for alternative community-based media in some parts of the world;[2] and basic struggles for freedom of expression and liberalization of state-controlled media in many parts of the world.

From UNESCO to the ITU to WSIS

In this context, what are the issues regarding media that ought to be considered in the debate on the information society? These can be essentially grouped in five categories:

- how to constrain the effects of growing concentration of commercial media ownership;
- how to enhance the place of mainstream public media;
- how to foster and promote independent, alternative media initiatives;
- how to promote freedom of expression and communication through the media, especially in situations of authoritarian state control; and
- how to deal with this plethora of issues in the context of new technologies and new communication platforms such as the Internet.

As soon as one considers these issues, two things become immediately clear:

---

[2] Full coverage of the sheer variety of examples, legal status and approaches to alternative media would require a separate article. For example, in Latin America, most "community" broadcasters are in fact licensed and regulated as commercial broadcasters. Only three Latin American countries recognize community broadcasting as a distinct sector and only one gives it meaningful support. Asian countries also present a range of different approaches, where the vocations of alternative and public service media sometimes overlap. Local community radio stations have appeared in a number of African countries in recent years with Mali and South Africa being the recognized leaders. In most of the former Soviet Union, alternative media are inherently oppositional to the governing parties. See, for some examples, Okigbo (1996); Roncagliolo (1996); Rosario-Braid (1996); and Girard (1992).

- efforts to intervene in the media require national initiatives hence depend on national sovereignty in the media sphere; and
- media issues are increasingly transnational, and will need to be dealt with by international conventions or other international measures.

Legal scholar Monroe E. Price (2002) has described the "taxonomy of influences" on national responses to media issues as including the existing regime structure, prevailing traditions of private versus state or public media, accessibility of new technologies, approaches to free trade, the country's situation with respect to global power realignments, its sensitivity to international norms and, increasingly, the influence of national security concerns (p. 234). According to this analysis, negotiating a regulatory space for media in this context may eventually lead to "a single over-arching international agency with regulatory powers, a glorified and empowered International Telecommunication Union" (Price 2002:248). If Price is correct, the outcome of WSIS could be important indeed for the future of media worldwide.

The most serious attempt so far to deal with these questions globally is to be found in the report of the World Commission on Culture and Development (WCCD), entitled *Our Creative Diversity* (1995), and the subsequent UNESCO *Draft Action Plan for Cultural Policies for Development* (1998).

In a broad review of cultural issues ranging from ethics to the environment, the WCCD, which was set up jointly by the United Nations and the United Nations Educational, Cultural and Scientific Organization (UNESCO), proposed an international agenda for developing global policy with respect to cultural development. Several chapters and proposals relating to media and new global issues in mass communication were framed by the following question: "How can the world's growing media capacities be channelled so as to support cultural diversity and democratic discourse?"

The WCCD recognized that while many countries were dealing individually with various important aspects of this question, the time had come for a transfer of emphasis from the national to the international level. "There is room for an international framework that complements national regulatory frameworks" (WCCD 1995:117).While many countries still needed to be incited to put in place or modernize existing national frameworks, there was growing justification for transferring attention to the global level.

Concentration of media ownership and production is becoming even more striking internationally than it is nationally, making the global media ever more market-driven. In this context, can the kind of pluralist 'mixed economy' media system which is emerging in many countries be encouraged globally? Can we envisage a world public sphere in which there is room for alternative voices? Can the media professionals sit down together with policy-makers and consumers to work out mechanisms that promote access and a diversity of expression despite the acutely competitive environment that drives the media moguls apart? (WCCD 1995:117).

These questions are even more relevant today than when they were formulated by the WCCD in 1995. The WCCD admitted that it did not have ready answers to these questions, but that answers had to be sought through international dialogue:

Many specialists have told the Commission how important it would be to arrive at an international balance between public and private interests. They envision a common ground of public interest on a transnational scale. They suggest that different national approaches can be aligned, that broadly acceptable guidelines could be elaborated with the active participation of the principal actors, that new international rules are not a pipe-dream but could emerge through the forging of transnational alliances across the public and private media space (WCCD 1995:117).

The WCCD's international agenda contained a series of specific proposals aimed at "enhancing access, diversity and competition of the international media system", based on the assertion that the airwaves and space are "part of the global commons, a collective asset that belongs to all humankind" (WCCD 1995:278).

This international asset at present is used free of charge by those who possess resources and technology. Eventually, 'property rights' may have to be assigned to the global commons, and access to airwaves and space regulated in the public interest (WCCD 1995:278).

Just as national community and public media services require public subsidy, internationally, the redistribution of benefits from the growing global commercial media activity could help subsidize the rest. As a first step, and within a market context, the Commission suggests that the time may have come for commercial regional or international satellite radio and television interests which now use the global commons free of charge to contribute to the financing of a more plural media system. New revenue could be invested in alternative programming for international distribution (WCCD 1995:278).

Competition policies, as exist in many countries, would need to be enacted in the international sphere to ensure fair practices. International public broadcasting services would need to be established "to help assure a truly plural media space". In general, the WCCD called for a new and concerted international effort, "an active policy to promote competition, access and diversity of expression amongst the media globally, analogous to policies that exist at the national level" (WCCD 1995:279).

The 1998 Intergovernmental Conference on Cultural Policies for Development organized by UNESCO in Stockholm took this a step further, adopting an *Action Plan for Cultural Policies for Development* (UNESCO 1998) and recommending a series of policy objectives to UNESCO's member states, in keeping with the general philosophical position that communication resources constitute part of "the global commons". Recognizing that "in a democratic framework civil society will become increasingly important in the field of culture", the conference endorsed a dozen principles including the fundamental right of access to and participation in cultural life, and the cultural policy objective of establishing structures and securing adequate resources necessary "to create an environment conducive to human fulfilment" (p. 2).

If one can consider media policy to be a subset of cultural policy, the conference made a number of contributions of direct relevance to the concerns of this paper, in affirming that:

- Effective participation in the information society and the mastery by everyone of information and communication technology constitute a significant dimension of any cultural policy.
- Government should endeavour to achieve closer partnerships with civil society in the design and implementation of cultural policies that are integrated into development strategies.
- In an increasingly interdependent world, the renewal of cultural policies should be envisioned simultaneously at the local, national, regional and global levels.
- Cultural policies should place particular emphasis on promoting and strengthening ways and means of providing broader access

to culture for all sectors of the population, combating exclusion and marginalization, and fostering all processes that favour cultural democratization (p. 3).

Among the relevant policy objectives recommended to UNESCO's member states, the conference proposed to "intensify co-operation between government, the business sector and other civil society organizations in the field of culture by providing the latter with appropriate regulatory frameworks" (p. 5). A number of proposals then dealt specifically with media and communication technologies. The conference asked member states to:

- Promote communication networks, including radio, television and information technologies which serve the cultural and educational needs of the public; encourage the commitment of radio, television, the press and the other media to cultural development issues, while guaranteeing the editorial independence of the public service media.
- Consider providing public radio and television and promote space for community, linguistic and minority services.
- Adopt or reinforce national efforts that foster media pluralism and freedom of expression.
- Promote the development and use of new technologies and new communication and information services, stress the importance of access to information highways and services at affordable prices (p. 6).

The appearance of such an action plan endorsed by 140 governments under the sponsorship of a world intergovernmental organization was certainly uplifting, but the subtext and context surrounding its adoption also pointed to the difficulties that lay ahead.

It took two-and-a-half years to organize the Stockholm conference, following the tabling of the WCCD Report on which the working documents presented in Stockholm were based. As mentioned earlier, that original report underscored the premise that communication media are an essential cornerstone of democracy and cultural development, as well as a part of the "global commons", and argued for extension of conventional national policy mechanisms to the global level. A global framework for media regulation, it suggested, could provide a framework for a more pluralist media system by, for example, enabling a tax levy on transnational commercial media activities, which could be used to generate financial support for global public service and alternative media. This proactive thrust, based on the use of existing policy mechanisms and the extension of the national policy logic to the global level, did not survive the diplomatic horse-trading that culminated in the action plan adopted in Stockholm.

Furthermore, the draft version of the action plan presented at the outset of the conference was far more affirmative in encouraging member states to provide public radio and television (rather than merely "consider" their provision), and in calling for international as well as national legislation to promote media pluralism. Significantly, a proposal that such legislation foster "competition and prevent excessive concentration of media ownership" was changed to refer instead to "freedom of expression". A proposal to "promote the Internet as a universal public service by fostering connectivity and not-for-profit user consortia and by adopting reasonable pricing policies" disappeared from the final text.

In terms of implementation, the Stockholm Conference recommended that the Director-General of UNESCO develop a comprehensive strategy for practical follow-up to the conference, "including the possibility or not of organizing a World Summit on Culture and Development". The WCCD Report had proposed such a summit, which was endorsed, among others, by participants in a forum of civil society organizations parallel to the intergovernmental conference in Stockholm. But Federico Mayor, then director-general of UNESCO, immediately ruled out the short-term organization of a world summit. In a statement to the Panafrican News Agency (PANA), at the close of the Stockholm conference, Mayor said it would take three or four years at least for the seeds sown at Stockholm to mature. Meanwhile, he said, the initiative should be left to the member states and regional organizations to implement the principles and commitments undertaken.

WSIS is the direct successor to this proposal. The only difference is that the lead organization for the summit is the International Telecommunication Union (ITU) and not UNESCO. The distinction is critical for issues of media democratization. Within the UNESCO logic, media are cultural institutions, part of the process of human development. Within the ITU logic, media are technical systems for information delivery. There was, in fact, a moment of overlap between the two approaches, in 1995, when a joint ITU-UNESCO study entitled *The Right to Communicate: At What Price?* (1995) wondered to what extent societal goals could be reconciled with commercial objectives in this context. This interagency report represented a rare effort to bridge the gap between technical and sociocultural sectors, insofar as UNESCO could be said to constitute a community of "public concern" for telecommunication services furnished by ITU members. The study noted the detrimental effects of economic barriers to access to telecommunication services, the lack of infrastructures in some countries, and the lack of an international universal telecommunication infrastructure.

This is often the result of historical circumstances, political requirements and monopolistic industry structures, the study recognized. A generous way to conceptualize WSIS is as an attempt to follow up on this set of concerns.

The problem, of course, is that history does not wait while all this talk goes on. Since the adoption of the Stockholm Action Plan, indeed, since the onset of the WSIS process, World Trade Organization (WTO) agreements have increasingly encroached on national government capacities to control their cultural and media space,[3] while transnational corporate capital has continued to successfully mobilize to promote its interests at the global level. Civil society, meanwhile, risks being confined once again to the role of bridesmaid, watching from the sidelines, observing from the margins, hoping there will be a next time, unless it can be more aggressive in formulating the agenda—at WSIS and elsewhere.

In some respects, the WSIS process can be seen as having updated and pragmatized the polemical approach of the New World Information and Communication Order (NWICO) debate of the 1970s and 1980s. At the risk of raising the hackles of those who see any historical reference to the NWICO as an attempt to rekindle the ideological confrontations of the Cold War, it needs to be recalled that a re-reading of the main texts of the NWICO debate, such as the UNESCO Mass Media Declaration of 1978 and the subsequent report in 1980 of the International Commission for the Study of Communication Problems, chaired by Sean MacBride, shows how timely and relevant that debate still is today. It is generally— and conveniently—forgotten that an ITU Independent Commission of the same vintage, chaired by Sir Donald Maitland, came to essentially the same conclusions as the MacBride report as to the unequal state and quality of communication development in the world (Independent Commission for Worldwide Telecommunications Development 1984). But there is a fundamental difference to be noted, in that the NWICO debate was strictly between states, and the interests represented by their respective governments, while today's information society debate (at least as it is being played out in WSIS) is significantly broader, not only in the themes and issues it covers, but in the range of actors who are trying to take part.

---

[3]   This has inspired a number of governments to create an International Network on Cultural Policy (INCP), with the express view of promoting the establishment of a "new international instrument on cultural diversity" to offset the impact of WTO agreements and generally keep culture off the table of international trade negotiations.

Media, Democratization and Regulation

The debate on media and democratization has always had a dual focus: democratizing media, as a positive value in and of itself, and fostering a role for media in the democratization of societies. For some, the media have tended to be seen as value-free containers of information, but they are in fact contested spaces, objects of contention in their own right. Media activists have struggled with how to problematize this, how to make the media a social issue, rather than something that people merely suffer, and how to broaden the public discourse on the media's role in democracy.

Historically, media issues have not had the same resonance among social activists as other themes such as the environment, gender issues and human rights. A 1999 statement by a group of media activists, *Voices 21*, sought to begin building a new social movement around media and communication issues. It proposed forming "an international alliance to address concerns and to work jointly on matters around media and communication". All movements that work toward social change use media and communication networks, *Voices 21* pointed out, it was therefore essential that they focus on current trends such as increasing concentration of media ownership in fewer and fewer hands (Voices 21 1999).[4]

The advent of the World Summit on the Information Society offers an opportunity to move in that direction. Media and communication issues are working their way on to broader social agendas (for example, through the World Social Forum). McChesney and Nichols (2002), among others, write about placing media democratization at the centre of a social movement: they present a programme for structural media reform in the United States. Among other things, the US media reform movement has successfully lobbied Congress to roll back some of the Federal Communication Commission's (FCC) more aggressive attempts to liberalize media ownership rules.

In short, there is a need to marry mainstream and alternative media reform initiatives with policy intervention, research and education. Media democratization will be based on the extent to which there can be a successful blending of five types of intervention, led by five sets of actors:

- ongoing critical analysis of media issues (researchers);
- media literacy efforts (educators);
- building and operating of autonomous media (alternative media practitioners);

---

[4] In the interest of transparency, it should be stated that the author is a member of Voices 21.

- progressive practices within mainstream media (journalists, editors, publishers, etc.); and
- policy intervention (media policy activists).

WSIS presents an opportunity to work on the issues raised in this paper within an institutional framework, and keeping in mind this five-pronged approach.

Furthermore, at the present time, formal attempts to influence media development can take four possible pathways.

The libertarian approach: This approach does not favour the regulation of media. With the spread of new digital technologies like the Internet, this approach is currently favoured by many national regulators (Australia is an important exception), mainly because they do not know what to do or how to do it. It is also largely favoured by many grassroots activists who are benefiting from this open communication system. But the history of older media technologies shows that, left to its own devices, this open access is not likely to last. A libertarian model of Internet governance will likely lead eventually to closed doors, restricted access and limited communication.

Self-regulation: This is the approach most often favoured by industry players, with the encouragement of national regulators. It is currently being touted as the solution to problems such as abusive content and the protection of rights on the argument that consumers will respond if they are not satisfied. But as we see with initiatives surrounding copyright and electronic commerce, even the promoters of self-regulation are recognizing the need for a global structural framework for communication activity, within which media self-regulation would take place.

The closed club, or top-down institutional model: This approach fills the vacuum created by the retreat of national governments from regulatory issues. Deals are negotiated in organizations such as the Organisation for Economic Co-operation and Development (OECD), Group of Eight (G-8), or the WTO, as well as in the new institutions emerging as the corporate sector. Here, the most powerful economic players would simply dictate the rules of the game to everyone else, and the media are perceived as businesses, entertainment vehicles and organs of tightly controlled public information.

The long march through the institutions: This is a process that is tied to the broader project of democratization of global governance, reflected in some of the initiatives around United Nations reform and in notions such as "cosmopolitan democracy". Access to global policy making through civil society participation in processes such as WSIS is crucial to this model, which has as a corollary the fostering of a plurality and diversity of media seen as facilitators of widespread participation in every aspect of public life.

In terms of media democratization—and the democratic role for the media—the latter path is clearly the only viable one. Transparency, public participation and a sociocultural approach to media governance are values that are now worth promoting transnationally.

A global policy approach along these lines would help redefine the role of the state with respect to the media, both domestically and in its new transnational guise, while providing leverage for addressing a range of specific issues that are currently well off the agenda.

In the current context of globalization, the media can be either a locomotive of human development or an instrument of power and domination. Which it will be has not been determined, and that is why the stakes of the WSIS debates are so high.

As issues involving the regulation of broadcasting go global, then, we need to begin thinking about appropriate global regulatory mechanisms. This would make it possible to begin thinking about intervening globally on a range of issues, such as the following:

- regulation of commercial media activities in the public interest, to guarantee equitable access and basic services;
- funding and institutional support for the creation and sustenance of public service and alternative media;
- placing limits on corporate controls resulting from transnational concentration of ownership in new and conventional media and telecommunications;
- providing incentives (through fiscal support measures, etc.) for production, distribution and exhibition of media content which meets public policy objectives;
- guarantees of access to available media channels on the basis of public interest criteria;
- development of universal codes and standards for curtailing the spread of abusive media content;
- facilitating networking capacity through use of media technologies by not-for-profit organizations; and
- provision of public media spaces for conflict resolution and democratic dialogue on global issues.

I am aware that this "regulatory approach" has important limitations. The extent to which so-called independent regulators in the liberal democracies have been captured by industry interests has been well documented.[5] Regulation, in some cases, acts as a thinly-veiled justification for state interference with media independence. Alternative-media activists have spent precious energy participating in meaningless

---

[5] See, for example, Center for Public Integrity (2003), which documents the successful lobbying activities of US media corporations vis-à-vis the FCC.

consultations and meeting regulatory requirements. Yet, allow me to make the counter argument.

Take, for example, the recent highly mediated decision by the FCC loosening US restrictions on cross-media and concentration of media ownership. A close look at this situation reveals that the US still has stronger rules than most Western countries regarding concentration of media ownership. Under the *new* FCC regulations, a network can own stations reaching up to 45 per cent of the national population, and a limited number of media in the same market. In neighbouring Canada— to cite an example of a country often believed to be very hands-on in regulatory measures—there are no restrictions regarding cross-media or national concentration; thus, one company (which happens to be the largest Canadian industrial corporation of all, Bell Canada Enterprises, or BCE) owns one of the country's two national newspapers as well as the leading national television network, whose stations reach 99 per cent of the English-speaking population.[6]

In the 1980s, riding the wave of deregulatory ideology ushered in with the election of Ronald Reagan, FCC chair Mark Fowler famously stated: "Television is just another appliance...a toaster with pictures". One does not regulate toasters, so why regulate television, the argument went. The point is, a radio, a television set or the Internet is not just a toaster with pictures. The point is to distinguish between "regulation" and "control": regulation must be aimed at providing an enabling framework within which the media can flourish and contribute to democratic public life and human development, and at enhancing freedom of expression *and* the right to communicate. As a leading US academic, Edwin Baker (2002), has written, media regulation has to be seen as legitimate, necessary and possible.

Independent regulatory authorities and public institutions such as public broadcasters have in fact protected the public interest from abusive state authority, be it the Richard Nixon, Ronald Reagan or George W. Bush regimes in the United States, the Margaret Thatcher regime in the United Kingdom or others. Despite declining audience shares (brought on by a combination of channel proliferation, cultural globalization and a slowness to adapt to the new context), public broadcasting still deserves widespread popular support wherever it has flourished historically. With the sole, interesting example of France, no developed country has "privatized" a national public broadcaster despite the rhetoric of a generation of neoliberal political leadership.

Regulation can be even more important for promoting a third sector in media, especially broadcasting—and possibly, shortly, the Internet.

---

[6] In fact, as this was being written, a Canadian parliamentary committee had just recommended a moratorium on further mergers until the government came up with a comprehensive policy on media ownership (Fraser 2003).

Regulation can guarantee a space in the environment for media that cannot force their way in by commanding either great financial resources or massive audience shares. Progressive fiscal regimes and funding programmes can provide assurances that alternative voices are heard.

The issue, as suggested above, is how to transfer these values to the international sphere—guaranteeing it where it exists (in the face of challenges from regressive international trade and copyright regimes), promoting it where it does not (in the illiberal countries of the world) and refocusing it in the new context of technological convergence and globalization.

In short, media regulation can address the following:

- licensing of public, privately owned and community broadcasting services (goal: competition, system administration);
- property transactions (goal: market pluralism, diversity);
- abusive content (goal: protection of societal norms);
- content quotas (goal: protection of and promotion of national culture);
- performance obligations (goal: public service, programming requirements);
- rates for free-to-air, subscriber, pay-per-view services (goal: consumer protection);
- access provisions (goal: equal opportunity for free expression);
- relation between public and private services (goal: system balance); and
- funding requirements (goal: promotion of priority services).

The role of media regulation is to determine the public interest, on an ongoing basis, and with regard to specific issues such as the ones mentioned above. This is too fine a job to be done by governments in the course of their general activities. It cannot be left to broadcasters alone, for they have necessarily vested interests (even in the case of public service broadcasters). The marketplace is too blunt an instrument. Citizens can individually and through their collective organizations articulate their expectations, but have no power for implementing them.

The success of a regulatory approach will therefore depend on the following:

- clear, but general, policy guidelines from the constituting authority;
- clearly defined powers, backed up by effective compliance mechanisms;
- the fullest possible transparency in all of its operations; and
- real, meaningful access to decision-making processes for all of the actors concerned, especially public interest organizations

which are otherwise relatively removed from the centres of power.

The role of a regulatory authority would be to:

- oversee system equilibrium: balance between the public, private and community sectors;
- guarantee the accountability of the public sector;
- specify the public service contribution of the private sector;
- facilitate the viability of the community sector;
- oversee system development (for example, introduction of new services);
- set general policy (between the macro level of broad state policy and the micromanagement of broadcasters' operations);
- oversee industry self-regulation;
- supervise licensing and renewal processes; and
- deal with complaints and content issues on the basis of established codes and standards.

Regulation can be seen as a brokering process between the interests of the state, the broadcasting industries and civil society. It is about framework structuring and enabling rather than, as is often assumed, about control. Seen in this way, WSIS can be a moment in the establishment of the new global media environment. It is an opportunity that should not be missed—but whose ultimate relevance needs to be carefully weighed and placed in its proper perspective.

References

Baker, C. Edwin. 2002. **Media, Markets and Democracy**. Cambridge University Press, Cambridge.

Center for Public Integrity. 2003. **Behind Closed Doors: Top Broadcasters Met 71 Times with FCC Officials**. www.publicintegrity.org/dtaweb/report.asp?ReportID=526&L1=10&L2=10&L3=0&L4=0&L5=0, accessed on 1 July 2003.

Council of the European Union. 1997. "Protocol on the system of public broadcasting in the member states". In **Draft Treaty of Amsterdam**. Brussels.

Downing, John. 2000. **Radical Media: Rebellious Communication and Social Movements**. Sage Publications, Thousand Oaks, CA.

Fraser, Graham. 2003. "Cross-ownership under attack". **Toronto Star**, 12 June, p. A4.

Girard, Bruce (ed.). 1992. **A Passion for Radio: Radio Waves and Community**. Black Rose Books, Montreal. http://comunica.org/passion, accessed on 1 July 2003.

Habermas, Jürgen. 1989. **Structural Transformation of the Public Sphere: An Inquiry into a Category of Bourgeois Society**. MIT Press, Cambridge, MA.

International Commission for the Study of Communication Problems. 1980. **Many Voices, One World**. Report of the International Commission for the Study of Communication Problems (chaired by Sean MacBride). UNESCO, Paris.

Independent Commission for Worldwide Telecommunications Development. 1985. **The Missing Link**. Report of the Independent Commission for Worldwide Telecommunications Development (chaired by Sir Donald Maitland). ITU, Geneva.

International Telecommunication Union (ITU) and United Nations Educational, Scientific and Cultural Organization (UNESCO). 1995. **The Right to Communicate: At What Price? Economic Constraints to the Effective Use of Telecommunications in Education, Science, Culture and in the Circulation of Information**. ITU and UNESCO, Paris.

Keane, John. 1991. **The Media and Democracy**. Polity Press, Cambridge.

McChesney, Robert W. and John Nichols. 2002. **Our Media Not Theirs: The Democratic Struggle against Corporate Media**. Seven Stories Press, New York.

McKinsey and Company. 2002. **Comparative Review of Content Regulation**. A McKinsey Report for the Independent Television Commission. Independent Television Commission, London.

Mills, C. Wright. 1956. **The Power Elite**. Oxford University Press, New York.

Okigbo, Charles. 1996. "Equatorial Africa: Broadcasting and development". In Marc Raboy (ed.), **Public Broadcasting for the 21st Century**. University of Luton Press, Luton, pp. 264–282.

Ó Siochrú, Sean and Bruce Girard. 2002. **Global Media Governance: A Beginner's Guide**. Rowman and Littlefield, Lanham, MD.

Price, Monroe E. 2002. **Media and Sovereignty: The Global Information Revolution and Its Challenge to State Power**. MIT Press, Cambridge, MA.

Price, Monroe E. and Marc Raboy (eds.). 2001. **Public Service Broadcasting in Transition: A Documentary Reader**. European Institute for the Media, Düsseldorf.

Raboy, Marc. 1997. "The world situation of public service broadcasting: Overview and analysis". In **Public Service Broadcasting: Cultural and Educational Dimensions**. UNESCO, Paris, pp. 19–56.

────── (ed.). 2002. **Global Media Policy in the New Millennium**. University of Luton Press, Luton.

Roncagliolo, Rafael. 1996. "Latin America: Community broadcasting as public broadcasting". In Marc Raboy (ed.), **Public Broadcasting for the 21st Century**. University of Luton Press, Luton, pp. 297–301.

Rosario-Braid, Florangel. 1996. "Philippines: Toward an alternative broadcasting system". In Marc Raboy (ed.), **Public Broadcasting for the 21st Century**. University of Luton Press, Luton, pp. 242–263.

UNESCO. 1998. **Action Plan for Cultural Policies for Development**. Adopted at the Intergovernmental Conference on Cultural Policies for Development (Stockholm, 30 March–2 April). UNESCO, Paris.

World Commission on Culture and Development (WCCD). 1995. **Our Creative Diversity**. Report of the World Commission on Culture and Development (chaired by Javier Perez de Cuellar). United Nations/UNESCO, Paris.

Voices 21. 1999. **A Global Movement for People's Voices in Media and Communication in the 21st Century**. www.comunica.org/v21/, accessed on 1 July 2003.

Human Rights for the Information Society

Cees J. Hamelink

Abstract

This paper proposes to explore how "informational developments" interact with the societies in which they take place. These developments refer to the growing significance of information products (such as news, advertising, entertainment and scientific data) and information services (such as those provided by the World Wide Web); the increasing volumes of information generated, collected, stored and made available; the essential role of information technology as the backbone of many social services and as the engine of economic productivity; and the input of information processing into transactions in trading and finance. The interactions between informational developments and societies have technological, cultural, political and economic dimensions, for which the international community has established human rights standards. These standards are analysed in the paper.

The major problem with these standards is the lack of implementation. No effective mechanisms have been established to deal with all the obstacles that hamper the realization of human rights in the field of informational developments. Moreover, current human rights provisions focus exclusively on "information" and ignore "communication". No human rights standard has been adopted to address communication as an interactive process. Communication tends to be seen as the "transfer of messages". This omission could be remedied by the adoption—as part of the existing human rights standards—of the "human right to communicate". This right is perceived by its protagonists as more fundamental than the information rights presently accorded by international law. The essence of this right would be based on the observation that communication is a fundamental social process, a basic human need and the foundation of all social organization. The right to communicate should constitute the core of any democratic system.

The paper concludes by stating that the World Summit on the Information Society (WSIS) could remind the international community of all that has been achieved already and stress the importance to seriously identify and remove major obstacles to the urgently needed implementation of existing human rights provisions. WSIS could also point out that the essential omission in "human rights for the information society" is the lack of human rights standards for communication as an interactive process. UN Secretary-General Kofi Anan stated the need for the right to communicate very explicitly in his message on World Telecommunication Day (17 May 2003) as he reminded the international community that there were millions of people in the poorest countries who were still excluded from the "right to communicate", which was increasingly seen as a fundamental human right.

Introduction

The information society is an elusive concept, which has no precise meaning and no established definition. Despite arguments over its intellectual flaws, this concept has become part and parcel of current international discourse in politics, economics and culture.

It can be questioned whether an information society exists anywhere in the world today. It may be more appropriate to suggest that some societies are confronted with "informational developments". This notion refers to the growing significance of information products (such as news, advertising, entertainment and scientific data) and information services (such as provided by the World Wide Web); the increasing volumes of information generated, collected, stored and made available; the essential role of information technology as the backbone of many social services and as the engine of economic productivity; and the input of information processing into transactions in trading and finance. The societal confrontation with informational developments occurs in different ways, at different levels, at different speeds and in different historical contexts. Societies design their responses to these developments through policies, plans and programmes both as centrally steered initiatives and as decentralized activities on national and local levels. Most of these initiatives are driven by economic motives and are strongly technology-centric. The actors involved are both public institutions and private bodies, and they increasingly operate through public/private partnerships. Societies may respond to informational developments with both legal arrangements and self-regulatory agreements.

This chapter proposes a typology of informational developments as interactions with societies, and asks how international human rights standards are pertinent to these interactions.

Why Human Rights?

The decision to analyse what the field of international human rights can offer informational developments is obviously a normative one. These developments can also be approached from the angle of international trade agreements or technical standardization conventions. This chapter is inspired by the thought that informational developments affect people on many different levels, and that these developments are shaped and governed by human initiatives. Future information societies will be sociopolitical configurations in which numerous individuals and social groups conduct their lives, carry out their labour, love and play, enjoy and suffer. Therefore, it would seem a legitimate option to look at how the future could be constructed in such a way as to serve people's interests.

An assessment of people's interests is a complex task because they cannot be expressed in a singular way at a clearly identifiable forum. Therefore, people's interests have to be inferred from an identifiable set of standards that are commonly agreed on. This would seem almost impossible, given that in a multicultural world with multilayered societies, people will have divided interests and will make different preferential normative choices. However, despite the temptations of a normative relativism and the justified suspicion of unitary value judgments, it is possible to infer people's interests from universally accepted standards. These are the standards of international human rights. Human rights currently provide the only universally available set of standards for the dignity and integrity of all human beings. It is in the interest of all people that they be respected. The provisions of international human rights law represent the interests of ordinary men, women and children, as individuals, as groups and as communities.

There is at present an international political consensus about human rights. The global political community has recognized the existence of human rights, their universality and indivisibility, and has accepted a machinery for their enforcement. In 1993, the Vienna World Conference on Human Rights managed to reinforce the universal nature of the human rights standard. This means that international human rights law represents—however ineffectually—a set of universally accepted moral claims. It therefore provides us with a legitimate normative guide for societies' response to informational developments.

Interactions Between Societies and Informational Developments

Societies and informational developments interact with each other in many different ways. These interactions can be differentiated by the following four dimensions.

There is a *technological dimension* to the interaction. Technology obviously plays a vital role in informational developments. The scope, volume and impact of these developments is to a large extent shaped by technolitical innovations and the opportunities they create. The interaction is a process in which social forces and interests also contribute to the shaping of technological innovations. With this dimension, issues are posed about the control over technology, the access to and benefit from technology, and the social risks that innovations and their applications entail.

There is also a *cultural dimension* to the interaction. The ways in which societies deal with the provision and processing of information is determined by cultural perspectives. Information contents are cultural products. Information is part of a society's cultural fabric. Among the important issues of this dimension are the sharing of knowledge and the protection of cultural identity.

There is a *sociopolitical dimension* to the interaction. Information and information technologies have an impact on a society's development, progress and its political system. Among the important issues are freedom of political speech, the protection against abusive speech and the information needs of societies.

There is an *economic dimension* to the interaction. Worldwide information markets have emerged. Economic interests are at stake in the protection of ownership claims to content. There are issues of corporate social responsibility and self-determination in economic development.

Dimensions and Human Rights Provisions

Which international human rights provisions are relevant to these four dimensions? Or, in other words, what does the normative framework that sets standards for the ways in which societies should respond to informational developments look like?

Each of the four dimensions is considered in turn in the following pages, describing in some depth the relevant provisions in the numerous international agreements. At the end of each section, the relevant instruments are listed.

On technology and human rights

Sharing benefits from the development of technology

The right of access to technology is provided in article 27.1. of the Universal Declaration of Human Rights (UDHR) where it is stated that "Everyone has the right to...share in scientific advancement and its benefits". This right is inspired by the basic moral principle of equality and the notion that science and technology belong to the common heritage of humankind.

Up until 1968 there was no serious debate in the international community about the relation between scientific and technological development, and the protection of human rights. The following statement was adopted at the Teheran International Conference on Human Rights in 1968:

> While recent scientific discoveries and technological advances have opened vast prospects for economic, social and cultural progress, such developments may nevertheless endanger rights and freedoms of individuals and will require continuing attention (United Nations 1968).

The conference recommended in resolution XI "that the organizations of the United Nations family should undertake a study of the problems with respect to human rights arising from developments in science and technology". The United Nations General Assembly followed this recommendation and asked the Secretary-General (UN General Assembly resolution 2450 of 19 December 1968) to focus in this study particularly on:

- respect for the privacy of individuals and the integrity and sovereignty of nations in the light of advances in recording and other technologies;
- protection of the human personality and its physical and intellectual integrity, in the light of advances in biology, medicine and biochemistry;
- uses of electronics that may affect the rights of persons and the limits that should be put in such uses in a democratic society; and
- more generally, the balance that should be established between scientific and technological progress and the intellectual, spiritual, cultural and moral advancement of humanity.

On 11 December 1969 the UN General Assembly adopted the Declaration on Social Progress and Development. In article 13 this declaration provides for:

- equitable sharing of scientific and technological advances by developed and developing countries, and a steady increase in the use of science and technology for the benefit of the social development of society;
- the establishment of a harmonious balance between scientific, technological and material progress and the intellectual, spiritual, cultural and moral advancement of humanity; and
- the protection and improvement of the human environment.

On the basis of the study that the General Assembly requested in 1968 and various related reports, the Commission on Human Rights gave considerable attention to the issue in its 27th session in 1971 and focused particularly on:

- protection of human rights in the economic, social and cultural fields in accordance with the structure and resources of states and the scientific and technological level they have reached, as well as protection of the right to work in conditions of the automation and mechanization of production;
- the use of scientific and technological developments to foster respect for human rights and the legitimate interests of other peoples and respect for generally recognized moral standards and standards of international law; and
- prevention of the use of scientific and technological achievements to restrict fundamental democratic rights and freedoms.

In the years 1971–1976, a series of reports was produced dealing with the problems of privacy protection, use of observation satellites, automation, procedures of prenatal diagnosis, introduction of chemicals into food production, deterioration of the environment and the destructive power of modern weapons systems.

In resolution 3026 (18 December 1972), the General Assembly asked the Commission on Human Rights to look at the possibility of an international legal instrument that would address the issue of strengthening human rights in the light of scientific and technological developments. In 1973 the General Assembly (UN General Assembly resolution 3150) called upon states to further international co-operation to ensure that scientific and technological developments are used to strengthen peace and security, the realization of people's right to self-determination and respect for national sovereignty, and for the purpose of economic and social development. The Secretary-General was invited to report on these matters. This report (presented in 1975) addressed the harmful effect of automation and mechanization on the right to work; the harmful effect of scientific and technological developments on the right to adequate food; and problems of equality of treatment in relation to the impact of scientific and technological development on the right to health. The report also analysed the deterioration of the environment, the problem of the population explosion and the special problem of the impact of atomic radiation on public health. Then, on 10 November 1975, the General Assembly resolved to adopt the Declaration on the Use of Scientific and Technological Progress in the Interests of Peace and for the Benefit of Mankind (UN General Assembly resolution 3384).

The key principles of the declaration are:

- International co-operation to ensure that the results of science and technology developments are used to strengthen international peace and security; to promote economic and social development; and to realize human rights and freedoms.
- Measures to ensure that science and technology developments satisfy the material and the spiritual needs of all people.
- A commitment by states to refrain from the use of science and technology developments to violate the sovereignty and territorial integrity of other states, to interfere in their internal affairs, to wage aggressive wars, to suppress liberation movements or to pursue policies of racial discrimination.
- International co-operation to strengthen and develop the scientific and technological capacity of developing countries.
- Measures to extend the benefits of science and technology developments to all strata of the population and to protect them against all possible harmful effects.
- Measures to ensure that the use of science and technology developments promotes the realization of human rights.
- Measures to prevent the use of science and technology developments to the detriment of human rights.
- Action to ensure compliance with legislation which guarantees human rights in the conditions of science and technology developments.

In September 1975, a meeting of experts in Geneva recommended establishing an international mechanism to assess new technologies from the point of view of human rights. This form of technology assessment would include the evaluation of possible side-effects and long-range effects of technological innovations and would weigh the advantages and disadvantages of such innovations. The General Assembly did not act upon this recommendation and merely asked the Commission on Human Rights to follow the implementation of the declaration with special attention. Since 1982, the Secretary-General reports regularly on the implementation of the provisions of the declaration to the General Assembly.

Over the past years the General Assembly and the Commission on Human Rights have adopted a series of resolutions that by and large endorse the principles of the declaration. Among them is resolution 1986/9 of the Commission on Human Rights (Use of Scientific and Technological Development for the Promotion and Protection of Human Rights and Fundamental Freedoms) which "[c]alls upon all States to make every effort to utilize the benefits of scientific and technological developments for the promotion and protection of human rights and fundamental freedoms".

Over the years, the United Nations Educational, Scientific and Cultural Organization (UNESCO) has been particularly concerned with the human and cultural implications of developments in science and technology. In a series of meetings of experts, UNESCO addressed problems related to the effects of science and technology on local cultures. In 1982 a seminar was convened by UNESCO in Trieste (under the auspices of the International Institute for the Study of Human Rights) to study the consequences of science and technology developments, particularly in the fields of informatics, telematics and genetic manipulation, for human rights. The principles set forth in articles 23 and 26 of the UDHR, and the Convention against Discrimination in Education (1960), as well as provisions in the two main human rights covenants (the International Covenant on Civil and Political Rights, and the International Covenant on Economic, Social and Cultural Rights) and the Convention on the Elimination of All Forms of Discrimination against Women (1979) are part of the preamble preceding the 1989 UNESCO Convention on Technical and Vocational Education, which entered into force in 1991. The convention provides for the right to equal access to technical education and pays special attention to the needs of disadvantaged groups.

Technology and the protection against harmful effects

Over the past decades, the UN Commission on Human Rights and the General Assembly have drawn attention to the fact that people not only benefit from advances in technology, but can also be negatively affected by them. There is an awareness of the potentially harmful effects of new technologies on the physical and mental integrity of people (through new forms of personal and bodily tests); on the privacy of their homes and confidentiality of their correspondence (through new forms of surveillance); on the deterioration of people's working environments (through automation techniques); and on the natural environment (as a result of the dumping of electric and electronic waste).

Technology and decision making

The idea of human rights has to extend to the social institutions (the institutional arrangements) that would facilitate the realization of fundamental standards. Human rights cannot be realized without involving citizens in decision-making processes about the areas in which human rights standards are to be achieved. This moves the democratic process beyond the political sphere and extends the requirement of participatory institutional arrangements to other social domains. The human right to democratic participation claims that technology choices should also be subject to democratic control. This is particularly important in the light of the fact that current political processes tend to delegate important areas of social life to private rather than to public control and accountability. Increasingly large volumes of social activity are withdrawn from public accountability, from democratic control, and from the participation of citizens in decision making. Against this, both the Universal Declaration of Human Rights and the International Covenant on Civil and Political Rights (ICCPR) stress the right of people to take part in the conduct of public affairs directly or through freely chosen representatives. This points to the need to develop forms of democratic governance for rights and freedoms provided for by these instruments.

The relevant instruments

- The Universal Declaration of Human Rights
- The International Covenant of Civil and Political Rights
- The Declaration on Social Progress and Development (UN General Assembly, 11 December 1969).
- The Declaration on the Use of Scientific and Technological Progress in the Interests of Peace and for the Benefit of Mankind (UN General Assembly resolutions 3384, 1975).
- The 1989 UNESCO Convention on Technical and Vocational Education

On culture and human rights

During the discussions preceding the adoption of the United Nations Charter in 1945, several Latin American states proposed the inclusion of cultural rights. This was not accepted at the time but in 1948, a reference to cultural rights was included in articles 22 and 27 of the Universal Declaration on Human Rights. Article 22 states that everyone is entitled to the realization of the economic, social and cultural rights indispensable for his dignity and the free development of his personality. Article 27 states "Everyone has the right freely to participate in the cultural life of the community".

In 1966 the International Covenant on Economic, Social and Cultural Rights (ICESCR) was adopted by the UN General Assembly, and cultural rights were provided in articles 1 and 15. Article 1 provides that "All peoples have the right of self-determination. By virtue of that right they freely determine their political status and freely pursue their economic, social and cultural development". And article 15 says that the States Parties to the present Covenant recognize the right of everyone:

- to take part in cultural life;

- to enjoy the benefits of scientific progress and its applications; and
- to benefit from the protection of the moral and material interests resulting from any scientific, literary or artistic production of which they are the authors.

UNESCO became the key specialized UN agency for the protection of these provisions. Over the past decades UNESCO produced several relevant instruments that address cultural rights.

In 1995 UNESCO received the report from the World Commission on Culture and Development (WCCD), titled *Our Creative Diversity*, which proposed an agenda for action on cultural rights. On 2 November 2001, the 31st General Conference of UNESCO adopted the UNESCO Universal Declaration on Cultural Diversity. As the UNESCO Director-General, Koichiro Matsuura, declared at the time of its adoption,

> This is the first time the international community has endowed itself with such a comprehensive standard-setting instrument, elevating cultural diversity to the rank of 'common heritage of humanity'—as necessary for the human race as bio-diversity in the natural realm—and makes its protection an ethical imperative, inseparable from respect for human dignity.[1]

Article 5 of the declaration provides that

> Cultural rights are an integral part of human rights. The flourishing of creative diversity requires the full implementation of cultural rights. All persons have therefore the right to express themselves and to create and disseminate their work in the language of their choice, and particularly in their mother tongue; all persons are entitled to quality education and training that fully respect their cultural identity; and all persons have the right to participate in the cultural life of their choice and conduct their own cultural practices.

The declaration states, in article 7, that all cultures should be able to express themselves and make themselves known and should have access to the means of expression and dissemination. Article 8 addresses cultural goods and services and demands special attention

> to the diversity of the supply of creative work, to due recognition of the rights of authors and artists and to the specificity of cultural goods and services which...must not be treated as mere commodities or consumer goods.

---

[1]   www.unesco.org/confgen/press_rel/021101_clt_diversity.shtml, accessed on 23 October 2003.

Added to the declaration is an action plan for its implementation. It proposes among others:

- To preserve the linguistic heritage of humanity.
- To promote digital literacy and mastery of the new Information and Communication Technologies (ICTs).
- To promote access to new ICTs in developing countries and countries in transition.
- To support the presence of diverse contents in the media and emphasize the role of public broadcasting.
- To increase the mobility of creative artists.
- To help enable the cultural industries of developing countries.
- To involve civil society in the elaboration of social policies that aim at the preservation of cultural diversity.

Within the international human rights regime the following essential cultural rights have been identified (Hamelink 1994:186 ff).

The right to culture

Several factors explain the emergence of cultural rights in the post-Second World War era. There was the rise of post-colonial states that sought their identity in the light of both imposed colonial standards and their own traditional values. The issue of cultural identity became very important in the decolonization process. The newly independent states saw the affirmation of their cultural identity as an instrument in the struggle against foreign domination. In their earlier battle with colonialism, cultural identity had played a significant role in motivating and legitimizing the decolonization movement.

The proliferation of the mass media offered possibilities of unprecedented cultural interaction as well as risks of cultural uniformity. The spread of a consumer society—largely promoted by the mass media—raised serious concerns about the emergence of a homogeneous "global culture".

The adoption of the right to culture as part of the human rights system with its inclusive emphasis on rights for "everyone" implied a shift away from an elite conception of culture to a view of culture as "common heritage". Actually, the UNESCO Declaration on Race and Racial Prejudice of 1978 (General Conference resolution 3/1.1/2) founded the right to culture on the notion of culture as "common heritage of mankind", which implies that all people "should respect the right of all groups to their own cultural identity and the development of their distinctive cultural life within the national and international context" (article 5).

In 1968 a UNESCO conference of experts considered the question of cultural rights as human rights. The conference concluded:

> The rights to culture include the possibility for each man to obtain the means of developing his personality, through his direct participation in the creation of human values and of becoming, in this way, responsible for his situation, whether local or on a world scale (UNESCO 1968:107).

The Intergovernmental Conference on the Institutional, Administrative and Financial Aspects of Cultural Policies (convened by UNESCO in 1970) decided that the right to participate in the cultural life of the community implies that governments have a duty to provide the effective means for such participation.

A series of regional conferences on cultural policies (in 1972, 1973 and 1975) provided important inputs into the formulation of a UNESCO recommendation on Participation by the People at Large in Cultural Life and Their Contribution to It, which was approved at the 19th session of the UNESCO General Conference on 26 November 1976. The recommendation aims to "guarantee as human rights those rights bearing on access to and participation in cultural life" and proposes that member states "provide effective safeguards for free access to national and world cultures by all members of society", "pay special attention to women's full entitlement to access to culture and to effective participation in cultural life" and "guarantee the recognition of the equality of cultures, including the culture of national minorities and of foreign minorities". Regarding the mass media, the recommendation states that they "should not threaten the authenticity of cultures or impair their quality; they ought not to act as instruments of cultural domination but serve mutual understanding and peace". The recommendation is especially concerned about the concentration of control over the means of producing and distributing culture and suggests that governments "should make sure that the criterion of profit-making does not exert a decisive influence on cultural activities". There was strong Western opposition to various elements of the recommendation, such as the mention of commercial mass culture in a negative sense, and the use of the term "people at large". In the preparatory meetings and during the UNESCO General Conference, several Western delegations expressed their concern that if implemented, the recommendation would restrict the free flow of information and the independence of the mass media. The strongest opponent was the United States.

The USA asserted a belief from the outset that access to and participation in cultural life were not fit subjects for international regulation, took minimal part of the drafting process, sent no delegation to the intergovernmental meeting, urged the General Conference to turn down the proposed text and, after its adoption, announced that it had no intention of transmitting the Recommendation to the relevant authorities or institutions in the USA (Wells 1987:165).

The recommendation uses a broad notion of culture as an integral part of social life and one of the principle factors in the progress of mankind. Culture "is not merely an accumulation of works and knowledge which an elite produces, collects and conserves...but is...the demand for a way of life and the need to communicate".

The main line of thought in the recommendation was reinforced by the 1982 World Conference on Cultural Policies held in Mexico City. The Declaration on Cultural Policies adopted by the conference reaffirmed the requirement that states must take appropriate measures to implement the right to cultural participation. In its various recommendations, conference participants claimed that cultural democracy should be based on the broadest possible participation by the individual and society in the creation of cultural goods, in decision making concerning cultural life, and in the dissemination and enjoyment of culture. Various assessments of the implementation of the recommendation on participation in cultural life over the past years showed that little had been done by many states and that these issues remained relevant.

In summary, it can be established that the recognition of the human right to culture implies the participation in cultural life, the protection of cultural identity, the need to conserve, develop and diffuse culture, the protection of intellectual property rights, and the recognition of linguistic diversity. Each of these themes is treated in the following paragraphs.

The right to participate fully in cultural life

Participation in cultural life has raised difficult questions about the definition of communities, the position of subcultures, the protection of participation rights of minorities, the provision of physical resources of access, and the links between cultural access and socioeconomic conditions. Underlying some of these difficulties is the tension between the interpretation of culture as public good or as private property. These interpretations can be mutually exclusive when historical works of art disappear into the vaults of private collections. The right to freely participate in the cultural life of one's community recognizes that a society's democratic quality is not merely defined by civil and political institutions but also by the possibility for people to shape their cultural identity, to realize the potential of local cultural life and to practise cultural traditions.

Participation rights also entail people's right "freely to participate in the cultural life of the community, to enjoy the arts and to share in scientific advancement and its benefits" (article 27 of the Universal Declaration of Human Rights). The participation claim requires the creation of social and economic conditions that will enable people "not only to enjoy the benefits of culture, but also to take an active part in overall cultural life and in the process of cultural development". The UNESCO Recommendation on Participation by the People at Large in Cultural Life and their Contribution to It that articulates this require- ment, also provides that "participation in cultural life presupposes involvement of the different social partners in decision making related to cultural policy". Participation extends beyond public participation in media production or media management into the areas of public decision making. The UNESCO Expert Consultation in Bucharest, Romania, in 1982 (UNESCO 1982) emphasized that it is essential "that individuals and groups should be able to participate at all relevant levels and at all stages in communication, including the formulation, application, monitoring and review of communication policies". This standard thus requires that political practices provide for people's participation in public policy making on the production of culture. People have the right to participate in public decision making on the preservation, protection and development of culture. This means that there should be ample scope for public participation in the formulation and implementation of public cultural policies.

The right to the protection of cultural identity

The protection of cultural identity became an especially sensitive issue during the debates in the 1970s on cultural imperialism. In 1973, heads of state at the Non-Aligned Summit in Algiers stated in their declaration that "it is an established fact that the activity of imperialism is not limited to political and economic domains, but that it encompasses social and cultural areas as well, imposing thereby a foreign ideological domination on the peoples of the developing world".

Cultural domination and the threat to cultural identity were also treated by the MacBride Commission, which was appointed by UNESCO. The commission saw cultural identity "endangered by the overpowering influence on and assimilation of some national cultures though these nations may well be the heirs to more ancient and richer cultures. Since diversity is the most precious quality of culture, the whole world is poorer" (International Commission for the Study of Communication Prob- lems 1980:31).

In its recommendations, the commission offered very little prospect for a multilateral approach to the issue of cultural domination. Its main recommendation was for the establishment of national policies "which should foster cultural identity. Such policies should also contain guidelines for safeguarding national cultural development while promoting knowledge of other cultures" (International Commission for the Study of Communication Problems 1980:259). No recommendation was proposed on what measures the world community might collectively take. The commission proposed the strengthening of cultural identity and promoted conditions for the preservation of the cultural identity, but left this to be implemented on the national level.

Ten years later, the South Commission also addressed the issue of cultural identity. According to its report, the concern with cultural identity "does not imply rejection of outside influences. Rather, it should be a part of efforts to strengthen the capacity for autonomous decision-making, blending indigenous and universal elements in the service of a people-centred policy" (South Commission 1990:132). The commission urged governments to adopt Cultural Development Charters that articulate people's basic rights in the field of culture. Cultural policies should stress the right to culture, cultural diversity and the role of the state in preserving and enriching the cultural heritage of society (South Commission 1990:133).

The notion of cultural identity remains a topic for much discussion. Among the unresolved issues is the question of how a society can protect the cultural identity of its constituent parts and at the same time maintain social cohesion.

The right to the protection of national and international cultural property and heritage

This cultural right is particularly relevant in times of armed conflict. It also has important implications for the recognition of the intellectual property of indigenous peoples.

In 1973, the United Nations General Assembly adopted a resolution (UN General Assembly resolution 3148 (XXVIII), 14 December) on the preservation and further development of cultural values. The resolution considers the value and dignity of each culture as well as the ability to preserve and develop its distinctive character as a basic right of all countries and peoples. In the light of the possible endangering of the distinctive character of cultures, the preservation, enrichment and further development of national cultures must be supported. It is important that the resolution recognizes that "the preservation, renewal and continuous creation of cultural values should not be a static but a dynamic concept". The resolution recommended to the director-general of

UNESCO to promote research that analyses "the role of the mass media in the preservation and further development of cultural values".

The resolution also urged governments to promote "the involvement of the population in the elaboration and implementation of measures ensuring preservation and future development of cultural and moral values".

On the protection of cultural property, governments adopted two UNESCO conventions: The Hague Convention for the Protection of Cultural Property in the Event of Armed Conflict (1954), and the Convention on the Means of Prohibiting and Preventing the Illicit Import, Export and Transfer of Ownership of Cultural Property (1970).

A specialized instrument on the protection of the world cultural heritage was adopted by the 17th session of the UNESCO General Conference in 1972: the Convention for the Protection of the World Cultural and Natural Heritage. The text noted that the world's cultural heritage is threatened, and that this impoverishes the world. Therefore, effective provisions are needed to collectively protect the cultural heritage of outstanding universal value. In the convention, the international protection of the world cultural heritage is understood to mean "the establishment of a system of international co-operation and assistance designed to support States Parties to the Convention in their efforts to conserve and identify that heritage".

In 1973 the United Nations General Assembly adopted a resolution on the Restitution of Works of Art to Countries Victims of Expropriation (UN General Assembly resolution 3187 (XXVIII), 18 December). The resolution sees prompt restitution of works of art as strengthening international co-operation and as a just reparation for damage done. To implement this, UNESCO established the Intergovernmental Committee for Promoting the Return of Cultural Property to its Countries of Origin or its Restitution in Case of Illicit Appropriation. Throughout the 1980s, the United Nations General Assembly stressed the issue, commended the work of UNESCO done in this field and called upon member states to ratify the relevant convention. In 1986 the General Assembly proclaimed 1988–1997 as the World Decade for Cultural Development. The following objectives were formulated for the decade: the acknowledgement of the cultural dimension of development; the enrichment of cultural identities; the broadened participation in cultural life; and the promotion of international cultural co-operation (UN General Assembly resolution 41/187, 8 December 1986).

Other approaches of the international community to the protection of cultural property include the safeguarding of traditional culture and folklore. In 1989 the UNESCO General Conference adopted a recommendation that stressed the need to recognize the role of folklore and the danger it faces. Folklore is defined as the totality of tradition-based creations of a cultural community. The recommendation urges measures for the conservation, preservation, dissemination and protection of folklore.

The UN Draft Declaration on the Rights of Indigenous Peoples (1994) refers explicitly to the cultural property of indigenous peoples. Article 12 states that

> Indigenous people have the right to practice and revitalize their cultural traditions and customs. This includes the right to maintain, protect and develop the past, present and future manifestations of their cultures, such as archaeological and historical sites, artefacts, designs, ceremonies, technologies and visual and performing arts and literature, as well as the right to restitution of cultural, intellectual, religious and spiritual property taken without their free and informed consent or in violation of their law, traditions and customs.

The right to use one's language in private and public

This cultural right recognizes that linguistic rights are a critical part of human rights. The language we speak and our mother tongue in particular is a crucial part of who we are as individuals. For a minority group, the loss of language threatens the existence of the group because it eventually assimilates with the group whose language it speaks.

The most far-reaching article in (binding) human rights law granting linguistic rights is article 27 of the International Covenant on Civil and Political Rights (1966), which states:

> In those states in which ethnic, religious or linguistic minorities exist, persons belonging to such minorities shall not be denied the right, in community with other members of their group, to enjoy their own culture, to profess and practise their own religion, or to use their own language.

Initially this article was seen as referring to individuals and not to collectives. This did not help immigrant communities, which were not seen as minorities. However, this changed with an interpretation of the article provided in a general comment on article 27, adopted by the UN Human Rights Committee on 6 April 1994. The committee sees the article as offering protection to all individuals on the state's territory or under its jurisdiction, including immigrants and refugees.

The UN Draft Universal Declaration on Rights of Indigenous Peoples formulates language rights strongly and explicitly, and requires the state to allocate resources. But the fate of the draft is still unsure—the latest version was completed 25–29 July 1994 and forwarded to the UN Sub-Commission on Prevention of Discrimination and Protection of

137

Minorities, which in turn submitted it to the UN Commission on Human Rights for discussion in February 1995. Work on it is still going on, and major changes can still be expected. However, there is some suspicion that indigenous peoples themselves may not have a lot of influence on these provisions. In connection with the recognition of their linguistic human rights, the draft declaration also provides in article 17 that indigenous people "have the right to equal access to all forms of non-indigenous media". And in addition, "States shall take effective measures to ensure that State-owned media duly reflect indigenous cultural diversity".

A World Conference on Linguistic Rights was held in Barcelona in June 1996, organized by the International PEN Club and a European Union-funded centre for linguistic legislation based in Catalonia. A Draft Universal Declaration of Linguistic Rights was approved, and UNESCO undertook to promote the work of submitting the declaration to national governments for endorsement, and to refine the text in collaboration with relevant associations. The text is a comprehensive document covering conceptual clarification, rights in public administration, education and the media, culture and the socioeconomic sphere.

While the document stresses the rights of what it calls "linguistic communities" (roughly corresponding to territorial minorities) to their mother tongue and to proficiency in an official language, it is of little help to non-territorial minorities and immigrant minorities.

The UNESCO Declaration on Cultural Diversity has some references to linguistic rights but does not highlight the language issue. In article 5 it provides that "All persons have therefore the right to express themselves and to create and disseminate their work in the language of their choice, and particularly in their mother tongue". Item 5 of the action plan proposes "Safeguarding the linguistic heritage of humanity and giving support to expression, creation and dissemination in the greatest possible number of languages", and item 6 states "Encouraging linguistic diversity—while respecting the mother tongue—at all levels of education, wherever possible, and fostering the learning of several languages from the youngest age". Item 10 recommends "Promoting linguistic diversity in cyberspace".

The relevant instruments

- The Universal Declaration of Human Rights (1948)
- The International Covenant on Social, Economic and Cultural Rights (1966)
- The International Covenant on Civil and Political Rights (1966)
- The UNESCO Hague Convention for the Protection of Cultural Property in the Event of Armed Conflict (1954)

- The UNESCO Convention on the Means of Prohibiting and Preventing the Illicit Import, Export and Transfer of Ownership of Cultural Property (1970)
- The UNESCO Convention for the Protection of the World Cultural and Natural Heritage (1972)
- The UNESCO Recommendation on Participation by the People at Large in Cultural Life and Their Contribution to It (1976)
- The UN Draft Declaration on the Rights of Indigenous Peoples (1994)
- The UNESCO Declaration of the Principles of International Cultural Co-operation (1966)
- The UNESCO Universal Declaration on Cultural Diversity (2001)

On politics, society and human rights

Freedom of expression

For the interactions between informational developments and the political systems of societies, the key human rights provisions refer to freedom of expression. These provisions are found in the Universal Declaration of Human Rights (article 19) and the International Covenant on Civil and Political Rights (article 19). The right to freedom of expression is also provided for children in the Convention on the Rights of the Child (article 13). The essential provision remains the formulation in article 19 of the Universal Declaration of Human Rights. The article reads, "Everyone has the right to freedom of opinion and expression; this right includes freedom to hold opinions without interference and to seek, receive and impart information and ideas through any media and regardless of frontiers".

In order to protect societies against possible abuses of the right to freedom of speech, international human rights law has also provided for a series of limitations on this freedom.

Among these are the prohibition of incitement to genocide. Article 3 of the 1948 Convention on the Prevention and Punishment of the Crime of Genocide declares that among the acts that shall be punishable is "direct and public incitement to commit genocide".

Article 4 states that "Persons committing genocide or any of the other acts enumerated in article III shall be punished, whether they are constitutionally responsible rulers, public officials or private individuals".

There are also provisions on the prohibition of discrimination. In the UDHR, article 2 states that "Everyone is entitled to all the rights and freedoms set forth in this declaration, without distinction of any kind, such as race, colour, sex, language, religion, political or other opinion, national or social origin, property, birth or other status".

139

Furthermore, according to the declaration no distinction shall be made on the basis of the political, jurisdictional or international status of the country or territory to which a person belongs, whether it be independent, trust, non-self-governing or under any other limitation of sovereignty. The essential principle here is equality. Differential treatment of people based on the features of persons or groups conflicts with the basic notion of human dignity. Article 2 is intended to provide a general protection against discrimination.

The equality standard entered international law for the first time with the United Nations Charter. The earlier Covenant of the League of Nations (1919), for example, did not provide such protection. The Preamble of the UN Charter calls for "the equal rights of men of women and of nations small and large". During the drafting work, discussion focused on the ground of discrimination, among others. One of the controversies was: should political opinion be included, or notions such as status, property and birth when they were objects of dissenting opinions? The phrasing "without distinction of any kind, such as..." implies that the enumeration should not be read as exhaustive.

The UDHR and ICCPR use the term "distinction", and the ICESCR uses "discrimination". However, the ICCPR uses the term discrimination in article 4.1 on derogation.

One of the most important treaties to codify the non-discrimination standard is the International Convention on the Elimination of All Forms of Racial Discrimination (1965). The most contested (and, for media, most pertinent) provision of this convention is found in article 4, which concerns the dissemination of ideas based on racial superiority.

The convention on racial discrimination has been ratified by an overwhelming majority of UN member states. Article 4 of this convention and article 20.2. of the International Covenant on Civil and Political Rights incorporate into domestic law the prohibition of the dissemination of ideas based on racial superiority and the incitement to racial hatred or advocacy of national or religious hatred. Article 20 of the covenant states in paragraph 2, "Any advocacy of national, racial or religious hatred that constitutes incitement to discrimination, hostility or violence shall be prohibited by law".

Other important provisions against discrimination are found in the Convention on the Elimination of All Forms of Discrimination Against Women (1979). Article 5 of this convention demands "the elimination of stereotyped representations of roles for men and women and prejudices based upon the idea of the inferiority or the superiority of either of the sexes". In article 10 on education, there is strong plea for the elimination of any stereotyped content of the roles of men and women at all levels and in all forms of education.

A limitation on the freedom of expression is also implied by the human rights standard on the protection of people's privacy against undue interference. The Universal Declaration of Human Rights provides in article 12:

> No one shall be subjected to arbitrary interference with his privacy, family, home or correspondence, nor to attacks upon his honour and reputation. Everyone has the right to the protection of the law against such interference or attacks.

The freedom to hold opinions

In article 19 of the Universal Declaration of Human Rights, the freedom to hold opinions without interference is recognized. When this provision was transformed into binding law through its incorporation in the International Covenant on Civil and Political Rights (article 19), an interesting development took place. In the covenant, the freedom of opinion and the freedom of expression are separated. The covenant provides for an absolute right to the freedom of opinion but allows certain restrictions on the freedom of expression, such as restrictions necessary for respect of the rights and reputations of others, and for the protection of national security or of public order (*ordre publique*), or of public health or morals, in paragraph 3 of article 19. The covenant also limits the freedom of expression through the provisions of article 20 that demand that any propaganda for war shall be prohibited by law and that any advocacy of national, racial or religious hatred that constitutes incitement to discrimination, hostility or violence shall be prohibited by law. The covenant emphasizes the special character of the right to freedom to hold opinions by rendering this a private right (related to the protection of privacy) that cannot be subject to any interference whatever.

On the public exposure of prisoners of war

International humanitarian law (which could be described as human rights for times of armed conflict) prohibits the exposure of prisoners of war to public curiosity (Third Geneva Convention relative to the Treatment of Prisoners of War, 12 August 1949).

News media violate this human rights provision when they publish pictures of captured prisoners of war and thus expose them to public curiosity. In various recent armed conflicts, this standard was violated in most of the world's news media. Well-known examples of such violations were the pictures of the Al Qaeda suspects in Guantanamo Bay and in Afghanistan, the TV station Al Jazeera showing British soldiers taken captive, and the video fragments of Iraqi military taken as prisoners of war that were broadcast around the world by Western media.

Providing information

International human rights law also points to the social responsibility to disseminate certain type of information. The preambles of the Universal Declaration of Human Rights and the two international human rights covenants (ICCPR and ICESCR) propose a general responsibility to contribute to the teaching of human rights. The UDHR states "That every individual and every organ of society, keeping this declaration constantly in mind, shall strive by teaching and education to promote respect for these right and freedoms". The preambles of both the covenants state "Realizing that the individual, having duties to other individuals and to the community to which he belongs, is under a responsibility to strive for the promotion and observance of the rights recognized in the present Covenant". The reference to "everyone" and "every organ of society" and to individual responsibility, would seem to logically imply that all information providers are among those individuals who are expected to contribute to the promotion and protection of human rights.

The Convention on the Rights of the Child also encourages the provision of a special type of information. In article 17 the convention provides that

> States Parties recognize the important function performed by the mass media and shall ensure that the child has access to information and material from a diversity of national and international sources, especially those aimed at the promotion of his of her social, spiritual and moral well-being and physical and mental health. To this end, States Parties shall:
>
> - Encourage the mass media to disseminate information and material of social and cultural benefit to the child and in accordance with the spirit of article 29;
> - Encourage international co-operation in the production, exchange and dissemination of such information and material from a diversity of cultural, national and international sources;
> - Encourage the production and dissemination of children's books;
> - Encourage the mass media to have particular regard to the linguistic needs of the child who belongs to a minority group or who is indigenous.

The relevant instruments:

- The Universal Declaration of Human Rights (1948)
- The Third Geneva Convention relative to the Treatment of Prisoners of War (1949)
- The International Covenant on Civil and Political Rights (1966)
- The Convention on the Prevention and Punishment of the Crime of Genocide (1948)
- The Convention on the Elimination of All Forms of Discrimination against Women (1979)
- The Convention on the Rights of the Child (1989)

On the economy and human rights

The right to self-determination and the right to development

With regard to informational developments and the development of local industries for the production and dissemination of information, it is important that article 1 of the International Covenant on Economic, Social and Cultural Rights provides for the right of self-determination. This implies that all societies are free to determine and pursue their economic development. This standard was further strengthened by the Declaration on the Right to Development, adopted by the UN General Assembly resolution 41/128 of 4 December 1986.

In article 2, the declaration provides that

> States have the right and the duty to formulate appropriate national development policies that aim at the constant improvement of the well-being of the entire population and of all individuals, on the basis of their active, free and meaningful participation in development and in the fair distribution of the benefits resulting therefrom.

This standard has obvious implications for the formulation of policies with regard to informational developments.

The right to the protection of moral and material interests of works of culture

This human rights standard has come to play an increasingly important role in the international economy. International rules for the protection of intellectual property rights originated in the nineteenth century. From the beginning, this protection has been inspired by three motives. The first motive was the notion that those who invested in the production of intellectual property should be guaranteed a financial remuneration.

With the establishment of the first international treaties on intellectual property protection (the Paris Convention for the Protection of Industrial Property of 1883 and the Berne Convention for the Protection of Literary and Artistic Works of 1886), a monetary benefit for the creator was perceived as a necessary incentive to invest in innovation and creativity. During the 1928 revision of the Berne convention, the second motive, the notion of moral rights, was added to the entitlement to economic benefits. The introduction of the moral value of works recognized that they represent the intellectual personality of the author. Moral rights protect the creative work against modification without the creator's consent, protect the claim to authorship and the right of the author to decide whether a work will be published. Early on in the development of intellectual property rights (IPRs), it was also recognized that there is a public interest in the protection of intellectual property. As a common principle and as a third motive, it was recognized that IPRs promote the innovation and progress in artistic, technological and scientific domains, and therefore benefit public welfare. Article 1 of the US Constitution, for example, articulates this as follows, "to promote the progress of science and the useful arts, by securing for limited time to authors and inventors the exclusive rights to their respective writings and discoveries". The protection of intellectual property rights is in fact a delicate balancing act between private economic interests, individual ownership, moral values, and public interest.

With the increasing economic significance of intellectual property, the global system of governance in this domain has moved away from moral and public interest dimensions, and in its actual practice mainly emphasizes the economic interests of the owners of intellectual property. Today, such owners are by and large no longer individual authors and composers who create cultural products, but transnational corporate cultural producers. The individual authors, composers and performers are low on the list of trade figures and, as a result, there is a trend toward IPR arrangements that favour institutional investment interests over individual producers.

The recent tendency to include intellectual property rights in global trade negotiations demonstrates the commercial thrust of the major actors. Copyright problems have become trade issues, and the protection of the author has ceded place to the interests of traders and investors. This emphasis on corporate ownership interests implies a threat to the common good utilization of intellectual property and seriously upsets the balance between the private ownership claims of the producer and the claims to public benefits of the users. The balance between the interests of producers and users has always been under threat in the development of the IPR governance system, but it would seem that the currently emerging arrangements benefit neither the individual creators nor the public at large. Its key beneficiaries are the transnational media conglomerates for which the core business is content. Several of their recent mergers are in fact motivated by the desire to gain control over rights to content as, for example, invested in film libraries or in collections of musical recordings.

Recent developments in digital technology, which open up unprecedented possibilities for free and easy access to, and utilization of, knowledge, have also rendered the professional production, reproduction and distribution of content vulnerable to grand-scale piracy. This has made the content owners very concerned about their property rights and interested in the creation of a global enforceable legal regime for their protection.

However, protecting intellectual property is not without risks. The protection of intellectual property also restricts the access to knowledge since it defines knowledge as private property and tends to facilitate monopolistic practices. The granting of monopoly control over inventions may restrict their social utilization and reduce the potential public benefits. The principle of exclusive control over the exploitation of works someone has created, can constitute an effective right to monopoly control, which restricts the free flow of ideas and knowledge. In the current corporate battle against piracy it would seem that the key protagonists are in general more concerned with the protection of investments than with the moral integrity of creative works or the quality of cultural life in the world.

In the currently emerging IPR regime, a few mega-companies become the global gatekeepers of the world's cultural heritage. At the same time the small individual or communal producers of literature, arts or music hardly benefit from international legal protection. Most of the collected money goes to a small percentage of creative people (some 90 per cent of the money goes to 10 per cent of the creative people) and most artists that produce intellectual property receive a minor portion of the collected funds (some 90 per cent share 10 per cent). Most of the money goes to star performers and best-selling authors. The media industry does not make money by creating cultural diversity as it gets its revenues primarily from blockbuster artists. If there was more variety on the music market, for example, the smaller and independent labels would compete with the transnational market leaders. Although this would fit into the conventional thinking about free markets, the industry in reality prefers consolidation over competition!

It becomes increasingly clear that the drive to protect media products against unauthorized reproduction leads to an increasing level of restrictions on reproduction for private purposes.

Intellectual property rights are recognized by the Universal Declaration of Human Rights as human rights (article 27), and this puts the protection of intellectual property in the context of other human rights, such as freedom of expression and right of access to information and knowledge. This human rights context should shape the political framework for all parties involved: producers, distributors, artists and consumers. The implication would be that the protection of intellectual property rights cannot be separated from the right to full participation in cultural life for everyone; the right of affordable access to information for everyone; the recognition of moral rights of cultural producers; the rights of creative artists; the diversity of cultural production, and the protection of the public domain.

A human-rights-based international agreement on intellectual property rights would recognize the needs of all people, the notion of common rights and the sharing of benefits (the World Trade Organization's Agreement on Trade-Related Intellectual Property Rights of 1993 recognizes in its preamble intellectual property rights only as private rights). Its primary purpose would be societal rather than commercial, and intellectual property rights would be seen as freedom rights more than as restrictive proprietary rights. In the initial conception of the protection of intellectual property as a human right, the restriction on the use of such property was seen only as temporary. This monopolization was seen as socially acceptable since the product would eventually be returned to the public domain. The current efforts to extend the duration of the protection (such as in the United States where recently protection was extended from 50 years to 70 years after the death of the author) point in the direction of an almost unlimited restriction.

Human rights and corporate responsibilities

Many of the operations of transnational corporations (TNCs) across the globe have human rights dimensions. The commercial activities of a growing number of TNCs affect such issues as global warming, child labour, genetically manipulated food or financial markets.

Following the widely accepted policies of liberalization and deregulation, the reach and freedom of TNCs have considerably expanded without a concurrent development of their social responsibility. TNCs, however, increasingly face public challenges to their moral conduct, and for some corporate actors, this has meant that they have begun to reflect on standards of good corporate governance.

Some companies also propose that voluntary compliance with human rights standards (through self-regulated codes of conduct) is good for business as it makes the company look good for consumers, helps to avoid legal cases, enhances risk management and increases worker productivity. In a statement to the United Nations, the non-governmental organization Human Rights Watch has proposed viewing the development of guidelines as a first step in the process of developing binding human rights standards for corporations. It believes "that there is a need for binding standards to prevent corporations from having a negative impact on the enjoyment of human rights. Such standards should not just be limited to transnational corporations but should apply to any corporation: local, national, or transnational".[2] The UNDP *Human Development Report 1999* also argues that TNCs are too important for their conduct to be left to voluntary and self-generated standards.

The issue of human rights with regard to private actors becomes more important now that public services are often performed by private actors. Once such formerly state-owned institutions, like the postal services, are privatized, the obligation, for example, to ensure that the human right to privacy is not violated, does not change. The protection of human rights implies that states should stop private parties from violating the human rights of their citizens. The Maastricht Experts Meeting Guidelines on Violations of Economic, Social and Cultural Rights (1997) states that: "The obligation to protect includes the States' responsibility to ensure that private entities or individuals, including transnational corporations over which they exercise jurisdiction, do not deprive individuals of their economic, social and cultural rights" (ICJ et al. 1997:9).

International human rights law does indeed provide for an obligation on the part of states to ensure that private business respects human rights. This is part of the indirect accountability of states. There are, however, also direct obligations for the conduct of commercial companies. There is an obligation for all parties (as the Preamble of the UDHR states) to promote human rights. This means to publicize and disseminate human rights principles and standards, to explain them, to help others to understand them and to use whatever influence one has to protect human rights. The committee for the ICESCR has been very outspoken about the inclusion of private actors in the protection of human rights. The committee has, among other things, pointed to the need for the right to privacy to be protected from violations by private entities. The committee has taken the position that the rights it is responsible for do indeed apply to private parties. Similarly, the tripartite ILO Declaration on Principles Concerning Multinational Enterprises and Social Policy (1977) refers in article 8 to the need to respect human rights for all parties (government, employers and trade unions) and mentions rights such as the freedom of expression.

The Sub-Commission on the Promotion and Protection of Human Rights (a body of the UN Human Rights Commission) has a working

---

[2]   http://208.55.16.210/Human-Rights-Watch-statement-31-July-2001.htm, accessed on 23 October 2003.

group on transnational corporations and human rights. In 1999 the working group began work on a code of conduct on corporations and human rights, which was approved for further development in 2000. The working group wants to eventually make the code a binding instrument. The US administration opposes this and has proposed the dissolution of the sub-commission.

Privacy and security

For international trading, the issue of security of online transactions has obviously become a major issue. The question arising from this is whether human rights provisions on the protection of privacy and the confidentiality of communication can be applied. The complication here is that industry tends to use a double standard. On the one hand there is a strong preference for robust protection of secure communications as an essential prerequisite for the growth of e-commerce, and on the other hand there is increasing corporate interest in the collecting and trading of person-related data.

Encryption technology is the obvious tool to ensure secure electronic communications. This technology has clear advantages for the users' privacy but also facilitates secret communication among members of criminal organizations. Most states claim the right to access information flows if they might endanger national security or in case the judicial process requires it. As a result they tend to hold ambivalent positions toward encryption. The dominant trend in the countries of the Organisation for Economic Co-operation and Development (OECD) is toward the liberalization of encryption and the general acceptance of coding techniques. An issue still to be resolved is the matter of whether the codes used for encryption should be deposited with third parties so that governments could access them in case they need this for security or law enforcement purposes. In March 1997 the OECD recommended regulation that demonstrated this ambiguity very clearly. The OECD Guidelines for Cryptography Policy form a set of non-binding principles on the use of cryptographic technologies. The essential regulatory principles are the trust in cryptographic methods, the choice of cryptographic methods, the market-driven development of cryptographic methods, the need for standards in cryptographic methods, the protection of privacy and personal data, lawful access, liability and international co-operation. The rules emphasize that national policies on cryptography should respect the fundamental rights of individuals to privacy, the confidentiality of communication and the protection of personal data. However, the principle of lawful access remains very vague and can be interpreted in ways that do not provide a robust protection of privacy. The OECD and other forums such as the chambers of commerce are inclined to adopt a system in which the encryption keys are deposited with trusted third parties. One question this raises is what it would mean in cases where law-abiding citizens comply but criminals design their own cryptographic systems.

In the European Union, most governments tend to allow the users of electronic traffic to use forms of cryptography, while requiring access when deemed necessary.

A Council of Europe recommendation (R(95)13) Concerning Problems of Criminal Procedure Law Connected with Information Technology stresses the need to minimize the negative effects of restriction on cryptography for criminal prosecution, while allowing the legitimate use of the technologies. On 8 October 1997, the European Commission issued a recommendation, Towards a European Framework for Digital Signatures and Encryption. The commission emphasized the significance of robust protection of the confidentiality of electronic communications because it was concerned that the restriction of encryption technologies negatively affected the protection of privacy. As a matter of fact, the commission felt that restrictions could make ordinary citizens more vulnerable to criminals, whereas criminals would probably not be hindered in using these technologies.

The individual preference to be left alone conflicts with the wish of public and private institutions to gather information about the individual. The development of digital ICTs has increased the tension of this conflict and has made it more urgent. The protection of personal data has always been a difficult challenge, but with recent developments such as the Internet, the effort has become very discouraging. Information about how people use the Internet is collected though a variety of means (such as the so-called cookies), and each act in cyberspace contains the real danger of privacy intrusion. Using electronic mail, for example, inevitably implies a considerable loss of control over one's privacy unless users are trained in the use of encryption techniques and as long as these are not prohibited by law.

When we engage in cyberspace transactions, we leave a digital trace through credit cards, bonus cards and client cards. And as online transactions grow, the collection of person-related data will increase. Not only is it attractive for entrepreneurs to know the preferences of their clients, it is also lucrative to sell such data to third parties. Acquiring data about people's biogenetical profiles as well as consumer data can be of great value to insurance companies, among others. The combined information about high blood pressure and the purchase of alcoholic beverages, for example, helps the insurer to define the level of risks and therefore the costs the client will pay for the insurance policy.

Person-related data are stored in what are known as data warehouses. With the assistance of increasingly intelligent information systems, all these data can be analysed and detailed profiles of subjects can be composed by combining data from various sources. This permits in-depth enquiries into the behaviour of certain categories of clients, which implies, on the one hand, that they can be better served through the marketing of the goods and services they need. It also implies that their privacy is progressively undermined. Collecting, analysing and interpreting of personal data has become a "data-mining" industry.

Corporate ownership

International human rights law does not contain any specific and direct provisions that address the issue of the ownership of information and communication institutions. There are no standards that regulate the possible monopolization or oligopolization of the production and/or distribution of information and communication goods and services. However, there is a multitude of provisions on the diversity of cultural content, the diversity of information sources, the social function of information, the equitable sharing of information and knowledge, and the specificity of cultural goods and services as more than mere consumer goods. It is difficult to see how such provisions can be combined with a monopolized or oligopolized control over information and communication markets. The implications of current human rights provisions seem to point toward the need for a variety of independent producers and distributors of information and communication goods and services, and a balanced mixture of privately owned, commercial corporate actors and publicly owned, not-for-profit institutions.

The relevant instruments

- The Universal Declaration of Human Rights (1948)
- The International Covenant on Economic, Social and Cultural Rights (1966)
- The ILO Declaration on Principles Concerning Multinational Enterprises and Social Policy (1977)
- The UN Declaration on the Right to Development (1986)

Societies and Informational Developments: Summary

The human rights provisions that are relevant to societies' interactions with informational developments can be summarized in the following table.

Table 1: Human rights provisions

Dimensions	Human rights provisions
Technology	Access to technical education
	Use of technology to promote human rights
	Equal sharing benefits of technology
	Protection against harmful effects
	Participation in public policy making
	Attention for the needs of disadvantaged groups
Culture	Self-determination of cultural development
	Diversity of creative work and media contents
	Participation in cultural life
	Recognition of cultural practices
	Sharing benefits of scientific developments
	Use of the mother tongue
	Protection of cultural heritage
	Involvement in cultural policies
Politics	Freedom of expression
	Freedom of opinion
	Protection against incitement to hatred and discrimination
	Protection of privacy
	Protection of prisoners of war
	Presumption of innocence
	Responsibility to provide information about matters of public interest
	Elimination of stereotyped contents
Economy	Self-determination of economic development
	Right to development
	Protection of intellectual property
	Corporate responsibility
	Privacy/security
	Corporate ownership

5. Implementation

The most important issue for the significance and validity of the human rights regime is the enforcement of the standards it proposes.

Enforcement

There is abundant evidence that these standards are almost incessantly violated around the world, and by actors with very different political and ideological viewpoints. If one studies the annual reports from Amnesty International, for example, there appears to be no country where human rights are not violated.

For moral philosophers this is actually not surprising. It concerns the classical gap between the moral knowledge possessed by human beings and their intention to act morally. The mechanisms the international community has developed to deal with the "moral gap" are largely inadequate.

Present procedures are based mainly upon the Optional Protocol (OP) to the International Covenant on Civil and Political Rights (1966) and resolution 1503 adopted by the United Nations Economic and Social Council (ECOSOC) in 1970. The protocol authorizes the UN Human Rights Committee to receive and consider communications from individuals from nationals of states that are party to the OP (presently 75 states) who claim to be victims of a violation by that state party of any of the rights set forth in the covenant. These complaints are published as part of the national human rights record. The OP provides for communications, analysis and reporting, but not for sanctions. ECOSOC resolution 1503 recognizes the possibility of individual complaints about human rights violations. It authorizes the UN Human Rights Commission to examine "communications, together with replies of governments, if any, which appear to reveal consistent patterns of gross violations of human rights". The 1503 procedure is slow, confidential and provides individuals with no redress.

In addition to the roles of the United Nations Commission on Human Rights, and the Human Rights Committee in monitoring the ICCPR, institutional mechanisms for implementation are the Committee on the Elimination of Racial Discrimination, the Committee on Economic, Social and Cultural Rights; the Committee on the Elimination of Discrimination Against Women; the Committee against Torture; and the Committee on the Rights of the Child.

Although the work of all these bodies is important, their powers to enforce human rights standards are very limited.

The UN Commission on Human Rights is a permanent body of ECOSOC. Its members are state representatives. Findings of the commission have a certain significance but are not binding.

The ICCPR Human Rights Committee consists of 18 experts supervising the implementation of the covenant. The work of the committee covers only parties that have ratified the covenant (presently 129 states) and provides international monitoring on the basis of reports provided by states. The committee's monitoring does not imply any sanctions, but it can generate some negative publicity on a country's human rights performance.

The Committee on the Elimination of Racial Discrimination has been established for the implementation of the convention on racial discrimination. The committee can receive complaints from states, but only 14 states authorize the committee to receive communications from individuals.

The implementation body for the 1979 Convention on the Elimination of Discrimination against Women is the Committee on the Elimination of Discrimination against Women. The committee is not authorized to receive individual communications.

The Committee on Economic, Social and Cultural Rights has no right to receive complaints from individuals or groups. In its submission to the 1993 UN World Conference on Human Rights the committee argued for a formal complaints procedure:

> As long as the majority of the provisions of the Covenant (and most notably those relating to education, health care, food and nutrition, and housing) are not the subject of any detailed jurisprudential scrutiny at the international level, it is most unlikely that they will be subject to such examination at the national level either (United Nations 1993a:paragraph 24).

In 1997 the 53rd session of the UN Commission on Human Rights discussed a draft protocol for a complaints procedure and, in a resolution, affirmed the interest of its members in the draft. This was the first step in the long process toward an optional protocol.

For the Convention on the Rights of the Child, the institutions and procedures for serious enforcement are largely ineffective. In 1991 states parties to the convention elected a monitoring body for the convention for the first time: the Committee on the Rights of the Child. The committee, which consists of 10 experts, meets three times a year to examine the implementation reports that are submitted by states parties that have accepted the duty (article 44 of the convention) to report regularly on the steps taken to implement the convention. However important the work of the committee is, its power to enforce the standards of the convention is severely limited. Moreover, the convention does not provide for individual complaints from children or their representatives about violations.

The obstacles

In addition to the weakness of the formal enforcement mechanisms (the "internal conditions"), the following "external conditions" that impede effective implementation of human rights provisions can be identified.

- The widespread lack of knowledge across the world about the existence of human rights. There are many commendable efforts in the field of human rights education, but at present the commitment of resources to such efforts is insufficient.

- The current worldwide suspension of fundamental human rights under the guise of the war on terrorism or the protection of national security.
- The lack of political will to commit adequate resources to the realization of human rights.
- The widening "development divide" between and within societies and the common refusal of policy makers to see the digital divide and its resolution as part of the lack of political will to resolve the wider problem.
- The existing and expanding international regime for the protection of intellectual property rights that hampers equitable access to information and knowledge.
- The trend to subject cultural goods and services to the rules of the WTO regime and to refuse exemption of culture from international trade policies that threaten cultural diversity.
- The appropriation of much of the world's technical knowledge under corporate ownership and the refusal by technology owners to agree on fair standards of international technology transfer.
- The monopolized or oligopolized corporate control over the production and distribution of information and communication goods and services.
- The worldwide proliferation of market-driven journalism which under-informs—if not misinforms—audiences around the world on matters of public interest.
- The limited perspective on human rights as mainly or even merely individual rights. This ignores the fact that people communicate and engage in cultural practices as members of communities, and hampers the development of indigenous sources of information and knowledge.

The Human Right to Communicate

No matter what way information societies will develop, we are likely to see different patterns for the traffic of information among people. Following a proposal by Bordewijk and Van Kaam (1982) four patterns can be distinguished.

- The dissemination of messages (Bordewijk and Van Kaam call this "allocution").
- The consultation of information (like in libraries or on the Web).
- The registration of data (for public or private purposes).
- The exchange of information among people (the modality of conversation).

A survey of the existing human rights standards relevant to "informational developments" shows that they cover mainly the dissemination, consultation and registration of information.

- Human rights for dissemination address the issues of freedom of speech and its limits.
- Human rights for consultation address the issues of access and confidentiality.
- Human rights for registration address the issues of privacy and security.

The following table provides the overview.

Table 2: Patterns for the traffic of information

Patterns	Human rights provisions
Dissemination	Freedom of expression
Consultation	Access to information
Registration	Protection of privacy

Although the first three patterns are covered, a striking omission in international human rights law is that provisions for the fourth pattern—conversation, or communication in the proper sense of that word—are missing. Practically all human rights provisions refer to communication as the "transfer of messages". This reflects an interpretation of communication that has become rather common since Shannon and Weaver (1949) introduced their mathematical theory of communication. Their model described communication as a linear, one-way process. This is, however, a very limited and somewhat misleading conception of communication, which ignores the fact that, in essence, "communicate" refers to a process of sharing, making common or creating a community. Communication is used for the dissemination of messages (such as in the case of the mass media), for the consultation of information sources (like searches in libraries or on the World Wide Web), for the registration of information (as happens in databases), and for the conversations that people participate in.

Existing human rights law, through article 19 of the UDHR and article 19 of the ICCPR, covers the fundamental right to freedom of opinion and expression. This is undoubtedly an essential basis for processes of dialogue among people but does not in itself constitute two-way traffic. It is the freedom of the speaker at Hyde Park Corner to whom no one has to listen and who may not communicate with anyone in his audience. The article also refers to the freedom to hold opinions: this refers to opinions inside one's head that may serve communication with oneself but do not necessarily bear any relation to communication with others. It mentions the right to seek information and ideas: this provides for processes of consultation and gathering news, for example, which is different from communicating. There is also the right to receive information and ideas, which is in principle also a one-way traffic process: the fact that I can receive whatever information and ideas I want does not imply that I am involved in a communication process. Finally there is the right to impart information and ideas: this refers to the dissemination/allocution that goes beyond the freedom of expression but in the same way does not imply exchange/dialogue. In sum, the provisions of article 19 address only the one-way processes of transport, reception, consultation and allocution, but not the two-way process of conversation.

A crucial question for this chapter is how this omission can be remedied. In 1969 Jean d'Arcy introduced the right to communicate by writing, "the time will come when the Universal Declaration of Human Rights will have to encompass a more extensive right than man's right to information. ... This is the right of men to communicate" (D'Arcy 1969:14). Communication needs to be understood as an interactive process. Adopted rules were criticized for focusing too much on the content of the process. "It is the information itself which is protected" (Fisher 1983:8). "The earlier statements of communications freedoms... implied that freedom of information was a one-way right from a higher to a lower plane" (Fisher, 1983:9). There is an increasing need for participation: "more and more people can read, write and use broadcasting equipment and can no longer, therefore, be denied access to and participation in media processes for lack of communication and handling skills" (Fisher 1983:9).

The right to communicate is perceived by the protagonists as more fundamental than the information rights as accorded by current international law. The essence of the right would be based on the observation that communication is a fundamental social process, a basic human need and the foundation of all social organization. This idea has been included in UNESCO's programme since 1974. The 18th session of the UNESCO General Conference, in its resolution 4.121, affirmed "that all individuals should have equal opportunities to participate actively in the means of communication and to benefit from such means while preserving the right to protection against their abuses".

The resolution authorized the then director-general "to study ways and means by which active participation in the communication process may become possible and analyse the right to communicate". In May 1978, the first UNESCO expert seminar on the right to communicate took place in Stockholm (in co-operation with the Swedish National UNESCO Commission). Participants identified different components of the concept of the right to communicate. These included the right to participate, the right of access to communication resources, and information rights. The meeting agreed "that social groups ought to have the rights of access and participation in the communication process. It was also stressed that special attention with regard to the right to communicate should be paid to various minorities—national, ethnic, religious and linguistic" (Fisher 1982:43). In summary, the Stockholm meeting concluded that

> the right to communicate concept poses 'big and messy' problems that require an outlook larger than that provided by any single cultural background, any single professional discipline, or any particular body of professional experience. And although some of the aspects of the concept were felt to be uncomfortable by some participants and observers, these same participants and observers also generally found the concept hopeful and encouraging (Fisher 1982:45).

Whereas the Stockholm meeting provided largely an analysis of the right to communicate on the levels of the individual and the community, a second expert seminar focused on the international dimension of the right to communicate. This was the Meeting of Experts on the Right to Communicate in Manila. The meeting was organized in co-operation with the Philippine UNESCO National Commission and took place from 15–19 October 1979. The participants proposed that the right to communicate is both an individual and a social right. As a fundamental human right it should be incorporated in the Universal Declaration of Human Rights. It has validity nationally and internationally; encompasses duties and responsibilities for individuals, groups, and nations; and requires the allocation of appropriate resources.

In its final report, the UNESCO-appointed MacBride Commission concluded that the recognition of this new right "promises to advance the democratisation of communication" (International Commission for the Study of Communication Problems 1980:173). The commission stated that

> Communication needs in a democratic society should be met by the extension of specific rights such as the right to be informed, the right to inform, the right to privacy, the right to participate in public communication—all elements of a new concept, the right to communicate. In developing what might be called a new era of social rights, we suggest all the implications of the right to communicate be further explored (International Commission for the Study of Communication Problems 1980:265).

The commission also observed that "Freedom of speech, of the press, of information and of assembly are vital for the realization of human rights. Extension of these communication freedoms to a broader individual and collective right to communicate is an evolving principle in the democratisation process" (International Commission for the Study of Communication Problems 1980:265). According to the commission, "The concept of the 'right to communicate' has yet to receive its final form and its full content...it is still at the stage of being thought through in all its implications and gradually enriched" (International Commission for the Study of Communication Problems 1980:173).

The 1980 UNESCO General Conference in Belgrade, in its resolution 4/19,14(xi), confirmed the concept of a right to communicate in terms of "respect for the right of the public, of ethnic and social groups and of individuals to have access to information sources and to participate actively in the communication process".

The UNESCO General Conference in Paris of 1983 adopted resolution 3.2 on the right to communicate:

> Recalling that the aim is not to substitute the notion of the right to communicate for any rights already recognized by the international community, but to increase their scope with regard to individuals and the groups they form, particularly in view of the new possibilities of active communication and dialogue between cultures that are opened up by advances in the media.

The 23rd UNESCO General Conference in 1985 in Sofia requested the director-general to develop activities for the realization of the right to communicate. In the early 1990s the right to communicate had practically disappeared from UNESCO's agenda. It was no longer a crucial concept in the Medium-Term Plan for 1990–1995. The right to communicate was mentioned but not translated into operational action.

In 1992 Pekka Tarjanne, Secretary-General of the International Telecommunication Union (ITU), took up the issue of the right to communicate and stated, "I have suggested to my colleagues that the Universal Declaration of Human Rights should be amended to recognize the right to communicate as a fundamental human right" (Tarjanne 1992:45). During the preparations for the United Nations World Summit on the Information Society (WSIS), to be held in 2003 in Geneva and 2005 in Tunis, the discussion on the right to communicate has been revitalized. This was due particularly to the activities of the Communication Rights in the Information Society (CRIS) campaign during the preparatory committee meetings (in July 2002 and February 2003). It is especially significant that the UN Secretary-General in his public message on World Telecommunication Day (17 May 2003) reminded the international community "that millions of people in the poorest countries are still excluded from the 'right to communicate', increasingly seen as a fundamental human right".[3]

In its evolution, the right to communicate has not been without its critics. Desmond Fisher wrote as early as 1982:

> The right to communicate embraces a much wider spectrum of communication freedoms than earlier formulations which failed to win general support because of uncertainty about their practical consequences. Inevitably, the new formulation will encounter even greater opposition (Fisher 1982:34).

Throughout the debate the objection was repeatedly raised that "communication is so integral a part of the human condition that it is philosophically unnecessary and perhaps wrong to describe it as a human right" (Fisher 1982:41). Another objection pointed to the possible use of the concept by powerful groups in society.

> The concept has to be interpreted, and this will be done by groups in power, not by the weak or oppressed. Limits will be fixed within which the right to communicate may be exercised. These borders will be defined on a political basis and will favour present power relationships in the world. The right to communicate is not a concept leading toward change; it is an attempt to give groups working for liberation a feeling of being taken seriously, while in practice the right to communicate will be used to preserve the present order in the world and to stabilize it even further (Hedebro 1982:68).

Opposition to the right to communicate has come from different ideological standpoints.

> The concept of the right to communicate is distrusted by the 'western' nations which see it as part of the proposals relating to new world information and communication orders, about which they are highly suspicious. ... In some socialist and Third World countries, opposition to the right derives from the fact that it could be used to justify the continuation of the existing massive imbalance in information flows and the unrestricted importation of western technology and information and, consequently, western values (Fisher 1982:34).

---

[3]   United Nations Secretary-General's message on World Telecommunication Day, www.itu.int/newsroom/wtd/2003/unsg_message.html, accessed on 23 October 2003.

The US government opposed the right to communicate in earlier debates and denounced the concept as a communist ploy. In this rejection the key feature was the link between the right to communicate and the notion of people's rights. Although the reference to people and to people's rights is very common in US political history, in the context of UNESCO this was seen as a defence of state rights and a threat to individual rights.

An important issue in the discussion on a human right to communicate is the question of whether expanding the human rights regime with a new right would endanger the existing provisions. International law is a living process, and the catalogue of human rights has considerably grown over past years to include new rights and freedoms without endangering the basic standards as formulated in the Universal Declaration of Human Rights. And, indeed, there should be no reason why adding the right to communicate would be a problem as long as one leaves the existing framework as is. The last thing that anyone should try to do is to break open the articles of the UDHR and amend them. That would be a very dangerous route to go because today the international community would certainly not adopt a document as far-sighted as the 1948 UDHR.

Another important point raised in current discussion on the right to communicate is whether this new right lends itself to abuse by governments. All provisions of international law can be abused by governments. Even the UN Charter can be interpreted by UN member states in abusive ways. Adopting an international standard on communication is in many ways more of a problem for anti-democratic governments than the right to freedom of expression. Allowing people to speak freely in Hyde Park Corner poses less of a threat to governments than allowing citizens to freely communicate with each other. The right to the freedom to communicate goes to the heart of the democratic process, and it is much more radical than the right to freedom of expression! The attempt to have a right to communicate adopted by the international community is therefore likely to meet with a great deal of resistance.

For the protagonists of the right to communicate there are various possible road maps.

First, there is the formal international law trajectory, where the intended end result is the incorporation of the right to communicate into the corpus of existing hard or soft international human rights law. This route implies the preparation of a formulation (in the form of a resolution or declaration) that would be adopted by an intergovernmental conference (such as WSIS) or by the general conference of a UN agency like UNESCO. Eventually, this approach could lead to a special UN conference to draft an international convention.

Second, there is the trajectory whereby representatives of civil society movements adopt a statement on the right to communicate as an inspirational document, an educational tool or as guidance for social action. They do not seek the consent of other stakeholders such as governments or business. An example of this approach is the People's Communication Charter.

Third, there is the option to expand the community of adopters by using the example of the Declaration of the Hague on the Future of Refugee and Migration Policy. This declaration emerged from a meeting convened by the Society for International Development (November 2002), and the signatories were individuals from civil society, government and business. Such a statement functions to remind the international community of relevant standards and suggests possible future action.

7. Conclusion

At the end of 2003 and again in 2005, the UN-convened World Summit on the Information Society will address some of the most important issues and concerns in the field of information and communication. The summit is inspired by the aspiration to find a common vision on the informational developments that currently affect most societies and that are conveniently bundled under the heading of "information society".

The most significant achievement of the international community since the Second World War is the articulation and codification of a broad range of fundamental human rights. It would therefore seem only logical that the normative framework of human rights standards should shape that common vision. As a matter of fact, over the past decades the international community has adopted and often confirmed as binding law an impressive variety of standards that relate to information and communication. This chapter has given an overview of these provisions and pointed to their major problem: the lack of implementation.

Following this analysis, WSIS could remind the international community of all that has been achieved already and stress the importance of seriously identifying and removing major obstacles to the urgently needed implementation of existing provisions. WSIS could also point out that the essential omission in "human rights for the information society" is the lack of human rights provisions for the conversational mode of communication, or communication as an interactive process. As UN Secretary-General Kofi Annan stated in his World Telecommunication Day (17 May 2003) message, the primary goal of WSIS is "helping all of the world's people to communicate".

If indeed all the world's people should be assisted in participating in the public and private conversations that affect their lives, the international community will have to secure the conditions under which such processes can take place. Conversational communication among individuals and groups—whether in public and or in private—should be protected against undue interference by third parties. It needs confidentiality, space and time, and requires learning the 'art of the conversation'. It also calls for resources for multi-lingual conversations; and for the inclusion of disabled people. All of this requires the commitment from the multistakeholder community of governments, intergovernmental organizations, civil society and business. A WSIS statement on the 'right to communicate' could broadcast to the world a strong signal for the mobilization of this commitment![4]

References

Bordewijk, J.L. and B. Van Kaam 1982. **Allocutie**. Bosch and Keunig, Baarn.

Council of Europe. 1995. **Recommendation (R(95)13), Concerning Problems of Criminal Procedure Law Connected with Information Technology**. Strasbourg.

D'Arcy, J. 1969. "Direct broadcasting satellites and the right to communicate." **EBU Review**. No. 118, pp. 14–18.

European Commission (EC). 1997. **Towards a European Framework for Digital Signatures and Encryption**. EC, Brussels.

Fisher, D. 1982. **The Right to Communicate: A Status Report**. UNESCO Reports and Papers on Mass Communication, No. 94. UNESCO, Paris.

Fisher, D. and L.S. Harms (eds.) 1983. **The Right to Communicate: A New Human Rights**. Boole Press, Dublin.

Hamelink, C.J. 1994. **The Politics of World Communication**. Sage, London.

Hedebro, G. 1982. **Communication and Social Change in Developing Nations**. Iowa State University Press, Ames.

---

[4] United Nations Secretary-General's message on World Telecommunication Day, www.itu.int/newsroom/wtd/2003/unsg_message.html, accessed on 23 October 2003.

International Commission for the Study of Communication Problems. 1980. **Many Voices, One World**. Report of the International Commission for the Study of Communication Problems (chaired by Sean MacBride). UNESCO, Paris.

International Commission of Jurists (ICJ), Urban Morgan Institute on Human Rights and Maastricht University. 1997. **The Maastricht Guidelines on Violations of Economic, Social and Cultural Rights**. Maastricht University, Maastricht.

Organisation for Economic Co-operation and Development (OECD). 1997. **Guidelines for Cryptography Policy**. Paris.

South Commission. 1990. **The Challenge to the South**. Oxford University Press, Oxford.

Tarjanne, P. 1992. "Telecom: Bridge to the 21st century." **Transnational Data and Communications Report**, Vol. 15, No. 4, pp. 42–45.

United Nations. 1968. **Proclamation of Teheran: Final Act of the International Conference on Human Rights**. (Teheran, 22 April–13 May). (UN Doc. A/CONF. 32/41 at 3). www1.umn.edu/humanrts/instree/l2ptichr.htm, accessed on 23 October 2003.

United Nations Educational, Scientific and Cultural Organization (UNESCO). 1982. **Right to Communicate: Legal Aspects**. UNESCO, Paris.

———. 1968. **Meeting of Experts on Cultural Rights as Human Rights**. Final report (Paris, 8–13 July). UNESCO, Paris.

Locating the Information Society within Civil Society: The Case of Scientific and Scholarly Publications[1]

Jean-Claude Guédon

Abstract

The phrase "information society" appears innocuous enough; yet, a deeper analysis demonstrates that it involves strategic aims which, in effect, serve to control the political debates surrounding the production, storage and reception of information. The limited, yet symptomatic, case of scholarly and scientific publishing helps to unveil some of these issues. Furthermore, it helps understand how anyone with some concern for the health of civil society might think about the information society and how it relates to civil society. In effect, the question raised is: how do we put the information society in its place?

Introduction

How does civil society relate to the information society? Despite parallel grammatical constructions, the two terms do not simply correspond to two different facets of society or two ways of looking at it. Rather than harmoniously complementing each other, the juxtaposition of civil society and information society raises a number of issues and problems. This paper proposes an understanding of their "orthogonal" relationship. The term conveys a tension between convergence and divergence. It also connotes the idea of a historical discontinuity. In other words, orthogonality reflects a contest between two viewpoints where, ultimately, one tries to override the other.[2]

History is full of such transitions. In a sense, two successive paradigms—in the Kuhnian sense[3] of the term—are orthogonal to each other because they cannot be compared to each other and, in a sense,

---

[1] The author would like to thank Bruce Girard, Mike Powell, Suroor Alikhan and the anonymous reviewers for their insightful comments and suggestions.
[2] The creation of the Royal Society is a useful example. In Europe in the seventeenth century, science emerged as an empirical form of knowledge, separate from political and religious forms of discourse. Modern science, it could be said, initially emerged orthogonally to politics and theology before trying to subsume them both. See Poovey (1998), especially chapter 3.
[3] See Kuhn's *The Structure of Scientific Revolutions* (1996).

speak past each other. More fundamentally, shifts in the very epistemological foundations of whole cultures can also conform to this kind of transformational scheme. The very term information society implies a degree of historical discontinuity, something revolutionary, which would replace what was there before. Civil society as an organizing paradigm has been portrayed by the information society apologists as a precursor to the information society, which would mean that civil society was subsumed and transcended by the information society. Conversely, because of the growing vigour of the associations, networks and other forms of human collectives, civil society claims its own existence and a strong capacity for drawing upon information. As a result, civil society can also be seen as a form of future for the information society, rather than its superseded past.

Positioning civil society in the past or the future of information society is a useful way to characterize the current struggle between these two methods of mobilizing organization. The point of this chapter, in fact, will be to explore how civil society can emerge against and through information society in such a way as to integrate it within a civil society framework. If the information society (as a concept) is to survive at all, it ought to be within the framework of civil society, and not the reverse.

The point of locating the information society within civil society is to subvert the functions generally assigned to the former. The phrase information society can be taken as a concept; and information, taken as a scientific term, conveys the idea that social problems are best resolved scientifically. From this perspective, politics is seen as something best avoided. Many discussion lists found on the Internet and relating to Internet policy are laced with comments such as: "may we keep the politics out of this question". Ultimately, the point that must be raised with regard to the information society is whether it is not often called upon precisely to neutralize political debates, and thus to help foster a particular, but hidden, political agenda under the banner of objective, rational and quantifiable knowledge.

Simply rejecting the notion of information society is of little value to oppose apparently scientific or objective justification: counter claims of irrationality quickly follow. Positioning information society within civil society appears more useful to respond to this kind of challenge; moreover, it facilitates the possibility of translating political objectives into a variety of policy frameworks and into a number of operational projects.

The issues just raised are obviously complex and cannot be fully covered within these few pages. The text that follows will limit itself to exploring some of these questions through a case study of scholarly and scientific publishing. Although this publishing area directly touches only a tiny minority of people in the world, it locates itself at the heart of research and, as such, at the core of data, information and knowledge production. At present, it has been transformed by globalization, including corporate mergers, like many other spheres of the world economy. As a result, it offers concrete, yet rich, insights into the whole notion of the information society, even though it has little to say about mass media in general or the massive commoditization of cultures. While it has a global effect, it is structured enough to lend itself to a relatively limited analysis. Finally, its complexity, while not overwhelming, is sufficient to allow it to touch most of the key elements that can help in thinking about how to position the idea of information society within civil society.

Scientific Information and Civil Society: A Cautionary Tale

Replacing excellence by elitism

Although scientific and scholarly publishing shares many characteristics with publishing in general, it also sports a number of interesting specificities as well. Unlike general commercial publishing, scientific and scholarly publishing fulfils several specific functions at once: while it serves as a communication system between peers that are both authors and readers, it also acts as a living memory and a kind of jurisprudence for science. Through scientific publishing, an author can point to a date of reception, revision or, at the very least, of publication to establish priority claims and the paternity of discoveries, observations or inventions. Finally, scholarly publishing is carried out through a wide range of journals whose prestige, visibility, authority and so on, range from the barely credible to the highly prestigious. In other words, publishing also acts as a "branding device" for scientific authors. In scientific publishing, unlike most other forms of publishing, direct financial profit is not of primary importance for the authors. Even for publishers, financial considerations would take second place, particularly in the case of learned societies and other largely non-profit organizations, although sometimes commercial publishers did find a symbolic value in publishing scientific journals.

In the last 30 years or so, however, the situation changed radically to the point that today, some of the highest profit levels encountered in the publishing industry are found within scientific and scholarly publishing.[4] The transformation of the economic sphere of scientific and

---

[4] As an illustration, the 2000 Report from Reed-Elsevier revealed that its STM (science, technology and medicine)-adjusted operating profit margin was 36 per cent, well above the company-wide level of 21 per cent profit. Source: message sent to the Reedelscustomers list

scholarly publishing is all the more striking since scientific authors are almost never paid for their contributions,[5] and peer review is generally done for free. At the same time, the research results published in scientific and scholarly publishing are the results of efforts financed primarily by public or foundation funds. Finally, scientific publications are bought mainly by libraries, which are also generally supported by public or non-profit funds. As the price of scientific and scholarly publishing goes up, the proportion of subscriptions paid by individuals tends to diminish—a situation easy to understand when the annual subscription to a science journal usually exceeds $1,000.

Traditionally, in the eighteenth and nineteenth centuries,[6] scientific journals were linked with scientific societies or academies, and the publication costs were borne mostly by the parent institution (see Kronick 1976). A small fraction of that cost was recovered by a number of private subscriptions, but bartering was also practiced on a large scale, so that, with a few dozen copies of the local journal and through judicious exchanges, a rather significant collection of publications could be developed. In effect, each scientific institution was promoting the best work of its own scientists by bearing the financial burden of the local journal, memoir or transaction. By attracting papers from recognized foreign scientists, its reputation was further enhanced. In this fashion, the validation and circulation of scientific ideas was achieved at a cost that was closely related to production costs. Being universal in nature (and apolitical in content), scientific knowledge could generally percolate across political boundaries and ideological or religious differences without much difficulty.

From the middle of the nineteenth century onward, the rapid growth of research communities translated into an equally rapid growth of scientific journals: a few dozen periodicals gradually grew into hundreds of titles. In parallel, learned societies found themselves involved in a publishing process where speed and efficiency became ever more important: securing priority in an increasingly competitive context demanded being published as quickly as possible. The failings of scientific societies and associations in this regard opened a window of opportunity to commercial activities, but it did so in a particular fashion. Commercial publishers knew that while scientific and scholarly

hosted at the University of Texas by Bob Michaelson (Northwestern University Library) on 27 March 2001.
[5] They generally carry out their research within the context of an academic or research position and they are paid a salary for this. Interestingly, if most researchers have managed to preserve an "author" status despite a context that could have easily led to a "work for hire" situation, it is largely due to the fact that no money is involved in scientific publishing, unlike patents.
[6] It is generally agreed that modern scientific publishing began with the appearance of the *Transactions of the Royal Society of London* in 1665.

publishing could not really be profitable in itself, these publications could be prestigious and therefore adorn a publishing catalogue. Moreover, they facilitated good relations with scientific authors who might decide to write more than mere scientific articles, for example manuals or treatises, which could be profitable.

Until the Second World War, scientific and scholarly publishing remained essentially stable, and commercial publishers remained valuable minority partners in a venture that was still largely disconnected from profit motives, even though financial concerns were never absent. The presence of commercial publishers imposed a useful, even healthy, check on learned institutions that, otherwise, might have quickly succumbed to various forms of complacency translating into unacceptable publication delays and unpalatable forms of corporatist censorship.[7] The situation, however, evolved rapidly after the Second World War. The rapid growth of scientific research led to a rapidly expanding system of scientific publications, and this quantitative mutation brought about its own series of problems, in particular, a growing concern about retrieving scientific information. There was concern in the 1950s that bibliographic methods in science had fallen so far behind that science would drown in its own documentation. Emblematic among many, the famous *Chemical Abstracts* published by the American Chemical Society had always relied on a network of volunteers and was falling further and further behind. In the context of the Cold War and the growing commercial competition with European firms, such difficulties triggered a flurry of research activity into new retrieval methods.

It is in this context that Eugene Garfield was prompted to study new approaches to scientific literature, resulting in the Science Citation Index (SCI). However, Garfield's solution to the problem of scientific information retrieval unwittingly set a series of unintended consequences in motion, the results of which were anything but positive.

Garfield managed to translate Bradford's law of distribution[8] into a law of concentration, thereby giving himself the possibility of approximating the whole of scientific publishing with a core collection of journals that, at first, stood around a thousand titles.[9] While statistically, the approximation can be defended, it translated into the defining of a core set of scientific journals, with definite boundaries, and provided a

---

[7] For example, statistics (for political reasons) and phrenology (for more substantive and epistemological reasons) were both subjected to censorship in nineteenth century Britain.

[8] Bradford's law of distribution states that, in a search for journal articles on any one subject, a small group of core journals will provide one-third of the articles, a larger group of "less-core" journals will provide another third, and a large number of peripheral journals will provide the remaining one-third.

[9] On Eugene Garfield, see Wouters (1999).

private institution—the Institute for Scientific Information (ISI), Garfield's own company—with the enormous power to select which journals would be included in SCI, and which, conversely, would be excluded. In other words, the pecking order of scientific journals that had always continuously extended from mediocrity to excellence had been surreptitiously transformed into a two-tier system: journals inside ISI and journals outside it. Excellence had been covertly redefined as elite— a substitution that was apparently highly satisfactory to a number of institutions that were already in the habit of viewing themselves in that light.[10]

The first unintended consequence of the SCI was the creation of this elite, which upset what used to be a competition for excellence.[11] However, the elite-producing mechanism started by SCI was about to be reinforced quickly and thus induce a far more negative consequence. The Garfield approximation being presented as representing "core science", libraries began to use it as a benchmark, with the result that many of them began to acquire roughly the same collection of journals. As the core set gradually increased to several thousand titles, most libraries eventually settled for buying all or most of this set. In effect, the major research libraries of North America had begun to view the ISI core set as the "indispensable" set of journals.

Such a co-ordinated concentration of interests could not go unobserved for long, and indeed large commercial publishers began to take note of the fact that the scientific and scholarly publishing market, long viewed as a marginal, if prestigious, activity, had turned into an inelastic market with all the profit possibilities attached to this notion.[12] This was the second unintended consequence of the idea of a core set of journals. Beginning in the late 1960s, commercial publishers began to acquire a variety of journals that belonged to the enchanted ISI set with a view to recouping these investments as quickly as possible through steep price rises. Thus emerged the so-called "serial pricing crisis", which began

---

[10] As the words "excellence" and "elite" are often used as synonyms, it is important to underscore the difference maintained here. Excellence is an ideal that everyone is supposed to strive for. In so doing, a continuous hierarchy or pecking order develops, based on the competitive qualities of the scientists; by contrast, elite is marked by one or several procedures aimed at including some and excluding others, thus creating a discontinuity among scientists. Being part of an institution or not, being listed in SCI or not, are examples of elite-creating procedures. See also note 11.

[11] At least nothing indicates that it was conceived as anything more than a pragmatic response to the problem of tracing in a credible way, some manageable subset of all the scientific citations published in all the scientific journals in the world.

[12] An inelastic market is one where demand is little affected by rises in costs. It allows monopolistic behaviour to flourish. One of the first individuals to size up the potential of the emerging situation was Robert Maxwell who created Pergamon Press in 1951 (Cox 2002).

affecting the workings of research libraries. This crisis deeply affected the globalization of scientific research results in the following ways.

Libraries are now buying a smaller fraction of the scientific literature than they did 20 or 30 years ago. This is happening despite significant increases in their acquisition budgets and despite the transfer of funds from monograph budgets to scientific periodicals.

This in turn has affected the market for scholarly monographs, which form the main vehicle for scholarly publications in the humanities and the social sciences. This, in turn, has made university presses more fragile and, as a result, more cautious in their editorial choices. One of the consequences of this state of affairs is that young scholars in the humanities and the social sciences are finding it more difficult to publish their first monograph on which their promotion and/or tenure depend.

Libraries in poorer institutions, and especially in poorer countries, have essentially been cut off from the current flow of scientific information with sometimes dire results. For example, until the World Health Organization (WHO) stepped in with the Hinari Project, core literature dealing with malaria was essentially inaccessible in many countries where malaria strikes and kills. How many lives have been lost because of this situation, no one knows, but it cannot have been insignificant.

Scientific societies, upon observing the price increases imposed by large publishers, began to take advantage of the new situation in order to better finance their various activities, including those related more to professional goals—for example, lobbying efforts—than to scientific aims.

The sharply rising price of journals led to major cancellations of subscriptions on the part, first, of individuals, and then of libraries. With the decreasing number of copies sold, prices began to increase even faster and, as a result, the quality of access to scientific information began to be concentrated in a decreasing number of rich institutions. If rich institutions adopt a cynical viewpoint, this situation may appear positive since it provides a new kind of competitive advantage to their own researchers. In a knowledge-based economy, where high returns accrue to the development phase—itself closely tied to fundamental research—such a concentration of the knowledge base in a few institutions, located mainly in countries of the Organisation for Economic Co-operation and Development (OECD), may not have been seen as such a bad thing after all.

The end result of these trends is clear: what could have been legitimately described as a "republic of science" before the Second World War has, since about 1970, turned into a form of growing elitism[13] that

---

[13] Again, to clarify what elitism means here, it is important to underscore that practicing science has always been an elitist activity. Science always set itself apart from the rest of society, for example by relying on a set of credentials (diplomas) needed to ensure basic

has replaced the earlier competitive quest for excellence; as this elitism is now kept in place and even intensified by financial means, it can be said that the republic of science has now given way to a scientific plutocracy—hardly a positive outcome!

Digitization and networks

At the very end of the 1980s, the Internet began what might be termed its public life. Starting with the universities and reaching a wider audience after 1995, the Internet, acting as a kind of trade language for all types of computer networks—a kind of meta-network in fact—began to take on the appearance of a materialized communication system of global proportions. As could be expected, scientific publishing took notice, and commercial publishers proceeded to explore ways to preserve and even improve their financial situation within the new digital context. Tulip (The University Licensing Program), the experimental project led by Elsevier from 1991 until about 1995, is emblematic of these efforts. The "l" in Tulip stands for "license", and it represents the most significant shift in this experiment. Elsevier had taken a leaf from the book of software companies and transposed it to journal publishing. Digital content appeared simply too volatile to be sold in the way printed journals had always been sold. For example, the "first sale" doctrine in copyright law allows the owner of a book to lend it to others and to sell it at will; however, this provision obviously put the control over the circulation of digitized scientific information at risk. Making a perfect copy of digital materials is very easy and not costly enough to limit the replication of sold materials. If the menacing perspective of a worldwide network is added, through which the copies can spread everywhere at little or no cost, it becomes clear that the publishers' revenue streams could disappear very quickly. In short, from a publisher's perspective, the traditional transactional framework of the print world was unfit for a digitized and networked environment. Something else had to be found, and licensing was the answer.

Because scientific documents are generally small enough to go easily through narrow bandwidth and because academics had early access to the Internet, scientific and scholarly publishing experienced the future early, so to speak.[14] The difficulties, however, were in no way limited to scientific publishing; and other forms of cultural documents—first music

---

credibility. What is new here is that a new order of elitism has appeared *within* science, marginalizing the old continuum from mediocrity to excellence. In science, a number of mechanisms including the ones affecting scientific and scholarly publishing and adumbrated here, have contributed to setting off a number of institutions and individuals sharply apart from the others. See footnote 9.

[14] Although the comparison is technically inaccurate, it would not be false to point to Paul Ginsparg's early physics database at Los Alamos as the philosophical prototype of Napster.

recordings and more recently movies—have since encountered similar difficulties. In a sense, for the publishing, recording and film industries, scientific publishing was a little like a canary in a coal mine.[15]

Already the photocopy machine had shown that scientific articles could no longer be chained to a particular issue of a journal. However, photocopying still required physically accessing the original issue and physically bringing it to a photocopy machine, which took some time and, generally, some money. Also, the copies, although usable, were less than perfect. In short, photocopies did not threaten sales, particularly to libraries, and the habit of photocopying mainly reflected the desire to keep the literature permanently close to one's place of work—office or laboratory. More recently, desktop access to digitized literature has capitalized on that very point, as it is local accessibility that makes it so appealing to scientific investigators.

Photocopying books was far less appealing: the process was cumbersome and sometimes costlier than the book itself, while the result was always a bit unwieldy: storing such "books" has always been somewhat awkward. In short, publishers could rest content with the notion that book photocopying was at worst a marginal phenomenon with limited financial consequences.[16]

Initially, music recordings were better protected against copying than books: tape recorders were cumbersome and significantly degraded the quality of the source. But now, with digital recording, CD burners copy the source perfectly. At the same time, the growing efficiency of the compression schemes allows transmitting songs through the networks relatively comfortably. The result has been what is know as the peer-to-peer phenomenon, first spectacularly illustrated by Napster and now more discreetly extended by secure, decentralized and anonymous exchange schemes, such as Freenet. With CDs carrying over a hundred songs and even movies, local networks of friends bypass the electronic networks altogether. In short, we are fast coming to the point where no material is immune to perfect copying and transmission—a situation that scientific and scholarly publishing has known for the better part of a decade by now.

---

[15] Coal miners had the habit of carrying a canary in the mines because, being more susceptible to carbon monoxide than human beings, the bird acted as an early warning system.

[16] However, some French publishers have led a campaign against the so-called "photocopillage", a pun on "photocopiage" where the connotation of "pillage" is introduced probably because of its metonymic relationship with piracy. However, these publishers, such as Galilée, publish slim essay volumes with relatively high prices. The public's anger against this practice, coupled with the relative ease and low cost of copying, obviously conspire to encourage photocopying, however illegal it may be.

Front lines and their contours

If we take digitized and networked scientific and scholarly publishing as the canary of information industries, its evolution allows us to observe the shape of things to come and it provides some fascinating insights. In responding to the challenges of the digital context, publishers have essentially explored three independent routes: one legal, one technical and one social. The hope is that, together, these three avenues can form a new publishing device where full control over the circulation of the published materials can be fully restored and, as a result, electronic commerce of electronic materials can be made profitable.

Moving to a licensing scheme is part of the legal move: it allows locating all informational transactions within contract laws rather than the copyright or authors' rights framework. As a result, annoying clauses such as "first sale" can be dismissed. For example, librarians discover that they must negotiate interlibrary loans because access and use are restricted to the local constituency in the license. Moreover, as libraries are essentially dispossessed of actual ownership of the materials, librarians have very little to say about the organizing of the documentation (for example, through cataloguing schemes[17]) and its preservation. Obviously, such reworking of the framework of informational transactions affects access, navigation and, ultimately, the appropriation of knowledge.

At the same time, there is a worldwide movement to extend copyright and authors' rights: the United States has recently lengthened copyright laws to 70 years beyond the author's death to bring it in line with many European countries (and to 90 years beyond first publication in the case of a corporate "creation" such as Walt Disney's Mickey Mouse). Moreover, several new copyright laws, such as the Digital Millennium Copyright Act (DMCA) in the United States, try to protect technical copy protection schemes by essentially prohibiting reverse engineering on them.[18] All this is supported by a very aggressive

---

[17] By creating a cataloguing order that maps knowledge and its divisions in a certain way (such as the Dewey, Cutter, or LC cataloguing systems) and by creating research aids and bibliographic tools, librarians add an applied dimension to the understanding of the structure of knowledge. To some extent, phrases such as "epistemological engineering" or "applied epistemology" convey this important element of librarianship.

[18] The question of reverse engineering in favour of interoperability generally remains valid in Europe but at best constitutes a murky point in the new US law. An example of this is deCSS (Decryption of Contents Scrambling System), a piece of code allowing circumvention of the DVD protection scheme that divides the world into various incompatible zones so as to facilitate various regional pricing strategies. According to its author, the cracking of this particular code was not done with the idea of piracy in mind, but to allow DVDs to be played on computers using the Linux operating system, which happened only after the industry had refused to release suitable drivers for this system or even to collaborate to help code such drivers.

surveillance system aimed at bringing to court anyone skirting the boundaries of the new laws.

On the technical side, new forms of technical "locks" are being tested in attempts to reconstruct the material stability of the printed or analogue universe. Ranging from outright cryptographic approaches to covert "tattooing" (steganography[19]), these methods either try to prevent unauthorized copying or to increase accountability by providing ways of determining the source of an allegedly pirated copy. Present dispositions of the law, such as the right to make copies for private use, complicate these efforts, but the aim of the content industry is to push back such rights as far as possible by constant (and costly) recourse to the courts, leveraging financial clout into favourable judicial jurisprudence. At the same time, armies of lobbyists work to influence new legislation where it really counts: Washington and Brussels.[20]

However effective the legal and technical measures may be, policing on the ground remains important and may even be the most important link in the whole control machinery. Enforcement, in the end, depends on the efficiency of the systems designed to watch, discipline and punish.

Here again, scientific and scholarly publishing provides an interesting example of how this is done. Faced with the question of how to protect their content, publishers have used the legal framework to assign responsibility for the terms of the contract to those buying the access rights—namely, the librarians. As a result, librarians are being asked to perform a series of tasks, many of which were previously alien to them, such as to positively identify that a particular person is a legitimate member of the constituency and to verify that this person is doing only what he or she is allowed to do. Relying on the physical space of a library is no longer sufficient to define access rights and librarians have had to negotiate hard to protect what amounts to (local) open access in general.[21] As a general rule, anyone able to walk into the library can access the materials located within the building; once outside the library, however, various schemes such as proxy servers or passwords are used to ensure that readers are actually members of the institution that paid for access rights.

Obviously, content owners try to protect their content while shifting the burden and cost of enforcement onto others. In this regard, asking a

---

[19] A form of cryptography that hides information by embedding messages within other, seemingly harmless messages. See www.jjtc.com/Steganography.

[20] For example, Reed-Elsevier is rumoured, from well-informed sources, to have 20 full-time lobbyists in Washington.

[21] The Bibliothèque nationale de France offers an amusing counterpoint to this theme: having digitized a number of works that are still protected by the *droit d'auteur* (authors' rights—the continental flavour of copyright) laws of the country, they limit access to these digital documents to people who are within the walls of the institution, thus defeating one of the advantages of the digital document, namely, ubiquitous access.

fraction of one's customers (librarians) to watch another (scholars or scientists) is brilliantly Machiavellian. At the beginning, these shifts were poorly monitored because they appeared simply insignificant, compared to the vast technical and legal transformations then affecting the librarians' work. As a result, a measure of acquiescence could be secured without even a debate. Quite subtly, a whole series of rights were surreptitiously eroded in the midst of brave talk about unending technical progress and the wonderful advent of an information society providing a bright future to "information services" that used to bear the simpler name of libraries.

It is precisely in this kind of context that the term "information society" comes in handy. Marketing professionals invoke it to focus everybody's attention on the ease of management that the new technologies offer to librarians and on the improved desk access for the end users. In effect, the marketing divisions of the large commercial publishers have been able to create language that serves their ends without revealing them too openly to the mesmerized listener or reader. Moreover, they can claim that this wonderful new technology costs quite a bit in research and development, and therefore, customers must understand that these wonders come at a price. In a nutshell, and in the context of scientific publishing, the information society appears as a device designed in such a way as to serve commercial ends while hiding more political (and sensitive) questions such as those of access. It substitutes itself for the real questions around issues such as collection building and preservation, optimizing access for local users, and creating the navigational aids that differentiate an average library from an excellent one. And it does all of this in the name of progress. Of course, the obvious presence of technical progress gives credence to the argument, but at the cost of a deplorable confusion between itself and social improvement.

Interpretation dilemmas and their meaning

How should such events be interpreted? While they certainly reflect the aggressive strategies deployed by the publishers to conquer new markets, they also reflect their deep-seated fear that long-standing business plans that have provided steady revenues for decades are coming to an end. Some publishers—generally the rich and technically savvy ones—forge ahead and invent new models designed to assure financial success in the new digital context; other publishers—generally smaller and less technically competent—may just try and simply behave in what can be seen as a reactionary manner. Faced with the uncertainties of the future, and seized by a fear of disappearing, these publishers unconsciously ape the French nobility before the Revolution, trying to shore up their weakening economic base by restoring, firming up or extending laws that had fallen into disuse for decades. That phase of French history, known as the *réaction nobiliaire*, or the reaction of the nobility, not only turned out to be ineffective, but even became counter-productive: by increasing popular resentment against a system of inequities that was becoming ever more unbearable, it precipitated the advent of the revolutionary events of 1789. Likewise, some publishers in search of extended forms of revenue have advanced rather strange arguments, including the alleged loss of revenues generated by library loans of books.[22]

Whether the present trends in copyright laws reflect a kind of *réaction nobiliaire* on the part of the publishers, or whether they are the expression of a growing greediness on the part of capitalistic companies, the very difficulty in determining which is which indicates that it is a contest that has not yet ended. In other words, looking at scientific and scholarly publishing reveals a confusing field where the early advantage enjoyed by commercial publishers continue to be exploited although it no longer guarantees them final victory. New alliances are emerging that bring into view possible forms of publishing that radically depart from the older models. Large, commercial publishers still hold the upper hand, but the frantic pace of mergers is not simply a quest for size, clout and efficiency of scale; it also reflects doubts and uncertainties and the need for defensive moves.

How segments of civil society made themselves heard

The combination digitization/network also attracted the attention of a number of scientists and scholars who began to design new communication tools—in effect new "electronic" journals. In so doing, they began to uncover some of the hidden dimensions of scientific and scholarly publishing that had long remained hidden, thanks in part to the work of librarians that had been only too efficient at creating the illusion of free (or costless) access. Scientists such as Stevan Harnad began looking more closely at the new technical possibilities. They began to consider that, from the perspective of publishing scientists or scholars, locking their writings behind a subscription scheme was counterproductive, if not downright stupid. However, scientists also need journals to establish that their work has been subjected to the peer review process, and, even more importantly, to benefit from the reputation bestowed by a given journal.

One of the options looked at was the freeing of content after a short while, a concept that is now being discussed in terms of a "moving wall" system; David Shulenburger's "NEAR" (National Electronic Archive Repository) concept proposed a three-month delay, and the Public

---

[22] French publishers, once again, have been engaged in this type of battle for the last couple of years. The fact that most are not very large or technically oriented may partially account for their tense, essentially reactive, attitude.

Library of Science (PLoS) petition in 2000 proposed a six-month delay. However, these suggestions were still trying to establish a compromise with the existing system. A more radical option was to grant immediate open access.

Scientists, fundamentally, want peer review, prestige *and* free access. The library scheme in effect provides a kind of institutional entitlement to reading rights, and most scientists have acted as if it were equivalent to free access. However, this entitlement does not directly or even satisfactorily respond to the desire for optimal visibility, which, in turn, may fuel authority and prestige. Only with true open access can scientists and scholars hope to move beyond the Faustian bargain[23]— giving one's copyrights to publishers in exchange for their branding capacity, all the while allowing them to milk (largely) public institutions and enjoy rather extraordinary profit margins.

Initially dispersed and unco-ordinated, these various expressive forms of protracted resistance began to converge, thanks to a meeting that took place in Budapest in December 2001. At the invitation of the Open Society Institute, about a dozen scholars, scientists and librarians convened to discuss these issues and explore action plans. The importance of the Budapest Open Access Initiative (BOAI) that emerged from this meeting lies in the fact that it began to bring direction and strategic coherence to the various groups trying to reform scientific publishing. It also focused squarely on the issue of free access, creating a new clarity of vision as well as some language to counteract the statements coming out of the discourses relating to "information society".

Among the initiatives that preceded the Budapest meeting was that of Harold Varmus, a Nobel Prize winner, who tried to convince medical journals to free their content into PubMed Central, a database sponsored by the United States National Institutes of Health (NIH). The reaction of medical journals, especially the *New England Journal of Medicine*, was anything but acquiescent. As a result, the PubMed Central project was quietly transformed into an open access repository for refereed, open access journals. It also became a guaranteed preservation site for open access publications.

A commercial outfit from Britain, BioMed Central (BMC), took advantage of PubMed Central to increase the credibility of its own venture. In BMC's scheme, authors retain their copyright, articles are in open access and NIH's PubMed Central guarantees preservation. The business plan of the venture rests on the idea that each article accepted and published will cost $500. The cost can be borne by a granting agency, an institution or even a foundation. Special, lower prices have been established for poorer countries, and subscription rates for unlimited

---

[23]   Stevan Harnad's phrase (Harnad 1995).

access to publication have been designed for various institutional sizes. PubMed Central provided the institutional guarantee that BioMed articles would remain in open access, no matter what happened to the commercial venture.[24]

With the multiplication of open access journals in the Web, the advent of BioMed Central, and, more recently, the announcement of an important grant ($9 million from the Moore Foundation) to PLoS to create two large, prestigious and open access journals in biology and medicine, the issue of open access began to gain visibility and credibility. As a result, a growing number of organizations, both public and private, are studying the question, and it has become a hot topic in the academic world, as many recent conference programmes testify. At a recent meeting at the Hughes Medical and Health Institute—a foundation financing medical research—representatives of the Wellcome Trust, NIH and the Max Planck Gesellschaft, as well as several foundations attended. The issue was open access and how best to promote this in the biomedical world. The meeting resulted in the Bethesda Statement, which committed the participants, including librarians, scholars, and public and private funding agencies, to support open access.[25]

The importance of open access is that it completely overturns the usual publishing pattern used by scholarly and scientific journals. Instead of adopting a sales model that, in the case of research results, appears both artificial and somewhat ill-adapted to the finalities of scientific communication, open access effectively liberates content, not in the sense of placing it in the public domain—open access schemes all rely on traditional copyright and to that extent remain impervious to changes in copyright laws[26]—but in letting it circulate according to the wishes of scientific authors. At the same time, it proposes a sustainable economic model and this could lead to two important consequences: redirecting the role of scientific publishers in new ways, and introducing a degree of transparency with regard to publishing costs and pricing.

It redirects the publishers' functions because it brings about the need to clearly delineate the border between editorial and publishing functions. In scientific research, a large part of the editorial function is

---

[24] The purpose of BioMed Central and its future can indeed be questioned: is it a real commercial business or is it simply a commercial venture testing a new business model in order to sell it? Should its viability be clearly demonstrated? Could it even be a front for a test covertly financed by some large commercial publisher(s)? The future will tell, but, whatever the answer, BMC was the first to tie up the question of open access with financial (and even commercial) sustainability and that represented a very crucial step in the evolution of open access thinking.

[25] www.earlham.edu/~peters/fos/bethesda.htm.

[26] Even if intellectual property were to reach the state of perpetuity, just like ordinary property—a dream pursued by publishers since at least the sixteenth century—it still would not prevent owners from placing it in open access. Legally, granting open access to a document is not equivalent to giving it away or placing it in the public domain.

covered by peer review and the publisher's role is actually quite limited. This is particularly true in a digital context where the publishers' contribution essentially corresponds to file markup, database construction, cross-referencing and similar tasks. The share of the work done by the publisher may even decrease with time, as open (and free) publishing platforms are increasingly available, enabling any reasonably savvy user of a computer to be quickly empowered into a full-fledged publisher.

Costs will be affected too. If open access publishing really takes root, collections will be have to be interoperable—a hypothesis that is already strongly supported by the existence and vigour of the Open Archive Initiative (OAI). OAI actually refers to standardized sets of meta-data allowing for the one-stop harvesting of distributed sites; it also allows identification of these sites, separating them from the general anarchy of the Web. As such, OAI is indeed fundamental if all these sites are not to become so many intellectual ghettos.

Once this interoperable point is reached, those who pay—institutions, granting agencies or foundations—will naturally try and balance visibility and prestige versus cost, and the "bang for the buck" syndrome will kick in. There will also be competition between various types of repositories, and it will be directly conditioned by the amount publishers charge for publishing and reviewing as well as their prestige and authority. Unlike the "core journal" system and its inelastic market, which allows publishers to divorce pricing from production costs, the new system will reintroduce cost as a factor. For example, if BMC does not manage to grant as much branding value as PLoS, it will have to keep its publishing fee below that of PLoS to attract a second-tier category of authors. And if PLoS raises its fees too high, new players will quickly step in to provide equivalent branding at a lower cost.

Obviously, the stakes are high, which explains why a number of publishers, including learned societies and publishing associations, are beginning to look into this issue with a great deal of attention (and trepidation). Open access experiments are clearly converging toward one single and simple objective: how can they construct excellent (and recognized) branding and evaluation systems in order to create the best "symbolic capital"—to use a concept borrowed from the French sociologist, Pierre Bourdieu—within a viable economic framework?

Curiously, open access does not necessarily work against commercial and even monopolistic interests. In fact, should a publisher like Reed-Elsevier or Taylor and Francis decide to capitalize on its branding capacity potential through its journals, it might decide to go down the open access road and, with the help of its well-established branding devices, price its products so as to maintain or perhaps even improve its revenue stream. The success of this strategy will depend on the entry cost for competitors. If $4–5 million are really required to start a successful open access journal, such as the two journals launched by PLoS, such a high entry cost should reassure the big commercial publishers to the point that they might even see open access as a viable business plan. Alternatively, if very credible and ultimately prestigious journals can be created for a very reasonable price, then traditional commercial publishers will face a new and very threatening form of competition.

In short, the transformations and the consequences that will result from open access are so complex and difficult to predict that commercial publishers will probably tend to play safe for a while. But they are also so profound that they cannot be neglected. It is not by chance that new experiments are originating in universities or with venture capitalists: only milieux such as these are conducive to such daring experiments. This is why the BMC and PLoS experiments are so important. This is also what makes the entire open access movement strategically crucial to anyone interested in the future of scientific publishing.

And if scientific publishing really acts as a canary, it points to fundamental elements in the contest between civil society and the information society. In particular, it shows that commercial discourse, laced with progressive terms as it is, cannot simply be opposed by a counter-strategy such as open access; rather, open access appears as a symptom. It points to the reconfiguration of a contest between public good and private interest. This reconfiguration has largely been invented and (so far) explored by supporters of the public good, in effect by civil society elements. However, its usefulness is not beyond the reach of private interests. In fact, nothing prevents the adoption of an open access model by commercial publishers and, consequently, the elaboration of an information society discourse in addition to it. We can even anticipate its emergence in the near future.

Tightened property rights, protection and enforcement, or overturned business models are the dilemmas in scientific and scholarly publishing at present. If scientific publishing is indeed going to act as the canary in the information society that we are moving into, it is worthwhile to take stock of this contest. The established publishers have generally shown limited originality and a largely reactive attitude. While it is true that relocating information transactions within a contractual framework was inventive, tightening copyright laws, designing better locks and strengthening the enforcement personnel are nothing but regressive. The publishers' aim, as we have seen, is essentially to transpose, thanks to the licensing scheme, all the advantages already held in the print world, and even increase them wherever and whenever possible through a clever use of networked technologies.

However, we have also observed other actors who are rethinking the business model of scientific and scholarly publishing, realigning it in such a way as to enable it to fulfil its primary function more efficiently, while designing an economic model that provides for sustainability (and perhaps even profit in the case of BMC). These efforts are far more creative and are certainly closer to the primary concerns of scientists. Open access publishing appears more efficient, less costly and just as good, if not better, in terms of providing good foundations for sound scientific evaluations. Whether it fits in with publishers' goals will probably vary greatly with each publisher. For example, existing or future publishers close to scientists (such as scientific societies, university presses or even libraries) will find these new models interesting. More traditional (and more powerful) publishers presently enjoying a steady revenue stream and good profit rates from the existing business models will be far more cautious—why kill the goose that lays the golden eggs? But the potential competition emerging from this unexpected sector is sufficiently credible—and even threatening—to warrant a close watch. Elsevier's Chemweb[27] is but one example of this monitoring.

Scientific and scholarly publishing is evolving in a most intriguing way. It displays a growing competition between two fundamentally opposed forms of publishing. On the one hand, traditional publishers merge, change the transaction framework, and try to maintain or even improve their revenue stream so as to improve their bottom line. On the other, new models based on free access mix private and commercial interests with non-profit, goal-oriented ventures, while trying to reform the science communication system to bring it more in line with the needs of all scientists and not just a small elite.

What is interesting in all of this is that the commercial publishers have traditionally and quite spontaneously tended to use the language of the information society as applied to their own field of activity. Technical progress (and its inherent cost) was supposed to justify both its deployment and the increased expenses. Desktop accessibility was pushed centre stage while increased control and reduced rights were kept in the background. For their part, open access groups have tended to emphasize the better alignment of the publishing context with the social and institutional needs of scholars and scientists. Rather than pretending to solve the problems of scientific communication in one sweep, with the use of technology, open access supporters have kept their attention trained on the true needs of scientists and scholars and have looked for ways to take advantage of the new technologies to achieve these goals. As a result, their discourse does not forget technology, but it subordinates it to more political and functional concerns. In short, they

---

[27] Chemweb was originally an experimental open-access repository of chemical preprints with a number of various functions attached to it, in particular discussion groups. It has turned into a sort of alert system for articles and is toll-gated.

speak a language that is also encountered in civil society circles. It is a language that does not shy away from technology, but which, conversely, does not fall into the trap of believing that any problem can be solved through a technical fix, preferably allocated through market mechanisms.

To return to an earlier hypothesis of this paper, if scientific communication can be seen as the canary of the whole information sphere as it is developing nowadays, present trends demonstrate the ways in which the language of the information society can be subsumed in a wider, stronger form of discourse where human beings remain squarely at the heart of the issue, where technology does not appear as a magic wand that can be waved at any social problem, and where issues of power are placed clearly in evidence rather than hidden behind apparently objective technical parameters of all kinds.[28]

Taking Stock of Scientific and Scholarly Publishing

What does the story of scholarly electronic publishing tell us about civil society and its relationship with the information society? The answer to this question lies in some of the interesting social details. It must be remembered that it all started in the context of a fast-growing scientific enterprise—characterized by the term "Big Science" by science historian Derek de Solla Price. It must also be remembered that the difficulty of ensuring efficient information retrieval through up-to-date bibliographic tools led to innovations that inadvertently modified the market characteristics of scholarly publishing. Some publishers—Robert Maxwell among them—duly noted the shift and ushered in a new phase in scientific publishing, which initially brought no response, except from the library community that was bearing the financial brunt of this change.

Unlike the first phase, the advent of digital publishing coupled with global networks led to the emergence of new players from the scholarly and scientific ranks. Quickly spotted and supported by librarians—the earlier public discussions about electronic publishing often took place within library meetings—these developments were also followed by the commercial publishers. As a result, two essentially divergent movements began to evolve. On the one hand, as we saw earlier, the licensing scheme of the publishers was first experimented with and then commercially deployed around 1996, causing libraries to react to the new, unfamiliar demands by creating consortia to negotiate favourable terms for Web site

---

[28] This is not to say that objective technical parameters can never be used; it only means that they must be put in their place and used within the confines of their true operational reach.

licenses. On the other hand, various groups of scholars began to band together to invent an alternative to the dominant, commerce-inspired, model of scientific journals bought and sold through subscriptions. In these early movements, led since 1991 by the likes of Paul Ginsparg and Stevan Harnad, one can recognize the rise of civil society actors and concerns. Toward the end of the decade, the Public Library of Science movement managed to draw the support of 30,000 signatories in the biomedical sciences worldwide.

Librarians, of course, followed this just as attentively as publishers, as they had always hoped to see some movement that would support their own approach based on open access to information for the widest numbers. It may be said that their action throughout the 1990s was to keep alive the various discussions and debates surrounding what they called the serial pricing crisis, while recognizing that these discussions aimed at creating new forms of publishing rather than merely addressing the rise in journal prices.

It must also be noted that early discussions had more to do with the potential of the new technology than with the political economy of scholarly knowledge. Ironically, early supporters of electronic publishing—including the author of this chapter—harboured a somewhat naive belief that technology alone would bring about all the benefits that are now recognized as being part of a truly societal struggle. One might say that in this first phase, the supporters of electronic publishing were trying to attain a civil society objective while speaking almost the same language as the one being used by commercial publishers—the difference being that the "pioneers" kept advancing cost figures which the publishing industry kept denying (and still denies). The point, of course, was that the pioneers hoped to convince sceptical colleagues or administrators through the apparent rationality of economic arguments. However, the real objective was also to reform the means and processes of scientific communication since the technology was transparent enough to reveal all sorts of possibilities that would obviously subvert many instituted social and institutional relations. Various bottlenecks such as time delays in publishing, fixed lengths for articles, and an inability to carry on debates were all regularly mentioned as being part of the potential of a digital environment.

The resistance to the status quo has fuelled a gradual move toward a more political vision of the situation. Examining how the scientific publication system really worked kept revealing new layers of power, involving administrators, scientists and commercial publishers. The branding process, in particular, the creation of symbolic value which can be cashed in for jobs, promotions, nominations to committees, grants and prizes, gradually demonstrated that commercial publishers, through their ability to support an editorial committee, or create new gatekeeping roles by establishing new journals, were in fact very much involved with the core of science. So much for purity and disinterestedness! The social dimension of science becomes only too clear when looked at from this perspective of publishing.

What has become clear in recent years is that two different types of concepts have emerged from this analysis. On the one hand, there are new non-profit, civil-society-type organizations and tactics. Libraries have pushed for institutional repositories as a way to create what might be called "conditions of possibility" for new forms of scientific publishing. Foundations have become involved in pushing for open access, and money has consequently been diverted to create new kinds of open access journals. The Moore Foundation grant to the Public Library of Science falls into this category, and so does the Open Society Institute financial support for various open access activities. The Rockefeller Foundation, the MacArthur Foundation and other similar institutions have all made concrete gestures of varying magnitude in favour of open access publishing. All this, supported by growing networks of scientists and increasing numbers of learned societies, can be said to correspond to the kind of dynamics fostered by civil society.

However, and more importantly, some members of commercial enterprises, while continuing to speak the language of the information society, are actively pursuing the goal of establishing new kinds of business within the open access paradigm. BioMed Central, of course, is the prime example here, but other publishers are beginning to test the open access waters with variously sized experiments. Open access is being closely monitored by many outfits, some of whom hover in the grey area between profit and non-profit, mirroring shifts in a society between its learned and professional side. The latter may be non-profit, but it values profits if only to support other kinds of activities, such as lobbying for better status and working condition for its members. Medical associations readily fall into that category.

The latter development may be the most interesting from which to draw more general lessons for civil society when confronting something like the information society. As a first approximation, or a first reaction, some might think it discouraging to see a noble, pure ideal such as open access appearing to be tainted by commercial interests. However, the very presence of entrepreneurs in this context can also point to a different vision that is far more sustainable over the long run: sainthood and purity may be the true ideals we should hold, but the costs of maintaining an impassable interface between the two worlds are enormous. As most churches know, maintaining communities of monks and nuns behind closed walls is viable only in the presence of very precise social conditions. Change only a few of these and the walls crumble. Likewise, the dream of creating a pure, autarchic, open access publishing probably requires social and institutional conditions that will never be attained completely for long. An occasional grant might create the illusion of possibility, but the more rigorous demands of sustainability reassert themselves promptly with unambiguous results.

This last point is important for the more general topic of civil society's relation with the information society. As science cannot maintain a completely pure profile despite its claims (which nonetheless form an essential part of its credibility and social efficacy), civil society cannot really hope to be a viable, working concept if it sees itself as being purely external to any concept of the information society. The realities (and power) of the commercial world are such that it must exist within a number of tenets, often summarized under the catch-all label of information society. But conversely, abandoning all the ground to the information society would mean simply to subscribe to the myth that the alleged superior efficiency of the capitalist system coupled with the inherent wisdom of the market leads to the best possible world—namely the one we have and into which we are rushing, even as these words are being written.

The important lesson to be drawn from BioMed Central is that, propelled by visions and actions generated by groups that clearly form part of civil society, a group of entrepreneurs decided to try their luck within the wider objectives and values of the open access movement. This example demonstrates two things:

- civil society can indeed subsume elements of the information society; and
- the real debate then may no longer be one based on opposition from the outside, but on defining the legitimate hierarchies and boundaries for each segment of society.

The answer to these questions will have to be limited within the scope of this paper, as it brings in entirely new levels of ideas that would take us too far afield to develop here. The point to keep in mind, however, is that whenever new technology is brought to bear on any social situation, a new question arises which translates the question of common good into a new entity—that of an open infrastructure. In this new perspective, the question of where the infrastructural level begins and ends becomes the most fundamental one. To develop this point, we will briefly discuss the area of "free" or "open source" software.

The Question of Infrastructural Goods

It is interesting to note that the free source code movement in software, like the open access movement in scientific publishing, is divided between commercial and non-commercial players. In the case of software, commercial firms are often unable to compete directly with various software giants, in particular Microsoft, or to identify a safe niche for themselves. Given this situation, they adopt a different strategy and develop a layer of services, in addition to software that is easily accessible and can be freely analysed. They can do so because, although the software is free (in the sense of free speech), its inherent complexity can make its handling somewhat difficult. In many ways, this is exactly what BioMed Central is exploring in scientific publishing as it tries to build a layer of services (Faculty of Thousand, citation linking and so on) on top of an essentially free-access system. It is, in effect, trying to redefine the boundaries between the infrastructural commons and the proprietary domain.

For their part, some non-commercial software ventures also strive to develop alternative models, for example, Debian in the GNU/Linux world does so because it has portrayed itself as the guardian of a certain free source code software orthodoxy. However, quality is also of the essence and through a somewhat conservative and slightly slower pace of development, Debian has secured a strong reputation for very well thought-out solutions with a high degree of robustness to the point that some companies use Debian as a base for their own distribution. We may be witnessing similar developments in science publishing. In a way, PLoS fits this image, and so do institutional repositories organized by various libraries and university presses. Like Debian, they strive to create an image of excellence; they work on the best branding instruments they can devise. But they also push back the limits of the infrastructure by beginning to provide alternatives to commercial services that may limit the latters' field of action.

The conclusion of this small digression into the area of software is that the distinction between commercial and non-commercial ventures is important, but the fixity of the boundary between the two worlds is not the real problem. What is fundamental is the way in which the commons are defined and how economic activity locates itself with respect to these commons. While it is obviously in Microsoft's interest to lock up the operating system (DOS, Windows) and then use this as a competitive advantage against other companies, it is likewise to the advantage of other companies to help develop alternative operating systems, betting that their free status and their quality will eventually make them attractive to users. In so reacting, these companies are helping redefine both commons and infrastructure, which, of course, must be equally accessible for all. Likewise, open access in scientific and scholarly publishing is trying to redefine what counts as free and universally accessible infrastructure. The attitude of commercial companies, in this regard, is derived not from altruism—which would be unsustainable for most—but from an intelligent understanding of what is minimally needed to design a reasonably viable business plan. A measure of commons is needed for competitive markets to remain relatively stable. The boundary between the infrastructural commons and the commercial, privatized world is deeply dynamic and can move a great deal from one situation to another.

These developments also provide insights into ways in which civil society and commercial interests (hiding behind the information society discourse) can position themselves with respect to one another. The difference lies in whether the notion of open or free infrastructures is not only legitimate, but also essential for the workings of a healthy economy. Quite often, those who believe in the information society will be easily recognized by their promptness to invoke the famed "tragedy of the commons"—an argument that claims that goods that are not owned privately tend to be badly managed and overused—despite the fact that information, by definition, can never be overused.[29] While we should not be confused by allusions to economic situations that do not apply to the cases examined, the possibility of reshaping commercial objectives from a civil society perspective appears probable, resting ultimately on redefining what counts as essential infrastructures or commons.

Information Society and Information Theory: A Deeper Mystification

Upon reflection, the term information society is really an odd one: it seems to limit itself to describing a society dominated in some sense by information—a situation presumably introduced by new kinds of technologies, which appears to introduce a level of conceptual sophistication that, on first glance, appears quite compelling. Where does this rhetorical strength, this ability to convince, come from?

The reason lies largely with the connotations carried by the term "information". Information theory, as developed by the likes of Claude Shannon and Norbert Wiener, once held the promise of a fundamental rewriting of most knowledge, similar perhaps to the formulation of the theory of relativity by Albert Einstein. Along with the nascent science of cybernetics, the mathematical formalization of information by Shannon revealed its connections with the older concept of entropy used in thermodynamics. As a result, the early 1950s seemed to promise that humanity was on the verge of some gigantic new synthesis. When geneticists began to interpret DNA as a code and, therefore, as information for producing living organisms, it even began to look as if information, energy and matter were all that were needed to account for

---

[29] On this point, Lawrence Lessig is an indispensable reference. See Lessig (2001).

the entire universe. Consilience was well on its way, to use a word revived in a recent work by E.O. Wilson.[30]

Actually, these developments echo an older tradition, linked in part to the Saint-Simonian movement in nineteenth-century France.[31] It had already linked communication technologies and human progress: the rhetoric surrounding the deployment of the telegraph and the railroad had enjoyed a fair measure of success in the late nineteenth and early twentieth centuries, and so had the digging of canals such as Suez and Panama. Jules Verne in France and, to a lesser extent, H.G. Wells in Britain popularized such notions, and world fairs, with their celebration of the telephone and electricity, certainly did their part to popularize the conflation of social and technical progress.[32]

The rise of new communication technologies in the 1970s and 1980s (Videotex in several countries, Internet in the United States) catalyzed a new round of interest in communication, which reached a frenzied pitch in the early 1990s. The term information highway was on everyone's lips, even though no one knew what it really meant. In France, a super-Minitel based on a full deployment of optic fibre seemed in the offing, while in Canada, telephone companies were floating the idea of a consortium named Sirius accompanied by billions of dollars of investments. The Internet was but one contender then and even as late as 1995–1996, asynchronous transfer mode (ATM) was regularly presented by various companies as a new technology that would encompass the Internet, rather than the reverse. Remarkably, it did not matter which side of the technology was presented since all relied on the aura of information theory. In fact, part of the information frenzy was probably no more than the echo of the commercial competition going on between telecommunication companies and Internet firms.

It is in this context that the expression information society took hold. The fundamental nature of Claude Shannon's concept of information, which Wiener had located as the centre of his cybernetic theory, seemed to ensure an equally fundamental positioning within a promised "new economy", variously known as the *knowledge* or *information economy*. It was a kind of magical economy where no one needed to be encumbered with material concerns, traditional accounting—for example, tangible assets—and common-sense limits on the workings of labour and capital. For example, the leader of Massachusetts Institute of Technology's (MIT) Media Lab, Nicholas Negroponte, has contrasted the new world of information bits to the old industrial world of physical

---

[30] Wilson 1998. The term conscilience refers to a coming together of knowledge across different disciplines to create a common ground of explanation.

[31] Saint-Simon developed a theory that rested on the conflation of social and technical progress. On the Saint-Simonian roots of network philosophy, see Musso (1997).

[32] Two books cover this story well: Standage (1998); Mattelart (1992).

atoms, and proceeded to argue that the present civilizational shift he claims to observe is in effect the result of bits substituting for atoms. This kind of "information transform" seemed to promise, as in the case of various mathematical counterparts (such as the "Laplace transforms" used to solve differential equations) a quick, painless solution to whole classes of very complex problems. Those familiar with the TV series *Star Trek* will recognize in this the "Beam me up, Scotty" syndrome, in which transmitting information about solid bodies takes the place of actually moving these bodies through space.

Interestingly enough, the two currently dominant technologies, the Internet and the mobile phone, underscore a fact that early Videotex and network experiments had already revealed—these technologies are appreciated to the extent that they permit a peer-to-peer approach. People have displayed a greater recurring interest for communication than for information for its own sake. The information society has turned out to be at best a "communication society". In the wake of the latter, civil society, in the form of self-organizing groups, has grown with an ease and vigour rarely seen since the early days of print. Content (or software, as we have seen earlier) is created and copied with an efficiency that threatens to compete successfully with the established publishers and the software industry. It also greases the wheels of protest, particularly the anti-globalization movements that have been able to organize, thanks to their effective use of the Internet.

In short, the information society has been superseded by a communication society and the latter has been working only too well, but not with the expected results. Instead of fostering the deployment of tools aimed at ensuring passive, consumer-based behaviour on the part of users, it has spawned a climate of freedom, sometimes disparaged as "anarchic", where traditional forms of property, especially intellectual property, have been threatened, encouraging the rise of alternative forms of power.

Ironically, advertising for the communication industry had the vocabulary of a deep revolution, but no one had expected to see the content align itself with these venal claims. Yet, the new communication tools have seemed to unleash a generation of young individuals freed from the shackles that the mass media had imposed on collective perceptions for several decades. Curiously, through co-operative programming (but also co-operative pirating), young people are building new forms of governance and new societal structures that do not necessarily respect older structures and values. In other words, what had been advertised as an information society had veered off in a very unexpected direction.

The prospect of activist individuals who might even rediscover the joy of being active citizens has obviously been too much for a number of reigning plutocracies. In the case of scientific and scholarly publishing—our faithful canary—the trick discovered by large publishers was to change the legal framework of operation and to recreate a client-server structure that would ensure the continuation of the traditional economic recipes and domination systems. Likewise, since the mid-1990s, the objective has been to rein in the Internet despite its international, distributed structure that defies territorialized legal systems, and this, in part, has been the function (and meaning) of the Internet Corporation for Assigned Names and Numbers (ICANN). It also explains the intensity of the debates surrounding this controversial organization. In parallel, through the World Trade Organization (WTO), World Intellectual Property Organization (WIPO) and changes to intellectual property laws (DMCA in the United States, for example), efforts are being made to prevent "consumers" from reshaping the social relations that influence their social and economic status. What the evolution of scientific publishing reveals, therefore, is that while civil society is split between legal and not-so-legal activities (in part reflecting the credibility or lack of credibility of the political and economic systems in question), the commercial world is similarly split between traditional enterprises and enterprises trying to fit within the new perception of civil society.

Paths of Resistance

The constant theme of this essay has been that scientific and scholarly publishing provides an interesting early warning system to examine how the glittering but shadowy contours of information society are marshalled to favour the deployment of new oligopolistic forms of commerce and, as far as possible, to reduce citizens to the state of passive consumers. It also offers insights into possible strategies to resist and even reverse such trends. The lessons learned in this small area ought to be of great interest to civil society. Let us review some of the more fundamental results encountered earlier, but transposed to the wider society here.

Library consortia have done little more than emulate consumer organizations in the wider world; while they certainly help to keep prices in check and provide some leverage to control quality, they fail to change the basic consumer game and may even occasionally contribute to its reinforcement. Moreover, library consortia have revealed some vulnerability to external manipulation that turn out to be quite useful to the multinational companies they ostensibly challenge.[33] This consortium level of resistance is probably unavoidable and, to some extent, it can be of use; however it provides no real solution, especially over the medium

---

[33] See Guédon (2001).

to long term. While it squarely belongs to a civil society approach, it also reflects many of the weaknesses of this kind of reaction.

The issues that essentially revolve around the role of commons, open domains that may take the form of a public domain, have been more interesting.[34] Open access and free source code are the terms that reflect this debate respectively in scientific and scholarly publishing on the one hand, and in computer programming on the other. In the broader terms of civil society, it coincides rather well with the language of infrastructures conceived as the necessary basis for a healthy economy.

Locating the infrastructure and clarifying the border between infrastructure provision and service activities is more fundamental than the commercial/non-profit dichotomy. The point of locating an infrastructure is not so much to oppose commerce as it is to facilitate healthy forms of commerce, and resist monopolistic and oligopolistic forms of behaviour. The equilibrium between the infrastructural commons and the private sphere should be viewed as dynamic.

The best examples of successful infrastructural projects rest on a distributed philosophy, which displays particularly robust forms of social organizations while fostering results of particularly good quality—results that do not cease to astonish the factory-based forms of organization that currently dominate productive activities. What must be noted here is that this ability to network in a distributed manner is very much at the heart of the association style of civil society. In other words, in discussing the relationship of civil society with the information society, we must reach the conclusion that the best way—perhaps the only way—to develop a good, healthy economic system is to rely on the vitality of civil society and its ability to help people come together and work together, preferably in open networks. This is equivalent to stating that a healthy economic society must work on infrastructural bases that are best left under the responsibility of civil society.

In short, and in conclusion, technologies are being deployed according to various agendas, as always. In our age, the capitalist vision of large multinational companies usually dominates and is often couched in universalistic terms that also aim at reducing everything to one simple, basic principle: progress. The information society discourse appears to be one kind of language that has been used precisely to achieve these aims. As a result, to beat it back and not succumb to its seductive harmonies—unfortunately, the world's problems will not be

---

[34] It must be remembered that the GNU license, which applies to a number of free source-code software, is not equivalent to public domain. It is a license, but a license so conceived as to ensure free access across its successive modifications. In that regard, it acts very much like scientific knowledge that must belong to someone, yet can be retrieved and used to nourish further scientific work.

solved by the mere ability to inform, or even to communicate[35]— it is important to construct a different vocabulary capable of feeding the actions of civil society. That language must foreground societal issues, but doing this alone is not enough; one must also point to some desired contours of this civil society. Stressing the need for infrastructural commons and, perhaps, addressing anew the whole notion of individualism—another point this paper could have addressed but which would have taken us too far afield—are some of the reference points to rebuild a language where something like an information society, if the term is to survive at all, must fit within humane objectives such as those expressed by civil society.

References

Benkler, Yochai. 2002. **Coase's Penguin, or, Linux and the Nature of the Firm**. www.benkler.org/CoasesPenguin.html, accessed on 14 October 2003.

Cox, Brian. 2002. "The Pergamon phenomenon (1951–1991): Robert Maxwell and scientific publishing". **Learned Publishing**, Vol. 15, No. 4, pp. 273–278.

Guédon, Jean-Claude. 2001. **In Oldenburg's Long Shadow: Librarians, Research Scientists, Publishers, and the Control of Scientific Publishing**. Association of Research Libraries. www.arl.org/arl/proceedings/138/guedon.html, accessed on 14 October 2003.

Harnad, S. 1995. "Electronic scholarly publication: Quo vadis?" **Serials Review** Vol. 21, No. 1, pp. 70–72. (Reprinted in **Managing Information**, Vol. 2, No. 3, 1995.)

Kronick, David A. 1976. **A History of Scientific and Technical Periodicals: The Origins and Development of the Scientific and Technical Press, 1665– 1790**, second edition. The Scarecrow Press, Inc., Metuchen, NJ.

Kuhn, Thomas. 1996. **The Structure of Scientific Revolutions**. University of Chicago Press, Chicago.

Lessig, Lawrence. 2001. **The Future of Ideas. The Fate of the Commons in a Connected World**. Random House, New York.

Mattelart, Armand. 1992. **La communication-monde: Histoire des idées et des strategies**. Éditions La découverte, Paris.

---

[35] The converse is not true: the lack of communication or information tools can bring about much misery. Absence hurts, but presence does not necessarily help.

Musso, Pierre. 1997. **Télécommunications et philosophie des réseaux: La Postérité paradoxale de Saint-Simon**. Presses Universitaires de France (PUF), Paris.

Poovey, Mary. 1998. **A History of the Modern Fact: Problems of Knowledge in the Sciences of Wealth and Society**. University of Chicago Press, Chicago.

Standage, Tom. 1998. **The Victorian Internet: The Remarkable Story of the Telegraph and the Nineteenth Century's On-Line Pioneers**. Walker and Company, New York.

Wilson, Edward O. 1998. **Consilience: The Unity of Knowledge**. Knopf, New York.

Wouters, Paul. 1999. **The Citation Culture**. Doctoral thesis, University of Amsterdam.

A Brief Descriptive Glossary of Communication and Information (Aimed at Providing Clarification and Improving Mutual Understanding)[1]

Antonio Pasquali

Abstract

This glossary was put together in response to an increasing technological and linguistic Tower of Babel effect in the communications field. It offers an initial filtering of the terminology based on a re-examination of information and communication "basics".

The first term, the notion of human relations, signifies a phenomenon that is ontologically impossible in the absence of the communicating act, and the quality of which is a reflection of the model of communication governing it. The chapter examines the following terms: deontologies, morals and ethics, which are reassigned their true meanings, underlining the inherence of "moral" and "communication", and of "intersubjectivity" and "society". Inform and communicate are concepts that can be derived by schematization from the group of relational categories in order to bring out the vertical, causative, desocializing and imperfect nature of the former, and the synthetic, reciprocal, socializing and perfect nature of the latter, demonstrating that "inform" should be conceived of from the perspective of "communicate", and not the reverse. This thinking lays a foundation for the full legitimacy and precedence of communication rights, whose areas of application are described.

The chapter also discusses the aspect of these rights that provokes the most conflict today—the vicarious exercise of them—in order to demonstrate the need for new social contracts in this area. The term free flow of information, an essentially positive concept, though often improperly applied, needs to be recovered, because many current controversies reproduce old and unresolved diatribes regarding information in its other senses. The two antonymous terms access and participation are identifiable in communicational terms as "receiving" and "transmitting" of messages. These two notions, of great strategic importance, are often distorted, if not manipulated. Finally, the term information society is a triumphalist nickname used to legitimize the repudiation of better and more peaceful human relations that are

---

[1] Translated from the Spanish original by Paul Keller.

expressed in a communication society. Considering the information society in its current phase, the chapter criticizes its evident anomy, the abuses of dominant positions that plague it, its addiction to espionage and its criminal economic record.

Rationale

The following explanations of basic communication and information terms are intended as an *aide-mémoire*, to help people from different cultural backgrounds keep core concepts in focus and understand each other. These explanations do not constitute definitions, nor do they favour one system of hermeneutics over another. Rather, they provide a frame of reference to prevent misunderstandings. Our pocket vocabulary begins with the concept of "human relations". While the essential importance of this endeavour may not be immediately apparent, it is, in fact, the *raison d'être* of the communicative and informative process.

It has not been easy for the young communication and information sciences—or disciplines—to create their own vocabulary, given the brisk pace at which their applications are changing. They have been forced to borrow terms from other branches of knowledge to express essential concepts, and these terms are laden with prior meaning. The pre-existing meanings themselves are not always unequivocal, coming, as they do, from varying linguistic and cultural contexts from which different connotations arise. The Tower of Babel phenomenon, in which the relationship between signifier and signified becomes problematic, is thus more frequent in our field than we might wish.

Numerous international debates in the 1970s and 1980s, regarding "the free flow of information", for instance, proved in the end to be dialogues of the deaf because their participants, often without realizing it, had distinct, and indeed divergent, notions of information and of freedom in particular. Although they used the same words, they had different concepts in mind. Today, the supposed need to control information for security reasons is presented in the guise of anodyne clichés, such as information security and network security—vague terms used to avoid calling massive interception of messages by its real name—espionage.

The polysemy of important terms such as information and access continues to create problems, and it would have been wise for the secretariat of the World Summit on the Information Society (WSIS) to produce, in advance, an agreed terminological glossary to be distributed to prospective meeting participants in order to reduce semantic confusion. The very definition of information favoured by the International Telecommunication Union (ITU) is not shared by other intergovernmental agencies, information technology specialists or news professionals.

The proliferation of communication channels and of digitization, globalization and instantaneous electronic messaging, the increasing economic, military, political and cultural weight of information and communication processes, and interminable changes in production, conservation, dissemination, vectors, coding and monitoring of messages make information and communication ever more complex. The Tower of Babel effect grows, while the capability for semantic manipulation increases concomitantly. The following reflections attempt to contribute to terminological clarity, promote mutual understanding and facilitate comprehension of what we truly wish to say to each other in our dialogue about communication and information.

Human Relations

Improving human relations (in the basic, not the management, sense of the term) is the ultimate practical aim of the social sciences. However, this governing concept is not invoked as often as might be desired, and hence, though WSIS, as a forum for humanity, is intended to impact certain parameters of human relations considered essential today, it is not surprising that the term does not figure in the organization's final documents, with the exception of a brief mention in one or more of the "considering that" clauses.

The concept of relation is one of a small number of logically indefinable concepts in the empyrean of thought. Knowledge itself is the fruit of a proper relation between understanding and things. Western schools of philosophy have placed relation among the dozen higher concepts called "categories", and have dedicated themselves, in a descending process of structural schematization, to ordering the different compartments used to divide the whole, based on the manner in which relation manifests itself in each.

From the start, the human microcosm is perceived as the realm of the highest attained relationship. The human being is superior to all other beings, and even godlike, because humans are the only ones capable of relating consciously with their fellows and of creating community. The way in which relation manifests itself among rational beings is called *koinonía* (in Greek) or *communitas* (in Latin). It is inspiring, even today, to contemplate the first Western thinker who explored the problem. It is to Democritus of Abdera, in the fifth century B.C., that we owe the insight that it was the invention of communicative language which turned hominids into humans. Democritus declared that without communication, we would never have transcended the brute state of copresence that we shared with the animals, to move toward a state of coexistence, in which the other becomes a neighbour with whom we coexist, and in which we reach the only fully conscious form of relationship, namely, community. Twenty-six centuries ago, Democritus stated that there can be no community without communication. Happily, almost every modern language has preserved the verbal root *kóinos* (common) or *communis, communitas, communicatio*, reminding us forever of the inherence of communication and community.

If it is true that without the communicative function there is no community, then any change in the communicative behaviour of a social group will produce changes in ways of perceiving, feeling and treating the other in the context of practical human relationship, within the framework of the model of community in force. The words communication or information always, and necessarily, refer to the essence of community and human relations. Thus, it is unacceptable to reduce these terms to the level of a technical or economic discourse that seeks to minimize or devalue the social repercussions of the communicating *factum*. Hence, society has an inalienable ontological right to view, and participate in, any decision that affects its communication or information—activities that constitute the essence of human relations.

The world order today favours political and economic interests that seek to steer social change by controlling communication and information. The international community is opposing this abuse with increasing clarity, posing the question of who is really to exercise authority in communications—the most essential function of human coexistence.

The statement that any society is a reflection of its communication networks is not ideological, but it makes ideologically suspect any attempt to favour sterile and desocialized communication and information discourses, in which terminology is reduced to its semiological, scientific/technical or commercial dimensions.

We are living through a historical transition in which much decision-making power is deliberately being removed from consensual bodies—generally within the United Nations family of organizations—and placed in new centres of power. There has been a constant attempt, for decades, to discredit and block the United Nations ("Not a good idea poorly applied, but simply a bad idea," argued the *Washington Post* in March 2003), and to replace it by a more malleable parallel system. In the new club of mega-powers—the International Monetary Fund (IMF), World Bank, Organisation for Economic Co-operation and Development (OECD), World Trade Organization (WTO), and the Group of Eight (G-8), whose areas of authority are constantly expanding—the generous multilateral principle of "one country, one vote" is replaced by a management system based on weighted voting. (In the IMF, the wealthiest country's vote has 1,322 times the weight of that of the poorest.) Issues such as intellectual property and asbestosis are now WTO matters, and water—believe it or not—has become a matter for the World Bank. Much deliberative activity related to communication and information has also been compelled to migrate to bodies that are less and less intergovernmental in nature—more docile, privatized or inclined to favour technological and economic, rather than social, approaches to issues. What the interested parties gain in these relocations, civil society tends to lose in morale and social cohesion. The forced migration to the ITU of the major issue of communication, reduced to the sub-chapter of information, is obviously one of these cases. The ITU defines itself as an "organization specializing in information and communication technologies" (that is, specializing in hardware) and, among UN organizations, it is perhaps the most advanced in the privatization process, with 189 member states, 660 private sector members and not a single organization representing civil society. (Its unprecedented and important Reform Advisory Panel, or RAP, formed in Minneapolis, includes the International Chamber of Commerce, Cisco, AT&T and Nortel, and the list of its "guests" includes WorldCom, Global Crossing, Qwest, AOL Time Warner and Xerox, some of which have disappeared or declared bankruptcy.) Meanwhile, its official auditor was recommended to it by none other than Arthur Andersen. In March 2002, the "intergovernmental" ITU proudly announced, in Istanbul, that "the new telecommunications world is one that can be characterized as private, competitive, mobile and global". The Secretary-General of the United Nations has entrusted this organization (quite different from what it was when it published the hope-inspiring report of the Maitland Commission, *The Missing Link*, in 1985) with the task of organizing WSIS and with the mandate to "play a key role in it". Given the danger announced at its 2002 plenary session regarding major drops in contributions to its budget from countries in the North, perhaps the ITU is seeking to provide its RAP with satisfactory results. One can also imagine, among the future results of the summit, a package of ethereal statements that leaves the sector's macro realities untouched, or an astute reinvigoration of the giant industrial/commercial telecom beast, which is in a weakened state today due to catastrophic speculation in the Internet and in Universal Mobile Telecommunications System (UMTS) frequencies. (During the PrepComs, the perception of a number of NGOs was that there was a tendency to turn the summit into an "Internet promotion".)

Ultimately, the scenarios cannot be predicted, but one fact may be taken for granted: While it discusses aid for development, funding, rights, broadcast frequencies, digitization, security, codes, access and the Internet, WSIS will fall into the behavioural patterns of the so-called information society, and thus pave the way for future decisions that, sooner or later, for better or worse, will change the community of human beings. Those concerned about a teleology of more equitable relations among human beings, and who are struggling for a reasonably peaceful and unified human family, will resist all reductionism, and will continue to reflect on the results of WSIS, in terms of their effects on human relations.

Deontologies, Morals and Ethics

These terms are widely used in vague and ambiguous ways. Humanity's diminished moral vocabulary, overwhelmed today by glamorous technological and economic dictionaries whose vocabulary everyone tries to imitate, reveals a certain cacophony. The oft-heard call for an ethical and moral rescue fails, for example, to indicate what ethics or morals are. Is the idea to use ethics to improve the poor image associated with morals, or are we simply dealing with a verbal stereotype that people adopt unquestioningly because it sounds good? (Yesteryear's "global village" was such a phrase.) A minimum of terminological clarity is called for here, and in analysing communications, there are two reasons for clarifying terms of moral philosophy.

First, communication and morals are, anthropologically speaking, the two categories of relation with the greatest conceptual and historical links, since they both concern our treatment of the other. Once the human group found, in communication, the oxidant for its sociability, survival obliged it to ensure a minimum of harmony. It accomplished this through social contract. It provided itself with standards of behaviour to facilitate the process of coexistence. (This is why, for millennia, justice was considered the supreme moral virtue.) All subsequent standards grew out of an original moral plexus, and law systematically returns to it when confronted with unprecedented crisis. Communication is a moral act and an act of interpersonal relationship, as well as a political act and an act of social construction. Communication and standards of co-existence are two fundamental, essential and related ways by which people are linked in human relationship.

The second reason is that unprecedented communication rights, ensuring just and pluralistic distribution of the power to communicate, would not survive in the absence of a new communication morality, adopted by a majority of those subject to such relationship—more specifically, a new intersubjective morality conceived on the basis of higher standards of communicative and informative behaviour. Without such a new morality, it will be difficult to establish new communication law and policy, which are indispensable if today's common law rights—riddled, as they are, by authoritarian elements—are to be democratized. The meanings of three terms are therefore clarified, for possible use by WSIS.

Deontologies: This word needs to be revived in the moral discourse of all languages, in order to prevent various types of misunderstanding. Deontologies (or "professional morals") are consistent and specific sets of standards to promote self-regulation, self-esteem, good governance and respect for the beneficiaries of specific professional activities. They do not involve any provision for legal sanctions. They are normally reflected in deontological codes (of which the Hippocratic oath is the archetype). The frequently employed phrase "code of ethics" creates great confusion and should be abandoned. Deontologies can lend themselves to moral dishonesty when, in the name of group interests or freedoms, they attempt to remove the group from society's control, replacing it by a mere self-watchfulness. A world of praxis governed only by pure, contradictory and unsystematic sectoral deontologies or micro-level systems of standards would be a morally anarchical and politically Hobbesian one. Deontologies can provide useful and finer-toothed regulation of behaviour when they serve as sets of standards added to pre-existing moral and legal norms, based on external oversight. On the other hand, they can become an excuse when they attempt to elude existing norms and sidestep legal sanctions. In communications, this degraded version of the concept has prevailed.

Morals: Morals are consistent, generic, historical and systematizable sets of norms that are constantly evolving. For communities that share beliefs and principles, they provide axiological and practical criteria for all types of action. All human groups, without exception, are governed by unwritten or codified, simple or complex moral standards—a confirmation of the Cartesian principle that while survival without metaphysics is possible, survival without a coherent moral conception of the world is not. True moral systems are characterized by being systematic and non-contradictory, with some degree of hierarchy in their axiological structures. (A popular collection of proverbs with its diverse and contradictory moral proto-standards is not yet a system of morals.) The social morals cited in many constitutions express the fact that every society—national society, in this case—holds to one set of values and duties more than to others: what may be questionable or reprehensible for one system of social morals can be quite acceptable for another. Whether moral principles remain in force over time depends on their ability to provide norms of proper behaviour even in new situations. If they fail to do this, their credibility suffers and the social moral system begins to: (i) generate amoral responses to unfamiliar stimuli; or (ii) seek more inclusive principles that will make it possible to incorporate the new within the moral system. Science, technology and economics, which are experiencing a boisterous evolution, generate—and, today, may be said to favour—*amoral* behaviours (which are the first step on the short path to *demoralization* and *immorality*), rather than to promote concerted searches for superior moral principles. In communication and information, this phenomenon is clearly evident: as deontological codes are used to avoid social responsibilities, technological wonders are cultivated in the search for amoral consensuses, in order to avoid the need for an obstructive examination of authority and content.

Ethics: This term should be reserved for moral philosophy, which is a metaphysical-gnoseological systematization of actual historical morals. (The Kantian definition—metaphysics of moral habits—is still faultless.) Ethics only begins when reason asks why are there moral principles; what supreme, universal and timeless principles are found in all moral systems; why are humans the only moral beings; and what is the origin of the great moral principles. Thus, ethics only exist in the form of coherent parts of some philosophical system. Any other use of the term is inappropriate and fosters confusion.

We speak correctly of the ethics of Hume or of the Frankfurt School, of the morals of the Greek people or of Nazism, and of the deontology of communicators or physicians. The term ethics, with occasional exceptions, should be reserved for philosophical conferences. Deontologies prove suspicious when their defenders are also the possessors of large extra-moral interests, but this term is the one to use—the only one—when referring to the morals of the communicator. Morality is in serious need of updating—conceptually and semantically—if its great principles are to avoid becoming inapplicable, which would pave the way for economic, military, political, scientific or technological principles to supplant them.

Informing and Communicating

In light of the very substantial progress of the communication media, modern science has been forced to rescue the term communication from disuse during the recent period of slightly more than a century. However, "progress" here does not refer to the generic proliferation of artificial channels and their quantitative growth in the industrial age, but rather, to three precisely defined phenomena that have qualitatively transformed human relations:

- the massive technical reproducibility of messages;
- the progressive irrelevance of spatial and temporal "distance" as a significant variable; and
- in these relocations, the preservation of what was previously unpreservable, such as sounds, static images and moving images.

It was neither the musical notation of Guido d'Arezzo nor Gutenberg's movable type that led to the dusting off of the generic term, communication. Rather, it was a chain of inventions such as daguerreotype, the rotary press, wire telegraphy, the phonograph and cinematography, that produced a qualitative change in human relations, beginning in the nineteenth century.

Information, on the other hand, can be traced from the classical era, where it thrived as a philosophical concept denoting the interpenetration or imposition of a form, idea or principle with or in material that thus becomes "in-formed" or "formed". Thus, for instance, marble becomes statue. (This old meaning is irreplaceable. It continues to help us understand modern relationships, such as that between news and public opinion). Then, for centuries, the use of the term information was nearly monopolized by journalists. In our time, the multiple meanings of information, in addition to the unresolved ambiguities of communicating and informing, create a certain Tower of Babel effect when there is an attempt to agree on a definition of the ideal ought-to-be of an information society. There is the information of informatics (the mathematically measurable quantum of unpredictability in the message), the information of cybernetics (the command signal that feeds into or provides feedback to programmed systems), the information of the telecommunication engineer (that which is digitizable/transmittable), the information of the defender of human rights and freedoms (any knowledge that is in the public domain and accessible), and the information of the journalist (essentially, the newsworthy). To add to the confusion, the venerable Reuter's describes itself on its homepage in the following terms: "Best known for our expertise in journalism, we are also one of the largest information providers in the world, with annual sales of £3.6 billion", doing away with the old equivalence of information and news, and making information a synonym of "economic bulletin". WSIS's hosts and guests, with their different inclinations and interests, may favour one definition over another. This leads to a threat of "Babelization" that should be cleared up before voting on, and signing, documents.

A world summit dedicated to communication and information should be an occasion for some terminological clarification, creating an acceptable conceptual platform in which each person can see reflected the definition that he or she finds most convincing. This should be possible, provided that we go back to the abstract generic approach to the two concepts—to pure communicating and informing.

To create such a platform, we must in fact return to the most comprehensive and important category in our field, that of relation, and ask ourselves what type of relation, how much relation, and what quality of relation are needed to ensure that human beings have information and communication. To put it another way, what model of human relations do information and communication tend to support?

Pure philosophy has unfortunately not dealt with a schematization of the categories of relation at different anthropological levels, but it has clearly determined what such categories were for all possible schematizations. (Definitions in parentheses, below, are Kantian, and should be retained.)

- Inherence (relation between substance and accident)
- Causality (relation between cause and effect)
- Community (reciprocal action between agent and patient)

Brought down to the area of communications, these can be schematized as follows:

Inherence	=	Communion
Causality	=	Information
Community	=	Community

The first category, communion, would not seem to be applicable to the human community in any of its communicative modes, since it connotes an absolute inherence of one thing in another, erasing all distance and difference of identity between the merged subjects. Rather, it is applicable to the inanimate (the whiteness inherent in snow, the hardness of stone) or the supernatural (the communion of the saints). Metaphorically only, it can be used to refer to moments of religious, mystical or love-induced ecstasy, properly defined as "nothingness" and "loss of oneself in otherness", a state of pure unrelatedness. As the zero level of relation, communion denotes a state, which makes it unusable as a means of conceiving of communication relationships, which always, and in every case, imply distance and distinction between the subjects or parties involved.

Information and communication remain the two basic categories capable of defining communicative relations between human beings.

As categories, the dialectical laws that unite them are ineradicable. To speak of information always, and necessarily, brings us back to communication, and vice versa. It would be entirely irrational to attempt to understand one of the two processes in total separation from the other. They are mutually explanatory. Given this dialectic, it is strictly true that, in praxis, any increment in the informative necessarily generates a drop in the communicative, and vice versa.

Information is ontologically related to causality. It connotes the message/cause of an active transmitter who seeks to generate in a receiving patient an immediate or remote behaviour/effect.

Communication is ontologically related to community. It connotes a message/dialogue that seeks to produce unprogrammed response, reciprocity, consensus and shared decisions.

Hence, information categorically expresses a less perfect or balanced communicating relationship than does communication, and tends to produce more verticality than equality, more subordination than reciprocity, more competitiveness than complementarity, more imperatives than indicatives, more orders than dialogue, more propaganda than persuasion.

The foregoing are no more than conceptual schemes intended to classify or include each communicative situation in the genus to which it belongs. In the actual historical world of human beings, it is impossible to find a relation of pure information (like the thermostat-heater) or a relation of pure communication. One might as successfully seek justice, beauty or truth in the pure state. But these schemes make it possible to define and describe all communicative relations, to have a solid basis on which to affirm that the informative or communicative component is manifest or predominant in this or that relation.

Information refers to a predominantly informative message in which one of the poles always or predominantly functions as transmitter, while the other always or predominantly functions as receiver. The transmitter tends here to institutionalize his transmission capacity, which is a way of institutionalizing and fixing the mute receiving function at the opposite pole. The receiver faces increasing difficulty, or is unable to turn himself into transmitter, and the establishment of reciprocity is prevented. This is replaced by a pseudo-interactivity that masquerades as reciprocity, or the receiver is simply left without immediate return channels. It thus becomes easier for institutionalized transmitters to exploit for their own benefit their causal monologues before a mute and powerless receiver, becoming, in turn, at will, in an immediate way, a transmitter. This cause-determined, rather than dialogue-determined, relation makes the informative message partially or totally unquestionable. Even with the best possible intentions, such messages tend to become command messages that silence the receiver—propagandistic, informative messages.

This relation, which tends to be informative, may also usefully be called cybernetic or piloted (*kubernetés* meaning pilot in Homeric Greek). The term cybernetic should be reserved exclusively for functions that include a component of external control. Its use (or the use of cyber), in place of *tele*, as a synonym of distance, in terms such as cyberspace, cybersecurity, cybercrime, cyberlearning and cyberhealth, is quite inappropriate.

Two corollaries can be raised:

1. Modern mediatization has greatly favoured the information message, because of the predominance of one-way channels that have physically and temporally distanced the transmitter and receiver. This means that the transmitter becomes part of an elite, while the mute receiver is seen as a mass. Some media (more precisely, some artificial channels of communication) act as diodes: they channel the flow of messages in one direction but do not permit messages to flow in the other. This reinforces the institutionalization of the transmitter and the causal character of the informative relationship—that is, the propaganda effect of massive messages. (A fool with a microphone shapes public opinion today far more than a wise man speaking with his neighbours on the corner by his house.)

2. The information relation becomes an aspect of the distribution of labour, and can be the fruit of an unwritten social compact. Many positive information relations (such as reading, viewing art, education) are consensual. The receiver desists *a priori*, and voluntarily, from using his transmitting power and consciously assumes a receiver role that he intuits will not remove from him his power to dialogue. He is quiet because he knows that the transmitting source does not wish to make him mute. ("Only in true speech is true silence possible," said the philosopher Martin Heidegger.)

Communication, or predominantly communicative messages, or genuine dialogue, occurs when both poles encompass the foregoing up/down or cause/effect pattern and in principle share identical power as transmitter and receiver, with the same ability to shift instantaneously between the two; when the receiver is respected without any attempt to in-form him or induce his responses, but rather, to generate in him a rational understanding of ideas and facts in a climate of reciprocity; when all players are given the same active role and enjoy the use of the same channel, a situation that favours those channels that ensure instantaneous bidirectionality (and note that the delegation or contracting of some communicating capacity to a spokesperson does not violate the rule); when, through dialogue, in lieu of a process of persuading or ordering, a truth higher than the one initially held is reached, or an unpreconceived, shared and consensual decision is attained. To communicate means preserving an optimal "distance" from one's interlocutor, and being open to his propositions. This, in turn, means respecting his otherness without pretending to absorb, alienate or reify him by reducing him via a causal message. To communicate is to achieve a well-tempered relationship that allows harmony to germinate. The laconic and perfect Kantian definition of reciprocal action between agent and patient, however, remains insuperable.

Two further schematizations can be mentioned:

1. *In the sociopolitical area:* Only genuine and open communications can create a critical mass of reciprocities capable of giving life to authentic open and free communities and unmanipulated public opinion. Any attempt to make informative relations more efficient can only create a further accumulation of privileges in the transmitter, and a corresponding decline in communicability, reciprocity, sociability, pluralism and democracy. Only by tirelessly keeping alive areas of sufficient communicative reciprocity without a predominance of causative factors, is it possible to imagine the survival of genuine democracy—an unrenounceable model of human relations that would be smothered in an all-informative universe. Any attempt to replace a dialogue of equals with a more efficient but desocializing informational charge inevitably creates effects that tend to deconstruct the social plexus. In this order of ideas, the phrase information society is hardly more than a cosmetic contradiction in terms (since only communication creates society), while the phrase social communication is a tautology (since communication is, by its essence, social).

2. *In the instrumental and institutional area:* The constantly evolving panoply of artificial channels of communication, or media, as well as the human institutions that use them, should be organized in a hierarchy according to their ability to be vehicles for, or promote, either communication or information. Today, the hierarchy would no doubt be headed by the Internet and the telephone (in that order, for the Internet, by addressing many receivers simultaneously, has addressed the last gap that the telephone was unable to fill), which are the two great instruments of open bidirectionality, of simultaneous use of an identical channel—in a word, of reciprocity and democracy. Leading candidates for the bottom of the list would be television, or, best of all, press agencies, the last surviving dinosaurs of communications, constituting an ever more meagre bundle of ever more powerful transmitters, broadcasting 40 million words per day of uniform thinking—a historical embodiment of everything in today's informative relation that is univectoral, causative, manipulatory, imposing and propagandistic.

Given this situation, it is rationally transparent, morally just and politically desirable to make efforts to:

1. Favour communication, which generates more reciprocity and fosters community, over the still necessary mechanisms of information, which should be required, insofar as possible, to be used progressively more communicatively, and always in accordance with the principles of the communication rights.
2. Favour the use of channels that facilitate bidirectionality, or that are less involved in imposing technological and economic constraints on users while accumulating advantages for transmitters.
3. Increase, to the extent possible, the coefficient of pluralism, transparency and democracy among institutions that have excessive power over technology, broadcasting and oversight of infrastructure, channels, codes and messages.

Communication Rights

Gnoseologically speaking, communication is the synthetic category that encompasses all communication relations, while, ontologically, it is the *raison d'être* of human relations. Hence, communication rights are among the original and organic human rights. Without using them fully, the rational being could not be a political animal, choose the modality of being with the other, or ensure the greatest possible reciprocity.

Only with great international will—a scarce commodity at this millennial juncture—can this essential, and still unwritten, chapter of human rights take form. Jean D'Arcy was right, in the 1980s, to complain that "no principle of international law regarding communications has yet been established," and the Communications Rights in the Information Society (CRIS) movement is right, today, to state that "the right to communicate constitutes a universal human right that assumes, and is at the service of, other human rights".

If they act in good faith, neither those who would prefer to see these rights as deriving from other existing rights, nor those advocates of global deregulation who deny the need for more international declarations on the subject, have anything to fear. The right implies no limitation. Rather, it extends communicative freedom to more people.

Unless, logically and ontologically, one turns things on their head, no specific existing right can give birth to a communication right that is more generic and of greater scope. The old sectoral rights come to us from eras that were localistic and shaped by a single medium, eras that did not understand the key role of communication in relation, and that did not foresee the capacity for use and abuse that the fourth estate would accumulate throughout the world (Burke 1774). Nor did they imagine a media system like today's, which would collapse without the far from innocent hundreds of billions of dollars that advertising injects into it.

Communication and information, deregulated and monopolized by the establishment, are today's most pertinent illustration of the fact that there are freedoms that enslave and laws that liberate (Fontenelle 1686). Its multiple anomies are defended by large corporate media law firms, with Cold War arguments. We already know what it has meant—in terms of *laissez faire*—for the ITU, which is hosting WSIS 2003, to be acting without the good judgment and thought that many would wish—because it does not, for instance, have a charter that requires it to work to promote equity. We have unconnected but usable fragments of a future and coherent communication right. Principles of freedom of expression consecrated by the international community, free use of any medium to exercise this freedom, and a prohibition on harassing those who exercise it, continue to be solid building blocks for constructing a fundamental communication right. All other rights related to the communicative relation—first of all, the right to information (improperly called access to information)—should be considered subsidiary and as deriving from it. Anything imposed on them, which contradicts the original and fundamental principles of communication rights, should be considered invalid.

Episodes such as those that occurred during the Second World War, in which an occupying power prohibited the inhabitants of an invaded country from using their native tongue—that is, from making use of the pristine, fundamental and pre-media communicative function of one being with the other—can be considered among the most brutal violations of the basic and unrestrictable communication right. Seen against the background of today's myopic media interests, the episode shows that a future communication right will have to cover an area of praxis far greater than that covered by Article 19 of the 1966 International Covenant on Civil and Political Rights, or the highly totemized but nineteenth-century principle of "freedom of expression" (something increasingly virtual in a hypermedia age, without a corresponding "freedom of communication")—an area that absolutely cannot be reduced either to the economic-political-media casuistry in which it is usually put into neat categories, or to business's diatribe against a state that is a Leviathan and an enemy by virtue of its antonomasia of freedoms. Only when communication rights are codified will the postulate with which D'Arcy began a famous 1969 essay be satisfied: "The declaration of human rights that…establishes for the first time in its Article 19 the right of man to information, will some day have to recognize the existence of a broader right: man's right to communication".

Let us enumerate half a dozen ingredients of communication rights that can be deduced from what we have stated so far:

1. Communication is the transmitting/receiving between equipolar and reciprocal poles, in agreed codes, of knowledge or feeling translated into the form of a message.

2. It is an inalienable birthright of human beings, gifted like no other being for the coding/transmission and decoding/receiving of messages, for one to know the other, through intercommunication in codes and channels selected by them. Their capacity to interact and their elevation into political beings depend on the free exercise of this right to a communicative relation.

3. Since reciprocal action is the defining concept, by antonomasia, of communication, a communication right should first, insofar as possible, guarantee all parties in a communicative relationship the isodynamic character of the relation. In other words, they must have the same identical practical ability to code, select channels, and transmit and receive messages, thus preventing a communicative relationship from deteriorating into an informing relationship. Subsidiarily, communication rights will set the conditions for a partial, delegated and consensual ceding of such prerogatives and capacities (see below).

4. Human societies, ideally considered as a hierarchical continuum from open to closed, reflect the communicative relations prevailing in them and how their citizens exercise communication rights. Any change in the communicative model leads to social change; any communicative imbalance leads to degradation of communication into information; any obstacle put in the way of the free exercise of communication rights, in regard to codes, channels, content, moment, place, or choice of receivers, is an attack on the relational nature of human beings and should be considered a crime.

5. Individual and social rights to communication (when democratically defined) have the same dignity and must be harmoniously reconciled.

6. Communication rights are inalienable and can be delegated to vicarious communicators at will. However, the *realpolitik* that disfigured just delegation and permitted political-economic powers to hoard the majority of such rights without democratic consensus (even legalizing the immoral principle of first come first served) will have to be reviewed in its entirety. That confiscated right must be returned to human societies, and the maximum possible pluralism and equity must be restored to free communication.

The Free Flow of Information

The free flow of information inflamed the world for a time in the 1970s and 1980s, when the champions of a New World Information and Communication Order (NWICO)—derived from the preceding New World Economic Order, or NWEO—postulated a need to rectify information imbalances and open communicative opportunities to those lacking in communicative power. They were immediately dismissed as proponents of statization and as Soviet accomplices, and the English-speaking West responded with a tough defence of free flow, which (in Foster Dulles style) was declared an unrenounceable principle of democracy. The bellows of the Cold War did the rest. The most educational and objective document of the period is still resolution 4/19 of the United Nations Educational, Scientific and Cultural Organization (UNESCO) General Conference. It bears rereading.

In the area of freedom, an Aristotelian prudence is called for. We ourselves, and coming generations, will continue to debate this complex and metaphysical subject, and it is a healthy precaution to assume that those who claim to possess the perfect libertarian formula for communications (and want to impose it on everyone else) are ignorant, arrogant or paid. The problem of free flow re-emerges incessantly, though, and a conceptual refresher is in order.

Free flow stresses the notion of channel: it advocates the most absolute and unconstrained freedom of circulation for messages, especially across borders, with an absence of geopolitical, technological or legal obstacles, except as provided for in international treaties. It favours an information universe without gaps or blockages, a universe open to all, which explains the capital importance given to it in the West during the Cold War decades, when radio transmissions to Iron Curtain countries undermined people's belief in socialism and led the Soviet Union to consume a billion kilowatts annually—and futilely—to block the broadcasts.

With the Cold War officially over, an unfortunate conclusion forces itself upon us: an ephemeral East-West confrontation was used to sweep away a structural North-South disparity. All of the old imbalances have been aggravated: the strong communicators have accumulated more power, while the weak are weaker. An understandable aura of suspicion continues to surround the theoretically irrefutable principle of free flow, which the United States used for its own self-interest for decades, like a sort of free navigation treaty imposed by the United States or China on Bolivia or Switzerland to give the latter countries one more high-sounding freedom, while the former get all of the world's shipping. The South was declared free, but was deprived of the instruments to exercise its freedom (its own news agencies, movie industry laws, local cultural industries, and so on). The poor example provided by Roman Proconsul Titus Quintus Flaminius in 196 B.C., when he declared that occupied Greece was free, has apparently lost none of its inspiring charm.

Today, the notion of free flow has more subtle complexities as a result of network technologies, codes and filters that, on the one hand, have broadened personal freedoms for individuals (a total information blackout is difficult or impossible today, even in countries where communications are highly controlled), while, on the other, lending themselves (ever more docilely) to capillary espionage, an activity defined by the experts as systematic information theft. Indeed, we have entered a new age of globally surveilled freedom, a paradox by which we are sold more freedom to better surveil ourselves.

Unprecedented problems of free flow emerge from one moment to the next. Extreme freedom enthusiasts believe that each new technology opens the frontiers of a new Wild West for freedom to conquer. They do not want to understand that if paedophilia or apologies for Nazism are violations of criminal codes, these activities do not become innocent by virtue of being committed on the Internet. On the suspicious side, let us remember that:

- every new communication technology (frequently as a result of government demands on equipment manufacturers) increases the possibility of locating users, intercepting or emptying their digital memories and copying their messages;
- the free use of confidential codes, as well as open codes (more difficult to spy on and control), is under greater attack every day;
- the country that, for now, owns the Global Positioning System (GPS), the Internet, and hundreds of communication and espionage satellites is the only one with the unilateral ability to block the communications of some or all of humanity, while it deploys its best efforts to prevent other countries from acquiring their own GPS systems;
- information, precursor of power, is not only one of the most coveted goods today, but the most manipulated in its most remote terrain—and it does not take preparations for an invasion of Iraq to prove it (the work on the economics of information that won J.E. Stiglitz the Nobel prize dealt with the "information asymmetry" generated by economic agents who fraudulently accumulate more information than others);
- universal electronic espionage has become extremely efficient and is now a real phenomenon (through companies such as Echelon, Carnivore, Fluent and Oasis), especially since the attacks on the United States on 11 September 2001, and the Total Information Awareness (TIA), which controls people

through networks, is already a reality, while the Pentagon's Office of Strategic Influence is like a "007" of information, with license to lie.

This unappealing, massively manipulated and surveilled freedom is already a part of our information society, and will become more so. Despite the solemn declarations of libertarians, this society has turned privacy into a suspicious value that is in danger of extinction. These arguments should be remembered for when the panegyrics reach strident levels.

Despite all of this, free flow is a beautiful, positive principle that we must defend in conferences and in real life, though we must unceasingly denounce abuses of dominant positions committed in its name. It would be infinitely worse to have no free flow at all. But one condition must be insisted upon: reciprocity is necessary to help the weak be as free as the powerful. A freedom that does not free is egotism and privilege. The double standard of free information in the abstract, while information in the concrete world is managed under mercantile principles that make it possible to eliminate the competition, is relationally and communicationally dishonest.

Access and Participation

These two antonyms, to which UNESCO dedicated a conference in 1974, are sources of confusion for three reasons:

- the frequent use of the former in lieu of the latter;
- deliberate exclusion of the latter; and
- certain ideological uses of the latter in the past era of socialism/communism.

For example—with our excuses to their authors—let us read the two following paragraphs from WSIS preparatory documents:

Access to information and communications media as a public and international common good should be participatory, universal, broad in scope and democratic.

Key principles: 1. Access to information and free flow of information are fundamental human rights.

(The term "participation" does not appear in any of the ten principles enunciated here.)

In the first case, we have access with a desire that it be participatory. In the second (where the subjects involved in communication are considered only as "users of communication, information networks and the media"), the authors at no point use the term participation; and they implicitly repudiate various definitions of the present glossary, specifically those relating to communication rights and the free flow of information. They continue, in the Cold War mode, to consider that basic communication rights are access to information and free flow.

Where culture and communication are involved, we suggest assigning to those terms the following meanings:

- *Access:* exercised capacity to receive (decode, come to know, discover, investigate, demand, recover, or place in the public domain) messages of any kind.
- *Participation:* exercised capacity to produce and transmit (generate, code, provide a vehicle for, disseminate, publish or transmit) messages of any kind.

Taking a symphony orchestra to a working class neighbourhood facilitates access to live classical music (passive receiving); opening a music school in the neighbourhood creates a process of participation in musical life (active transmission). Those countries whose media live exclusively on access to exogenous sources of information, without their own agencies and correspondents participating in creating information, lose all endogenous capacity to understand and interpret the world autonomously.

The following equation is thus produced:

$$\frac{\text{access}}{\text{receiving}} = \frac{\text{participation}}{\text{transmission}}$$

Reciprocal complementarities and negations are produced between access and participation (as between information and communication).

Growing ease of access makes participation more difficult and can inhibit it (and vice versa), generating more dependency, paternalism and social cybernetization, which explains the fact that the word access abounds in the hegemonic business discourse, while participation scarcely appears.

A society's communicative health can be measured in terms of the complementarity and healthy equilibrium existing between the plurality and quality of the messages to which it has access, and in terms of its share of participation in message generation and transmission (for example, the entire Latin American continent fails to participate, with agencies of its own, in the global production of news, while the population of the United States is kept practically without access to cinema from other parts of the world).

Access and free flow, as mentioned earlier, are key words in the vocabulary of the current information/communication world. With the same passion that they use to defend free flow, the mentors of the information society preach access (even where there is an overabundance of it), while they hold firmly to the sin of omission where participation is concerned. Access, obviously, is construed in relation to the inputs and messages produced and put into motion by these advocates, while they maintain an embargo on elements that could facilitate a participatory process by which consumers would be transformed into producers. Such elements are free software, universal standards, open sources and codes, generosity as regards public domain and intellectual property, and so on. Thanks to this subtly engineered imbalance, many have erroneously been persuaded that an abundance of means of access, and of receivers, is equivalent to more communication and information, when the truth is the opposite. However, saturating the access function, to the point of dumping, yields high dividends. First of all, it discourages and inhibits any potential will to participate on the part of receivers. There is no lack of experiments in raising the access threshold, measuring how much messaging the user can still take in. (Urban neighbourhoods have been saturated with up to 500 television channels.) Meanwhile, a modest participatory project, such as a small, nearby television station managed by the community itself, would do what no overdose of access can ever do: improve relations, generate participation and promote genuine communication.

National laws regarding the right to information include a recent freedom of information bill in a large Asian country. The essential object is defined as being to "empower every citizen with the right to obtain information from the government". The very first article of the law restricts the right to one side of the coin: access. It guarantees citizens the power to know and use official information—we should say, in passing, that many private sources also prevent access to information—without even mentioning the positive, active and participatory side of the coin, which should also *a fortiori* be guaranteed: the right to generate and transmit information. In its official documents for WSIS, ITU assigns itself, as its main task, to "ensure universal access to the information society". The undesirable final product of this kind of semantic imprecision is that even in a document as important as the draft declarations and action plan of the second preparatory committee, the term access appears 47 times and the term participation only six—but not with the meanings discussed here (for example, "the participation of the private sector"). Thus, we can safely tally the score as 47 to 0. The notion of information, in and of itself limiting and desocializing, in relation to communication, receives a second limitation here by being reduced to mere access to the messages of others, amputating the participatory side, the creation and transmission of one's own messages.

An institutional reduction of the informative phenomenon when receiving others' knowledge and opinion without a counterpart, can only institutionalize the muteness of the receiver/consumer. This is a coherent goal only in the framework of economistic conceptions of communication, where the receiver/client hardly counts, where what counts is cost benefit, economies of scale, targets and return on advertising investment—criteria that communications policy has gradually made its own. Furthermore, our societies become information societies in proportion to their degree of connectivity. Its induced pro-access behaviours promote exaggerated and unnecessary consumption both of decoding terminals (landline and cellular telephones, fax, radios, televisions, computers, modems, scanners, antennas, connections, and so on) and telecommunications vectors, whose rates will continue to be very high until their providers reabsorb the losses of the gigantic end-of-millennium speculations. Thus, it is major economic interests (not to mention political interests) that are the most important sources behind the pro-access discourse of the information society.

With all of these omissions, the term participation has been dangerously swept from the communication and information vocabulary. Now that WSIS is imminent, it is important to revive the word and make it into a driving concept that can help to hold back access hypertrophy, which can lead to serious participatory atrophy. In the information environment that surrounds us, which is the object of so many panegyrics (the ITU itself does not hesitate to speak of humanity's greatest revolution), individuals and societies should not resign themselves to being a chorus, or mere spectators, but should seek a leading, participatory role. In an area as anomic as communication, without basic social contracts to govern it, there is room to envisage original forms of participation. Many have already been invented, and it is simple enough to apply or fortify them. For example:

1. Given that almost all political regimes, even in the great democracies, tend to generate unhealthy forms of collusion between the executive branch and the media, behind the backs of the people, the societies must unflaggingly denounce such abuse of dominant positions and demand that the other branches of government take measures to guarantee more participation and real pluralism (not just "more of the same") in the production/transmission of messages.
2. In the name of a free flow that can coexist with other free flows, cultural diversities and the so-called cultural exception must be tirelessly safeguarded, in the interest of humanity as a whole. Specifically, this means:

- ensuring sufficient and appropriate participation, that is, presence in the media of the creator, producer and local transmitter of messages (a difficult battle at the international level, especially when it takes place in culturally incompetent institutions, such as the WTO); and
- where possible, negotiating coproduction or reciprocity.

3. Technological mediatization makes collaborative participation in producing and transmitting messages economically impossible for many aspiring transmitters today. Fair taxation should be used to ensure that those who profit from information/communication by using public goods on a concession basis, finance, even if only partially, economically unprofitable information/communication that is in the public interest. They must, indeed, make major efforts to ensure that everyone who participates in informative activity as a transmitter has free and equal access, without obstacles, to inputs and technologies that could be used selectively to benefit some and not others. At the international level, the efforts of developing countries to create and develop their own hardware and software capacity must be facilitated, not hindered.

4. Throughout the world, even in countries with long-established democracies, civil society and users have not yet gained the guarantee of a full participatory presence, through the mechanism of "user representatives". This is an important power, and represents significant decision-making power in, and in relation to, international, national, regional and local bodies that deal with communication and information. These range from United Nations organizations to national and international regulatory agencies, audiovisual councils, supervisory bodies for radio concessions, public broadcasting services and certain deontological committees. This participatory precept is indispensable, inasmuch as bodies that were once intergovernmental or public have been incorporating representatives of the private communication and information industries in their organizations, reproducing at the inter-national level the type of collusion between government and business sectors that we have referred to on the national level. The immoral cohabitation of regulatory bodies and regulated sectors demands that the watchdog function of civil society be strengthened. The ITU, as organizer of WSIS, could provide a good example in that sense, creating a sort of Control Advisory Panel (CAP) made up entirely of users, to counterbalance the

Reform Advisory Panel (RAP), which is entirely devoted to the business sector.

5. Ensuring greater active citizen participation in communication processes should lead, among other things, to rediscovering the notion and benefits of public services in communications. Well-conceived and managed, these public services are still the best possible example of genuine participation, in three different ways:

- by guaranteeing opportunities conducive to cultural creativity and diversity;
- by being primarily financed with public funds (in some cases, fees and other contributions from the users themselves); and
- by admitting elected user representatives into their decision-making bodies *ex officio*.

There are countries, especially in the Southern hemisphere, that have never experienced public services in the communications area, or whose experience was not positive. In some cases, such bodies degenerated into organs for government propaganda. It is a moral duty of those societies that know the advantages of efficient public services (such as post, telecom, radio and television) to take an educational role vis-à-vis the less fortunate. At a time when the privatization of world enterprise seems to have reached its upper limit, it would not be inappropriate for the following dreaded question to be posed at WSIS: Has the time not come for certain oligopolistic, anti-pluralistic, and totally unparticipatory information and communication services to be turned into (or turned back into) new-generation public services under strict civil society oversight, or even turned into user co-operatives?

The Information Society

Logically speaking (see above), "information society" is a contradiction in terms, a combining of the desocializing phenomenon of "information" with the strong, noble noun "society", which, in reality, relates only to communication. However, it is futile to impugn stereotypes that have become commonplaces. Let us adopt it with reservations, keeping it in mental quotation marks. Let us say, tolerantly, that information society here denotes that segment of a communication society in which, by pragmatic agreement, information relations predominate, but where the values and standards of communication, as formulated through communication rights, remain in full force.

Rather than an information society, ours is, more accurately, a "computerized" civilization, or an information-dependent one, to a degree directly proportional to the wealth of a country. In the past half-century, much knowledge has been democratized thanks to communications, and the production, conservation and dissemination of knowledge owes much to information and communication technologies. The Internet fulfilled telephony's age-old aspiration by further democratizing the medium: one can now address everyone simultaneously. The Web has not only achieved this, but has put the most efficient and unimaginable post office within everyone's reach, making it possible for anyone to produce his or her own newspaper and put it on display at that news-stand known as "the world".

This is a part of the "golden legend" to which we all clearly subscribe, though without letting ourselves be dazzled. However, a world summit is an almost unique occasion for comparing it with the "black legend"—not to replace the former with the latter (which would be infantile), but rather to seek a reasonable, middle path capable of protecting the vulnerable part of humanity from a deceitful and distracting show. This would make it possible to reach a consensus regarding a universally acceptable model of the information society, one that is clear in its teleology and with no tricks in its methods for achieving the agreed goals.

The first thing to note is that the so-called Pareto's Law has been reproduced or specifically schematized in communications. (Indeed, it would have been a miracle had this not been the case.) Eighty per cent of the world's wealth tends to accumulate, regardless of politics, in society's most favoured 20 per cent, though human avarice has recently broken through that ceiling, so that 87 per cent of the earth's wealth is now concentrated in that upper quintile. Communications (as Jipp's Law on the correspondence of telephone density and the gross domestic product, or GDP, showed decades ago) follow the same curve with exaggerated fidelity. In 2000, 91 per cent of Internet users (that is, 19 per cent of the world population) were concentrated in the OECD countries. During the months when Luxembourg was climbing to a density of 170 telephones per 100 inhabitants, Niger fell to 0.21 per 100 (a comparative ratio of 800 to 1 between the two countries). This suggests at least five major issues for the Geneva and Tunis meetings of WSIS to consider:

1. In the proper doses, with the proper amount of technology and the proper timing, communications and computerization undeniably improve quality of life. It would be wrong, however, to ignore the fact that the absolute dramatic priorities of 70 per cent of humankind continue to be protein, water, and a modicum of health and education, rather than an Internet connection. At

such scandalous levels of impoverishment, the idea of technology as saviour is unacceptable.

2. Assuming that one acts in good faith, one cannot change certain economic determinants. Connectivity will continue to be essentially a GDP-dependent variable. Humanity must first be relieved of its critical poverty, and along with this, access to information/communication can be improved.

3. Any attempt to violate this determining pattern is an error called "developmentalism". This approach failed in the 1960s, when it was thought that saturating the universe of the needy with the gadgets of the rich would be enough to make the needy act as if they were not.

4. The South is the last unsaturated reservoir of access. (There is almost no participation, which means an inability to compete.) It is the only place where strong market expansion is still possible, and it is also the part of the world with the highest telecommunication rates. This cocktail of ingredients explains why there is so much eagerness to provide more access terminals to the region.

5. Of all of the interlinked universes in which human relations move, the one that shows the least pluralism and democracy—the worst possible example of human relations—is, absurdly, today's communication universe. This is a perverse paradox, the result of an excessive confiscation and concentration of communicative power—a situation that must be ended. Any decision that does not democratize information/ communication on both sides—access and participation—is suspect and should be discarded. Otherwise, "universal access to the information society" could seem like selling glass beads to the poor, immortalizing the cartoon of the little farmhouse squashed under the weight of a much bigger satellite dish.

The second component of the black legend is sectoral anomy. The efforts, by those who generate almost all available information, to advance the information society in a context of more deregulation and an increasing legal vacuum, may be seen as another effort by maritime nations to impose a free navigation treaty on landlocked nations. It is essential that WSIS approve a first Universal Declaration on Communication Rights, of which a good draft is already in circulation. Let us limit ourselves to mentioning one of its aspects that is crucial today—that of the vicarious function in communications.

Ever since face-to-face communication was replaced by the media, which proliferated, but altered, intercommunication, almost all human communications have been "mediatized", depersonalized by the channel through which they pass. Some people were able to utilize the media effectively, while others who were kept at a distance from the media were not heard. The media simultaneously brought expansion and communicative imbalance to human relations. In communications and information, the only legitimization of the transmitter (and not a codified legitimization) is either to have arrived first, or to have enough political and economic power to accumulate knowledge and convert it into messages. No social contract or international pact governs the power of the fourth estate. This finding is not aimed to take freedoms away from the fourth estate, but because of a desire to expand the freedom to those who did not get there first, or who have fewer resources. From Adam Smith to Jürgen Habermas, the validity of the controls exerted over government by public opinion, through its media, has been reconfirmed. However, complicity between government and the media—even in the great democracies—is of such vast scope that the question of who is to control the controllers is a global issue. There are 6 billion of us, and soon there will be 10 billion. The idea of all of us being transmitters through the mass media is obviously a nightmare. The acceptance of the practice of a few vicarious transmitters communicating and informing in the name of many is what the best logic suggests, in terms of social economy and distribution of labour. Nevertheless—and this is the problem— citizens without any real media communication capacity should continue to be considered as permanent depositories of that same unrenounceable power (see Heidegger's "silent does not mean mute") that they entrust to others to exercise in their name as a vicarious function. Communication rights should now lead, for the first time, to a legal category that provides for granting vicarious communicative power—without conflict- ing, obviously, with other basic human rights. Thus, today's frequent abuses of dominant position in information/communications can be minimized and punished. The granting process will obviously be more demanding when the delegated person makes concessional use of public goods (such as broadcast frequencies and public infrastructure). In such cases, the community has the right to impose a set of obligations and quality standards on the vicarious communicator, in order to ensure that the community receives the service for which it has granted the right of public transmission.

Third, human societies and their community organizations will have to state clearly and fearlessly whether they accept the concept that the information society should be, structurally, a society of suspicion, surveillance and espionage, under a unilateral, rather than a universally shared, system of security criteria.

Fourth, it should be remembered that an information society is not a future entelechy. It exists already, has its history and its owners, and has amply demonstrated its potentials and limitations. What should be done, before designing another, better version, is to make a strategic accounting of the merits and demerits of the current system.

Our information society, for example, has already done things that, under the law, are not far from qualifying as criminal, namely, the two speculative bubbles used in an attempt to make of the Internet (in the United States) and UMTS telephony (in Europe) the mothers of all speculation. As of March 2000, Internet stock speculation had led to what was called "the greatest creation of wealth in the history of humanity". Less than three years later, $7 trillion had disappeared into an e-crack described as "the greatest destruction of wealth in peacetime". This loss was borne by millions of owners of savings who were bamboozled by dishonest managers, sales of pseudo-necessities, serious insider crimes, and criminal complicity by banks and firms providing analysis, auditing and financial advice. In short, they were defrauded by the system. In Europe, a powerful industrial lobby convinced the European Union (EU), in 1998, that EU countries could grant UMTS licenses, which a number of greedy governments hastened to do, collecting $314 billion in a few weeks. The technology was not ready, and countries that were already saturated with telephones bought in at prices more exorbitant than those paid for tulips in Holland in the seventeenth century. (In England, the cost of UMTS licenses reached the extravagant figure of $652 per inhabitant, while entire national telephone systems, such as Venezuela's, had been privatized at prices of $50–75 per inhabitant. Today, the countries with the greatest debt from telephony globally are those that bought UMTS at a high price.) The cost of these two speculations was transferred to users. It is calculated that for another entire generation, we will be paying for Internet and telephone service at artificially elevated prices in order to allow the firms involved to recover their losses. With deceptive Internet bubbles, malicious speculations of the UMTS variety, fraudulent bankruptcies on the Global Crossing model, and suspicious frauds such as the already forgotten millennium bug, it would be best for WSIS to place all of this out in the open and demand a minimum of guarantees to ensure that such things will not happen again.

References

D'Arcy, Jean. 1983. "An ascending progression." In Desmond Fisher and L. S. Harms (eds.), **The Right to Communicate: A New Human Right**. Boole Press, Dublin.

————. 1969. "Direct broadcast satellites and the right to communicate." **EBU Review**, No. 118.

Fontenelle, Bernard. 1686. **Entretiens sur la pluralité des mondes**. http://abu.cnam.fr/cgi-bin/go?plural3, accessed in October 2003.

Independent Commission for Worldwide Telecommunications Development. 1985. **The Missing Link**. Report of the Independent Commission for Worldwide Telecommunications Development (chaired by Sir Donald Maitland). ITU, Geneva.

Weill, Georges. 1934. "La presse anglaise et antinapoléonienne de 1789 à 1815. Lutte et progrès de la presse anglaise" In **Le journal: Origines, évolution et rôle de la presse périodique**. La Renaissance du livre, Paris.